T0212602

Lecture Notes in Computer Science

Lecture Notes in Artificial Intelligence **14133**

Founding Editor

Jörg Siekmann

Series Editors

Randy Goebel, *University of Alberta, Edmonton, Canada*
Wolfgang Wahlster, *DFKI, Berlin, Germany*
Zhi-Hua Zhou, *Nanjing University, Nanjing, China*

The series Lecture Notes in Artificial Intelligence (LNAI) was established in 1988 as a topical subseries of LNCS devoted to artificial intelligence.

The series publishes state-of-the-art research results at a high level. As with the LNCS mother series, the mission of the series is to serve the international R & D community by providing an invaluable service, mainly focused on the publication of conference and workshop proceedings and postproceedings.

Manuel Ojeda-Aciego · Kai Sauerwald ·
Robert Jäschke

Editors

Graph-Based Representation and Reasoning

28th International Conference
on Conceptual Structures, ICCS 2023
Berlin, Germany, September 11–13, 2023
Proceedings

 Springer

Editors
Manuel Ojeda-Aciego ⓘ
Universidad de Málaga
Málaga, Spain

Kai Sauerwald ⓘ
FernUniversität in Hagen
Hagen, Germany

Robert Jäschke ⓘ
Humboldt-Universität zu Berlin
Berlin, Germany

ISSN 0302-9743   ISSN 1611-3349 (electronic)
Lecture Notes in Artificial Intelligence
ISBN 978-3-031-40959-2   ISBN 978-3-031-40960-8 (eBook)
https://doi.org/10.1007/978-3-031-40960-8

LNCS Sublibrary: SL7 – Artificial Intelligence

This Springer imprint is published by the registered company Springer Nature Switzerland AG
The registered company address is: Gewerbestrasse 11, 6330 Cham, Switzerland

Preface

The 28th edition of the International Conference on Conceptual Structures (ICCS 2023) took place in Berlin, Germany, during 11–13 September 2023, and its proceedings are published under the title "Graph-Based Representation and Reasoning". Since 1993, ICCS has been a yearly venue for publishing and discussing new research methods along with their practical applications in the context of graph-based representation formalisms and reasoning, with a broad interpretation of its namesake conceptual structures. Topics of this year's conference include lattices and formal concept analysis, fuzzy logic and fuzzy sets, database theory and modelling and explanations.

The call asked for regular papers reporting on novel technical contributions, and 32 submissions were received (28 papers and 4 posters). The committee decided to accept 14 papers, which corresponds to an acceptance rate of 50%. Each submission received three reviews. In total, our Program Committee members delivered 96 reviews. The review process was double-blind, with papers anonymized for the reviewers and reviewer names unknown to the authors. We organized bidding on papers to ensure that reviewers received papers within their field of expertise. The response to the bidding process allowed us to assign each paper to reviewers who had expressed an interest in reviewing a particular paper. The final decision was made after the authors had a chance to reply to the initial reviews via a rebuttal to correct factual errors or answer reviewer questions. We believe this procedure ensured that only high-quality contributions were presented at the conference.

Next to the regular contributions, we were delighted to host three tutorials: the tutorial "Conceptual Structures for the Digital Humanities" by Tom Hanika (University of Hildesheim, Germany), Sergei Obiedkov (TUD Dresden University of Technology, Germany) and Robert Jäschke (Humboldt-Universität zu Berlin, Germany); the tutorial "fcaR, a computational tool for Formal Concept Analysis" by Domingo López-Rodríguez (Universidad de Málaga, Spain) and Ángel Mora Bonilla (Universidad de Málaga, Spain); as well as "Needs beyond ChatGPT: Teaching the Concepts of Knowledge Representation by Filling a Void" by Jan Krämer (Humboldt-Universität zu Berlin, Germany) and Lilian Löwenau (Humboldt-Universität zu Berlin, Germany). Furthermore, we were honoured to receive three keynote talks: "The Dynamics of True Belief - Learning by Revision and Merge" by Nina Gierasimczuk (Technical University of Denmark, Denmark), "What's in a story? How narratives structure the way we think about the economy" by Henrik Müller (TU Dortmund University, Germany), and "Semantic graphs and social networks" by Camille Roth (CNRS, Centre Marc Bloch, Germany). Note that this volume provides the abstracts of the keynote talks.

As general chair and program chairs, we thank our speakers for their inspiring and insightful talks. We would like to thank the Program Committee members and additional reviewers for their work. Without their substantial voluntary contribution, setting up such a high-quality conference program would not have been possible. We would also like to thank EasyChair for their support in handling submissions and Springer for their support in making these proceedings possible. Our institutions, the Universidad de Málaga, Spain, the FernUniversität in Hagen, Germany, and the Humboldt-Universität zu Berlin, Germany, also provided support for our participation, for which we are grateful. Last but not least, we thank the ICCS steering committee for their ongoing support and dedication to ICCS.

September 2023

Manuel Ojeda-Aciego
Kai Sauerwald
Robert Jäschke

Organization

General Chair

Robert Jäschke   Humboldt-Universität zu Berlin, Germany

Program Committee Chairs

Manuel Ojeda-Aciego   Universidad de Málaga, Spain
Kai Sauerwald   FernUniversität in Hagen, Germany

Steering Committee

Tanya Braun   University of Münster, Germany
Madalina Croitoru   Université Montpellier, France
Dominik Endres   University of Marburg, Germany
Simon Polovina   Sheffield Hallam University, UK
Uta Priss   Ostfalia University of Applied Sciences, Germany
Sebastian Rudolph   TUD Dresden University of Technology,
Germany

Program Committee

Simon Andrews   Sheffield Hallam University, UK
L'ubomír Antoni   Pavol Jozef Šafárik University in Košice, Slovakia
Tanya Braun   University of Münster, Germany
Peggy Cellier   IRISA/INSA Rennes, France
Pablo Cordero   Universidad de Málaga, Spain
M. Eugenia Cornejo Piñero   Universidad de Cádiz, Spain
Diana Cristea   Babes-Bolyai University, Romania
Licong Cui   University of Texas Health Science Center at
Houston, USA
Harry Delugach   University of Alabama in Huntsville, USA
Dominik Endres   University of Marburg, Germany
Jérôme Euzenat   Inria, Université Grenoble Alpes, France
Marcel Gehrke   University of Lübeck, Germany

Raji Ghawi	Technical University of Munich, Germany
Ollivier Haemmerlé	IRIT, University of Toulouse le Mirail, France
Tom Hanika	University of Hildesheim, Germany
Dmitry Ignatov	National Research University Higher School of Economics, Russia
Hamamache Kheddouci	Université Claude Bernard Lyon 1, France
Petr Krajča	Palacký University Olomouc, Czech Republic
Ondrej Krídlo	P. J. Šafárik University in Košice, Slovakia
Léonard Kwuida	Bern University of Applied Sciences, Switzerland
Domingo López-Rodríguez	Universidad de Málaga, Spain
Philippe Martin	University of La Réunion, France
Jesús Medina	University of Cádiz, Spain
Amedeo Napoli	LORIA Nancy, CNRS, Inria, Université de Lorraine, France
Carmen Peláez-Moreno	University Carlos III de Madrid, Spain
Heather D. Pfeiffer	Akamai Physics, Inc., USA
Uta Priss	Ostfalia University of Applied Sciences, Germany
Sebastian Rudolph	TUD Dresden University of Technology, Germany
Francisco J. Valverde-Albacete	Rey Juan Carlos University, Spain
Diana Şotropa	Babes-Bolyai University, Romania

Additional Reviewers

Abeysinghe, Rashmie
Aragón, Roberto G.
Haldimann, Jonas Philipp
Hao, Xubing
Huang, Yan
Lalou, Mohammed
Lobo, David
Ojeda-Hernández, Manuel
Ramírez Poussa, Eloisa

Abstracts of Keynote Talks

The Dynamics of True Belief: Learning by Revision and Merge

Nina Gierasimczuk(ID)

Technical University of Denmark, Kongens Lyngby, Denmark
nigi@dtu.dk

Successful learning can be understood as convergence to true beliefs. What makes a belief revision method a good learning method? In artificial intelligence and knowledge representation, belief revision processes are interpretable on epistemic models – graphs representing uncertainty and preference. I will discuss their properties, focusing especially on their learning power. Three popular methods: conditioning, lexicographic revision, and minimal revision differ with respect to their learning power – the first two can drive universal learning mechanisms, while minimal revision cannot. Learning in the presence of noise and errors further complicates the situation. Various types of cognitive bias can be abstractly represented as constraints on graph-based belief revision; we can then rigorously show ways in which they impact truth-tracking. Similar questions can be studied in the context of multi-agent belief revision, where a group revises their collective conjectures via a combination of belief revision and belief merge. The main take-away is that rationality of belief revision, on both an individual and a collective level, should account for learning understood not only as adaptation, but also as truth-tracking.

References

1. Gierasimczuk, N.: Learning by erasing in dynamic epistemic logic. In: Dediu, A.H., Ionescu, A.M., Martín-Vide, C. (eds) Language and Automata Theory and Applications. LATA 2009. LNCS, vol. 5457, pp. pp. 362–373. Springer, Berlin, Heidelberg (2009). https://doi.org/10.1007/978-3-642-00982-2_31
2. Gierasimczuk, N.: Bridging learning theory and dynamic epistemic logic. Synthese **169**, 371–384 (2009). https://doi.org/10.1007/s11229-009-9549-1
3. Gierasimczuk, N.: Knowing one's limits. logical analysis of inductive inference. PhD Thesis, Universiteit van Amsterdam, The Netherlands (2010)
4. Baltag, A., Gierasimczuk, N., Smets, S.: Belief revision as a truth-tracking process. In: Proceedings of the 13th Conference on Theoretical Aspects of Rationality and Knowledge TARK 2011, Groningen, The Netherlands, (Krzysztof Apt, editor), ACM, New York, pp. 187–190 (2011)
5. Baltag, A., Gierasimczuk, N., Smets, S.: Truth-tracking by belief revision. Stud Logica **107**, 917–947 (2019). https://doi.org/10.1007/s11225-018-9812-x
6. Papadamos, P., Gierasimczuk, N.: Cognitive bias and belief revision.: In: Proceedings of the 19th Conference on Theoretical Aspects of Rationality and Knowledge TARK 2023, Oxford, UK, (Rineke Verbrugge, editor), vol. 379, EPTCS, pp. 441–454 (2023)

What's in a Story? How Narratives Structure the Way we Think About the Economy

Henrik Müller

TU Dortmund University, Dortmund, Germany
henrik.mueller@tu-dortmund.de

Telling narratives is the mode in which humans make sense of an otherwise incomprehensibly complex world. Societies run on a set of narratives that serve as short-hand descriptions of the state of the nation. These stories shape expectations and drive economic and policy decisions. Journalism is a key player in shaping economic narratives. Furthermore, it adds an additional approach to economists' reasoning: narratives can be valuable complements to the statistics-focused approach pursued by economists, particularly in times of substantial structural change, when high levels of uncertainty prevail. What's more, modern text mining approaches lend themselves to detecting and quantifying the salience of narratives.

Semantic Graphs and Social Networks

Camille Roth (ID)

French National Centre for Scientific Research, Centre Marc Bloch, Berlin, Germany
roth@cmb.hu-berlin.de

The social distribution of information and the structure of social interactions are more and more frequently studied together, especially in fields related to computational social sciences. On the one hand, content analysis, variously called "text mining", "automated text analysis" or "text-as-data methods", relies on a wide range of techniques from simple numerical statistics (textual similarity, salient terms) to machine learning approaches applied at the level of sets of words or sentences, in particular to extract various types of semantic graphs – whether they are simple co-occurrence links between terms, "subject-predicate-object" triples, or more elaborate structures at the level of an entire sentence. These data and, sometimes, these semantic graphs, are also associated with actors whose various relations (interaction, collaboration, affiliation) are also frequently gathered in social graphs. This presentation aims at proposing an overview of approaches mixing contents and interactions, where digital public spaces and scientific communities represent frequent empirical grounds, being social systems where information and knowledge are produced and propagated in a decentralized way.

Contents

Modelling and Explanation

Semantic Web and Graphs

Posters

Complexity and Database Theory

Functional Dependencies with Predicates: What Makes the $g3$-error Easy to Compute?

Simon Vilmin[1,2]($\boxtimes$), Pierre Faure–Giovagnoli[2,3], Jean-Marc Petit[2],
and Vasile-Marian Scuturici[2]

[1] Université de Lorraine, CNRS, LORIA, 54000 Villers-lès-Nancy, France
`simon.vilmin@loria.fr`
[2] Univ Lyon, INSA Lyon, CNRS, UCBL, LIRIS, Villeurbanne UMR5205, France
`pierre.faure-giovagnoli@insa-lyon.fr`, `Jean-Marc.Petit@liris.cnrs.fr`
[3] Compagnie Nationale du Rhône, Lyon, France
`vasile-marian.scuturici@liris.cnrs.fr`

Abstract. The notion of functional dependencies (FDs) can be used by data scientists and domain experts to confront background knowledge against data. To overcome the classical, too restrictive, satisfaction of FDs, it is possible to replace equality with more meaningful binary predicates, and use a coverage measure such as the $g3$-error to estimate the degree to which a FD matches the data. It is known that the $g3$-error can be computed in polynomial time if equality is used, but unfortunately, the problem becomes **NP**-complete when relying on more general predicates instead. However, there has been no analysis of which class of predicates or which properties alter the complexity of the problem, especially when going from equality to more general predicates. In this work, we provide such an analysis. We focus on the properties of commonly used predicates such as equality, similarity relations, and partial orders. These properties are: reflexivity, transitivity, symmetry, and antisymmetry. We show that symmetry and transitivity together are sufficient to guarantee that the $g3$-error can be computed in polynomial time. However, dropping either of them makes the problem **NP**-complete.

Keywords: functional dependencies · $g3$-error, predicates

1 Introduction

Functional dependencies (FDs) are database constraints initially devoted to database design [26]. Since then, they have been used for numerous tasks ranging from data cleaning [5] to data mining [28]. However, when dealing with real world data, FDs are also a simple yet powerful way to syntactically express background knowledge coming from domain experts [12]. More precisely, a FD $X \rightarrow A$ between a set of attributes (or features) X and another attribute A depicts a *function* of the form $f(X) = A$. In this context, asserting the existence of a function which determines A from X in a dataset amounts to testing the validity of $X \rightarrow A$ in a relation, *i.e.* to checking that *every pair* of tuples that are *equal* on X are also *equal* on A. Unfortunately, this semantics of satisfaction

M. Ojeda-Aciego et al. (Eds.): ICCS 2023, LNAI 14133, pp. 3–16, 2023.
https://doi.org/10.1007/978-3-031-40960-8_1

suffers from two major drawbacks which makes it inadequate to capture the complexity of real world data: (i) it must be checked on the whole dataset, and (ii) it uses equality.

Drawback (i) does not take into account data quality issues such as outliers, mismeasurements or mistakes, which should not impact the relevance of a FD in the data. To tackle this problem, it is customary to estimate the partial validity of a given FD with a *coverage* measure, rather than its total satisfaction. The most common of these measures is the g_3-error [8,17,21,31], introduced by Kivinen and Mannila [22]. It is the minimum proportion of tuples to remove from a relation in order to satisfy a given FD. As shown for instance by Huhtala et al. [21], the g_3-error can be computed in polynomial time for a single (classical) FD.

As for drawback (ii), equality does not always witness efficiently the closeness of two real-world values. It screens imprecisions and uncertainties that are inherent to every observation. In order to handle closeness (or difference) in a more appropriate way, numerous researches have replaced equality by *binary predicates*, as witnessed by recent surveys on relaxed FDs [6,32].

However, if predicates extend FDs in a powerful and meaningful way with respect to real-world applications, they also make computations harder. In fact, contrary to strict equality, computing the g_3-error with binary predicates becomes **NP**-complete [12,31]. In particular, it has been proven for differential [30], matching [11], metric [23], neighborhood [1], and comparable dependencies [31]. Still, there is no detailed analysis of what makes the g_3-error hard to compute when dropping equality for more flexible predicates. As a consequence, domain experts are left without any insights on which predicates they can use in order to estimate the validity of their background knowledge in their data quickly and efficiently.

This last problem constitutes the motivation for our contribution. In this work, we study the following question: *which properties of predicates make the g_3-error easy to compute?* To do so, we introduce binary predicates on each attribute of a relation scheme. Binary predicates take two values as input and return `true` or `false` depending on whether the values match a given comparison criteria. Predicates are a convenient framework to study the impact of common properties such as reflexivity, transitivity, symmetry, and antisymmetry (the properties of equality) on the hardness of computing the g_3-error. In this setting, we make the following contributions. First, we show that dropping reflexivity and antisymmetry does not make the g_3-error hard to compute. When removing transitivity, the problem becomes **NP**-complete. This result is intuitive as transitivity plays a crucial role in the computation of the g_3-error for dependencies based on similarity/distance relations [6,32]. Second, we focus on symmetry. Symmetry has attracted less attention, despite its importance in partial orders and order FDs [10,15,27]. Even though symmetry seems to have less impact than transitivity in the computation of the g_3-error, we show that when it is removed the problem also becomes **NP**-complete. This result holds in particular for ordered dependencies.

Paper Organization. In Sect. 2, we recall some preliminary definitions. Section 3 is devoted to the usual g_3-error. In Sect. 4, we introduce predicates, along with definitions for the relaxed satisfaction of a functional dependency. Section 5 investigates the problem of computing the g_3-error when equality is replaced by predicates on each attribute. In Sect. 6 we relate our results with existing extensions of FDs. We conclude in Sect. 7 with some remarks and open questions for further research.

2 Preliminaries

All the objects we consider are finite. We begin with some definitions on graphs [2] and ordered sets [9]. A *graph* G is a pair (V, E) where V is a set of *vertices* and E is a collection of pairs of vertices called *edges*. An edge of the form (u, u) is called a *loop*. The graph G is *directed* if edges are ordered pairs of elements. Unless otherwise stated, we consider *loopless undirected* graphs. Let $G = (V, E)$ be an undirected graph, and let $V' \subseteq V$. The graph $G[V'] = (V', E')$ with $E' = \{(u, v) \in E \mid \{u, v\} \subseteq V'\}$ is the graph *induced* by V' with respect to G. A *path* in G is a sequence $e_1, \ldots, e_m$ of pairwise distinct edges such that e_i and e_{i+1} share a common vertex for each $1 \leq i < m$. The *length* of a path is its number of edges. An *independent set* of G is a subset I of V such that no two vertices in I are connected by an edge of G. An independent set is *maximal* if it is inclusion-wise maximal among all independent sets. It is *maximum* if it is an independent set of maximal cardinality. Dually, a *clique* of G is a subset K of V such that every pair of distinct vertices in K are connected by an edge of G. A graph G is a *co-graph* if it has no induced subgraph corresponding to a path of length 3 (called P_4). A *partially ordered set* or *poset* is a pair $P = (V, \leq)$ where V is a set and $\leq$ a reflexive, transitive, and antisymmetric binary relation. The relation $\leq$ is called a *partial order*. If for every $x, y \in V$, $x \leq y$ or $y \leq x$ holds, $\leq$ is a *total order*. A poset P is associated to a directed graph $G(P) = (V, E)$ where $(u_i, u_j) \in E$ exactly when $u_i \neq u_j$ and $u_i \leq u_j$. An undirected graph $G = (V, E)$ is a *comparability graph* if its edges can be directed so that the resulting directed graph corresponds to a poset.

We move to terminology from database theory [24]. We use capital first letters of the alphabet (A, B, C, ...) to denote attributes and capital last letters (..., X, Y, Z) for attribute sets. Let U be a universe of attributes, and $R \subseteq U$ a relation scheme. Each attribute A in R takes value in a domain $\mathsf{dom}(A)$. The domain of R is $\mathsf{dom}(R) = \bigcup_{A \in R} \mathsf{dom}(A)$. Sometimes, especially in examples, we write a set as a concatenation of its elements (e.g. AB corresponds to $\{A, B\}$). A *tuple* over R is a mapping $t \colon R \to \mathsf{dom}(R)$ such that $t(A) \in \mathsf{dom}(A)$ for every $A \in R$. The *projection* of a tuple t on a subset X of R is the restriction of t to X, written $t[X]$. We write $t[A]$ as a shortcut for $t[\{A\}]$. A *relation* r over R is a finite set of tuples over R. A *functional dependency* (FD) over R is an expression $X \to A$ where $X \cup \{A\} \subseteq R$. Given a relation r over R, we say that r *satisfies* $X \to A$, denoted by $r \models X \to A$, if for every pair of tuples (t_1, t_2) of r, $t_1[X] = t_2[X]$ implies $t_1[A] = t_2[A]$. In case when r does not satisfy $X \to A$, we write $r \not\models X \to A$.

3   The g_3-error

This section introduces the g_3-error, along with its connection with independent sets in graphs through counterexamples and conflict-graphs [3].

Let r be a relation over R and $X \rightarrow A$ a functional dependency. The g_3-error quantifies the degree to which $X \rightarrow A$ holds in r. We write it as $g_3(r, X \rightarrow A)$. It was introduced by Kivinen and Mannila [22], and it is frequently used to estimate the partial validity of a FD in a dataset [6,8,12,21]. It is the minimum proportion of tuples to remove from r to satisfy $X \rightarrow A$, or more formally:

Definition 1. *Let R be a relation scheme, r a relation over R and $X \rightarrow A$ a functional dependency over R. The g_3-error of $X \rightarrow A$ with respect to r, denoted by $g_3(r, X \rightarrow A)$ is defined as:*

$$g_3(r, X \rightarrow A) = 1 - \frac{\max(\{|s| \mid s \subseteq r, s \models X \rightarrow A\})}{|r|}$$

In particular, if $r \models X \rightarrow A$, we have $g_3(r, X \rightarrow A) = 0$. We refer to the problem of computing $g_3(r, X \rightarrow A)$ as the *error validation problem* [6,31]. Its decision version reads as follows:

Error Validation Problem (EVP)
Input: A relation r over R, a FD $X \rightarrow A$, $k \in \mathbb{R}$.
Question: Is is true that $g_3(r, X \rightarrow A) \leq k$?

It is known [6,12] that there is a strong relationship between this problem and the task of computing the size of a maximum independent set in a graph:

Maximum Independent Set (MIS)
Input: A graph $G = (V, E)$, $k \in \mathbb{N}$.
Question: Does G have a maximal independent set I such that $|I| \geq k$?

To see the relationship between EVP and MIS, we need the notions of *counterexample* and *conflict-graph* [3,12]. A *counterexample* to $X \rightarrow A$ in r is a pair of tuples (t_1, t_2) such that $t_1[X] = t_2[X]$ but $t_1[A] \neq t_2[A]$. The *conflict-graph* of $X \rightarrow A$ with respect to r is the graph $\mathsf{CG}(r, X \rightarrow A) = (r, E)$ where a (possibly ordered) pair of tuples (t_1, t_2) in r belongs to E when it is a counterexample to $X \rightarrow A$ in r. An independent set of $\mathsf{CG}(r, X \rightarrow A)$ is precisely a subrelation of r which satisfies $X \rightarrow A$. Therefore, computing $g_3(r, X \rightarrow A)$ reduces to finding the size of a maximum independent set in $\mathsf{CG}(r, X \rightarrow A)$. More precisely, $g_3(r, X \rightarrow A) = 1 - \frac{|I|}{|r|}$ where I is a maximum independent set of $\mathsf{CG}(r, X \rightarrow A)$.

Example 1. Consider the relation scheme $R = \{A, B, C, D\}$ with $\mathsf{dom}(R) = \mathbb{N}$. Let r be the relation over R on the left of Fig. 1. It satisfies $BC \rightarrow A$ but not $D \rightarrow A$. Indeed, (t_1, t_3) is a counterexample to $D \rightarrow A$. The conflict-graph $\mathsf{CG}(r, D \rightarrow A)$ is given on the right of Fig. 1. For example, $\{t_1, t_2, t_6\}$ is a maximum independent set of $\mathsf{CG}(r, D \rightarrow A)$ of maximal size. We obtain:

$$g_3(r, D \rightarrow A) = 1 - \frac{|\{t_1, t_2, t_6\}|}{|r|} = 0.5$$

In other words, we must remove half of the tuples of r in order to satisfy $D \rightarrow A$.

r	A	B	C	D
t_1	1	2	1	5
t_2	1	1	2	5
t_3	2	1	1	5
t_4	3	2	3	5
t_5	2	3	4	5
t_6	4	4	5	6

Fig. 1. The relation r and the conflict-graph $\mathsf{CG}(r, D \to A)$ of Example 1.

However, MIS is an **NP**-complete problem [13] while computing $g_3(r, X \to A)$ takes polynomial time in the size of r and $X \to A$ [21]. This difference is due to the properties of equality, namely reflexivity, transitivity, symmetry and antisymmetry. They make $\mathsf{CG}(r, X \to A)$ a disjoint union of complete k-partite graphs, and hence a co-graph [12]. In this class of graphs, solving MIS is polynomial [14]. This observation suggests to study in greater detail the impact of such properties on the structure of conflict-graphs. First, we need to introduce predicates to relax equality, and to define a more general version of the error validation problem accordingly.

4 Predicates to Relax Equality

In this section, in line with previous researches on extensions of functional dependencies [6,32], we equip each attribute of a relation scheme with a binary predicate. We define the new g_3-error and the corresponding error validation problem.

Let R be a relation scheme. For each $A \in R$, let $\phi_A \colon \mathsf{dom}(A) \times \mathsf{dom}(A) \to \{\texttt{true}, \texttt{false}\}$ be a predicate. For instance, the predicate ϕ_A can be equality, a distance, or a similarity relation. We assume that predicates are black-box oracles that can be computed in polynomial time in the size of their input.

Let Φ be a set of predicates, one for each attribute in R. The pair (R, Φ) is a *relation scheme with predicates*. In a relation scheme with predicates, relations and FDs are unchanged. However, the way a relation satisfies (or not) a FD can easily be adapted to Φ.

Definition 2 (Satisfaction with predicates). *Let (R, Φ) be a relation scheme with predicates, r a relation and $X \to A$ a functional dependency both over (R, Φ). The relation r satisfies $X \to A$ with respect to Φ, denoted by $r \models_\Phi X \to A$, if for every pair of tuples (t_1, t_2) of r, the following formula holds:*

$$\left(\bigwedge_{B \in X} \phi_B(t_1[B], t_2[B]) \right) \implies \phi_A(t_1[A], t_2[A])$$

A new version of the g_3-error adapted to Φ is presented in the following definition.

Definition 3. *Let (R, Φ) be a relation scheme with predicates, r be a relation over (R, Φ) and $X \to A$ a functional dependency over (R, Φ). The g_3-error with predicates of $X \to A$ with respect to r, denoted by $g_3^{\Phi}(r, X \to A)$ is defined as:*

$$g_3^{\Phi}(r, X \to A) = 1 - \frac{\max(\{|s| \mid s \subseteq r, s \models_{\Phi} X \to A\})}{|r|}$$

From the definition of $g_3^{\Phi}(r, X \to A)$, we derive the extension of the error validation problem from equality to predicates:

Error Validation Problem with Predicates (EVPP)
Input: A relation r over (R, Φ), a FD $X \to A$ over R, $k \in \mathbb{R}$.
Question: Is it true that $g_3^{\Phi}(r, X \to A) \leq k$?

Observe that according to the definition of satisfaction with predicates (Definition 2), counterexamples and conflict-graphs remain well-defined. However, for a given predicate ϕ_A, $\phi_A(x, y) = \phi_A(y, x)$ needs not be true in general, meaning that we have to consider ordered pairs of tuples. That is, an ordered pair of tuples (t_1, t_2) in r is a counterexample to $X \to A$ if $\bigwedge_{B \in X} \phi_B(t_1[B], t_2[B]) = \mathsf{true}$ but $\phi_A(t_1[A], t_2[A]) \neq \mathsf{true}$.

We call $\mathsf{CG}_{\Phi}(r, X \to A)$ the conflict-graph of $X \to A$ in r. In general, $\mathsf{CG}_{\Phi}(r, X \to A)$ is directed. It is undirected if the predicates of Φ are symmetric (see Sect. 5). In particular, computing $g_3^{\Phi}(r, X \to A)$ still amounts to finding the size of a maximum independent set in $\mathsf{CG}_{\Phi}(r, X \to A)$.

Example 2. We use the relation of Fig. 1. Let $\Phi = \{\phi_A, \phi_B, \phi_C, \phi_D\}$ be the collection of predicates defined as follows, for every $x, y \in \mathbb{N}$:

- $\phi_A(x, y) = \phi_B(x, y) = \phi_C(x, y) = \mathsf{true}$ if and only if $|x - y| \leq 1$. Thus, ϕ_A is reflexive and symmetric but not transitive (see Sect. 5),
- ϕ_D is the equality.

The pair (R, Φ) is a relation scheme with predicates. We have $r \models_{\Phi} AB \to D$ but $r \not\models_{\Phi} C \to A$. In Fig. 2, we depict $\mathsf{CG}_{\Phi}(r, C \to A)$. A maximum independent set of this graph is $\{t_1, t_2, t_3, t_5\}$. We deduce

$$g_3^{\Phi}(r, C \to A) = 1 - \frac{|\{t_1, t_2, t_3, t_5\}|}{|r|} = \frac{1}{3}$$

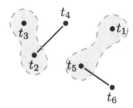

Fig. 2. The conflict-graph $\mathsf{CG}_\Phi(r, C \to A)$ of Example 2.

Thus, there is also a strong relationship between EVPP and MIS, similar to the one between EVP and MIS. Nonetheless, unlike EVP, the problem EVPP is **NP**-complete [31]. In the next section, we study this gap of complexity between EVP and EVPP via different properties of predicates.

5 Predicates Properties in the g_3-error

In this section, we study properties of binary predicates that are commonly used to replace equality. We show how each of them affects the error validation problem.

First, we define the properties of interest in this paper. Let (R, Φ) be a relation scheme with predicates. Let $A \in R$ and ϕ_A be the corresponding predicate. We consider the following properties:

(ref) $\phi_A(x, x) = \mathtt{true}$ for all $x \in \mathsf{dom}(A)$ (reflexivity)
(tra) for all $x, y, z \in \mathsf{dom}(A)$, $\phi_A(x, y) = \phi_A(y, z) = \mathtt{true}$ implies $\phi_A(x, z) = \mathtt{true}$ (transitivity)
(sym) for all $x, y \in \mathsf{dom}(A)$, $\phi_A(x, y) = \phi_A(y, x)$ (symmetry)
(asym) for all $x, y \in \mathsf{dom}(A)$, $\phi_A(x, y) = \phi_A(y, x) = \mathtt{true}$ implies $x = y$ (antisymmetry).

Note that symmetry and antisymmetry together imply transitivity, as $\phi_A(x, y) = \mathtt{true}$ entails $x = y$.

As a first step, we show that symmetry and transitivity are sufficient to make EVPP solvable in polynomial time. In fact, we prove that the resulting conflict-graph is a co-graph, as with equality.

Theorem 1. *The problem EVPP can be solved in polynomial time if the predicates used on each attribute are transitive (tra) and symmetric (sym).*

Proof. Let (R, Φ) be a relation scheme with predicates. Let r be relation over (R, Φ) and $X \to A$ be a functional dependency, also over (R, Φ). We assume that each predicate in Φ is transitive and symmetric. We show how to compute the size of a maximum independent set of $\mathsf{CG}_\Phi(r, X \to A)$ in polynomial time.

As ϕ_A is not necessarily reflexive, a tuple t in r can produce a counterexample (t, t) to $X \to A$. Indeed, it may happen that $\phi_B(t[B], t[B]) = \mathtt{true}$ for each $B \in X$, but $\phi_A(t[A], t[A]) = \mathtt{false}$. However, it follows that t never belongs to a subrelation s of r satisfying $s \models_\Phi X \to A$. Thus, let $r' = r \setminus \{t \in r \mid \{t\} \not\models_\Phi X \to A\}$. Then, a subrelation of r satisfies $X \to A$ if and only if it is an independent set of $\mathsf{CG}_\Phi(r, X \to A)$ if and only if it is an independent set of $\mathsf{CG}_\Phi(r', X \to A)$. Consequently, computing $g_3^\Phi(r, X \to A)$ is solving MIS in $\mathsf{CG}_\Phi(r', X \to A)$.

We prove now that $\mathsf{CG}_\Phi(r', X \to A)$ is a co-graph. Assume for contradiction that $\mathsf{CG}_\Phi(r', X \to A)$ has an induced path P with 4 elements, say t_1, t_2, t_3, t_4 with edges (t_1, t_2), (t_2, t_3) and (t_3, t_4). Remind that edges of $\mathsf{CG}_\Phi(r', X \to A)$ are counterexamples to $X \to A$ in r'. Hence, by symmetry and transitivity of the predicates of Φ, we deduce that for each pair (i, j) in $\{1, 2, 3, 4\}$, $\bigwedge_{B \in X} \phi_B(t_i[B], t_j[B]) = \mathtt{true}$. Thus, we have $\bigwedge_{B \in X} \phi_B(t_3[B], t_1[B]) = \bigwedge_{B \in X} \phi_B(t_1[B], t_4[B]) = \mathtt{true}$. However, neither (t_1, t_3) nor (t_1, t_4) belong to $\mathsf{CG}_\Phi(r', X \to A)$ since P is an induced path by assumption. Thus, $\phi_A(t_3[A], t_1[A]) = \phi_A(t_1[A], t_4[A]) = \mathtt{true}$ must hold. Nonetheless, the transitivity of ϕ_A implies $\phi_A(t_3[A], t_4[A]) = \mathtt{true}$, a contradiction with (t_3, t_4) being an edge of $\mathsf{CG}_\Phi(r', X \to A)$. We deduce that $\mathsf{CG}_\Phi(r', X \to A)$ cannot contain an induced P_4, and that it is indeed a co-graph. As MIS can be solved in polynomial time for co-graphs [14], the theorem follows. □

One may encounter non-reflexive predicates when dealing with strict orders or with binary predicates derived from $\mathtt{SQL}$ equality. In the 3-valued logic of $\mathtt{SQL}$, comparing the $\mathtt{null}$ value with itself evaluates to $\mathtt{false}$ rather than $\mathtt{true}$. With this regard, it could be natural for domain experts to use a predicate which is transitive, symmetric and reflexive almost everywhere but on the $\mathtt{null}$ value. This would allow to deal with missing information without altering the data.

The previous proof heavily makes use of transitivity, which has a strong impact on the edges belonging to the conflict-graph. Intuitively, conflict-graphs can become much more complex when transitivity is dropped. Indeed, we prove an intuitive case: when predicates are not required to be transitive, EVPP becomes intractable.

Theorem 2. *The problem* EVPP *is* **NP**-*complete even when the predicates used on each attribute are symmetric* (`sym`) *and reflexive* (`ref`).

The proof is omitted due to space limitations, it can be found in [33]. It is a reduction from the problem (dual to MIS) of finding the size of a maximum clique in general graphs. It uses arguments similar to the proof of Song et al. [31] showing the **NP**-completeness of EVPP for comparable dependencies.

We turn our attention to the case where symmetry is dropped from the predicates. In this context, conflict-graphs are directed. Indeed, an ordered pair of tuples (t_1, t_2) may be a counterexample to a functional dependency, but not (t_2, t_1). Yet, transitivity still contributes to constraining the structure of conflict-graphs, as suggested by the following example.

Example 3. We consider the relation of Example 1. We equip A, B, C, D with the following predicates:

- $\phi_C(x, y) = \mathtt{true}$ if and only if $x \le y$

- $\phi_A(x, y)$ is defined by

$$\phi_A(x, y) = \begin{cases} \text{true} & \text{if } x = y \\ \text{true} & \text{if } x = 1 \text{ and } y \in \{2, 4\} \\ \text{true} & \text{if } x = 3 \text{ and } y = 4 \\ \text{false} & \text{otherwise.} \end{cases}$$

- ϕ_B and ϕ_D are the equality.

Let $\Phi = \{\phi_A, \phi_B, \phi_C, \phi_D\}$. The conflict-graph $\mathsf{CG}_\Phi(C \to A)$ is represented in Fig. 3. Since ϕ_C is transitive, we have $\phi_C(t_3[C], t_j[C]) = \text{true}$ for each tuple t_j of r. Moreover, $\phi_A(t_3[A], t_6[A]) = \text{false}$ since (t_3, t_6) is a counterexample to $C \to A$. Therefore, the transitivity of ϕ_A implies either $\phi_A(t_3[A], t_4[A]) = \text{false}$ or $\phi_A(t_4[A], t_6[A]) = \text{false}$. Hence, at least one of (t_3, t_4) and (t_4, t_6) must be a counterexample to $C \to A$ too. In the example, this is (t_3, t_4).

Fig. 3. The conflict-graph $\mathsf{CG}_\Phi(r, C \to A)$ of Example 3.

Nevertheless, if transitivity constrains the complexity of the graph, dropping symmetry still allows new kinds of graph structures. Indeed, in the presence of symmetry, a conflict-graph cannot contain induced paths with more than 3 elements because of transitivity. However, such paths may exist when symmetry is removed.

Example 4. In the previous example, the tuples t_2, t_4, t_5, t_6 form an induced P_4 of the underlying undirected graph of $\mathsf{CG}_\Phi(r, C \to A)$, even though ϕ_A and ϕ_C enjoy transitivity.

Therefore, we are left with the following intriguing question: can the loss of symmetry be used to break transitivity, and offer conflict-graphs a structure sufficiently complex to make EVPP intractable? The next theorem answers this question affirmatively.

Theorem 3. *The problem* EVPP *is* **NP***-complete even when the predicates used on each attribute are transitive (**tra**), reflexive (**ref**), and antisymmetric (**asym**).*

The proof is omitted due to space limitations. It is given in [33]. It is a reduction from MIS in 2-subdivision graphs [29].

Theorem 1, Theorem 2 and Theorem 3 characterize the complexity of EVPP for each combination of predicates properties. In the next section, we discuss the granularity of these, and we use them as a framework to compare the complexity of EVPP for some known extensions of functional dependencies.

6   Discussions

Replacing equality with various predicates to extend the semantics of classical functional dependencies is frequent [6,32]. Our approach offers to compare these extensions on EVPP within a unifying framework based on the properties of the predicates they use. We can summarize our results with the hierarchy of classes of predicates given in Fig. 4.

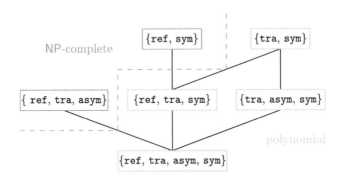

Fig. 4. Complexity of EVPP with respect to the properties of predicates.

Regarding the computation of the g_3-error, most existing works have focused on similarity/distance predicates. First, the g_3-error can be computed in polynomial time for classical functional dependencies [20]. Then, Song et al. [31] show that EVPP is **NP**-complete for a broad range of extensions of FDs which happen to be reflexive (ref) and symmetric (sym) predicates, which coincides with Theorem 2. However, they do not study predicate properties as we do in this paper. More precisely, they identify the hardness of EVPP for differential [30], matching [11], metric [23], neighborhood [1], and comparable dependencies [31]. For some of these dependencies, predicates may be defined over sets of attributes. Using one predicate per attribute and taking their conjunction is a particular case of predicate on attribute sets.

Some extensions of FDs use partial orders as predicates. This is the case of ordered dependencies [10,15], ordered FDs [27], and also of some sequential dependencies [16] and denial constraints [4] for instance. To our knowledge, the role of symmetry in EVPP has received little attention. For sequential dependencies [16], a measure different than the g_3-error have been used. The predicates of Theorem 3 are reflexive, transitive and antisymmetric. Hence they are partial orders. Consequently, the FDs in this context are *ordered functional dependencies* as defined by Ng [27]. We obtain the following corollary:

Corollary 1. EVPP *is* **NP**-*complete for ordered functional dependencies.*

Ordered functional dependencies are a restricted case of ordered dependencies [15], sequential dependencies [16], and denial constraints [4] (see [32]). The hardness of computing the g_3-error for these dependencies follows from Corollary 1.

The hierarchy depicts quite accurately the current knowledge about EVPP and the delimitation between tractable and intractable cases. However, this analysis may require further refinements. Indeed, there may be particular types of FDs with predicates where EVPP is tractable in polynomial time, even though their predicates belong to a class for which the problem is **NP**-complete. For instance, assume that each attribute A in R is equipped with a *total* order ϕ_A. We show in Proposition 1 and Corollary 2 that in this case, EVPP can be solved in polynomial time, even though the predicates are reflexive, transitive and antisymmetric.

Proposition 1. *Let (R, Φ) be a relation scheme with predicates. Then, EVPP can be solved in polynomial time for a given FD $X \to A$ if ϕ_B is transitive for each $B \in X$ and ϕ_A is a total order.*

Proof. Let (R, Φ) be a relation scheme with predicates and $X \to A$ a functional dependency. Assume that ϕ_B is transitive for each $B \in X$ and that ϕ_A is a total order. Let r be a relation over (R, Φ). Let $G = (r, E)$ be the undirected graph underlying $\mathsf{CG}_\Phi(r, X \to A)$, that is, $(t_i, t_j) \in E$ if and only if (t_i, t_j) or (t_j, t_i) is an edge of $\mathsf{CG}_\Phi(r, X \to A)$.

We show that G is a comparability graph. To do so, we associate the following predicate $\leq$ to $\mathsf{CG}_\Phi(r, X \to A)$: for each pair t_i, t_j of tuples of r, $t_i \leq t_i$ and $t_i \leq t_j$ if (t_i, t_j) is a counterexample to $X \to A$. We show that $\leq$ is a partial order:

- *reflexivity.* It follows by definition.
- *antisymmetry.* We use contrapositive. Let t_i, t_j be two distinct tuples of r and assume that (t_i, t_j) belongs to $\mathsf{CG}_\Phi(r, X \to A)$. We need to prove that (t_j, t_i) does not belong to $\mathsf{CG}_\Phi(r, X \to A)$, *i.e.* it is not a counterexample to $X \to A$. First, $(t_i, t_j) \in \mathsf{CG}_\Phi(r, X \to A)$ implies that $\phi_A(t_i[A], t_j[A]) = \texttt{false}$. Then, since ϕ_A is a total order, $\phi_A(t_j[A], t_i[A]) = \texttt{true}$. Consequently, (t_j, t_i) cannot belong to $\mathsf{CG}_\Phi(r, X \to A)$ and $\leq$ is antisymmetric.
- *transitivity.* Let t_i, t_j, t_k be tuples of r such that (t_i, t_j) and (t_j, t_k) are in $\mathsf{CG}_\Phi(r, X \to A)$. Applying transitivity, we have that $\bigwedge_{B \in X} \phi_B(t_i[B], t_k[B]) = \texttt{true}$. We show that $\phi_A(t_i[A], t_k[A]) = \texttt{false}$. Since (t_i, t_j) is a counterexample to $X \to A$, we have $\phi_A(t_i[A], t_j[A]) = \texttt{false}$. As ϕ_A is a total order, we deduce that $\phi_A(t_j[A], t_i[A]) = \texttt{true}$. Similarly, we obtain $\phi_A(t_k[A], t_j[A]) = \texttt{true}$. As ϕ_A is transitive, we derive $\phi_A(t_k[A], t_i[A]) = \texttt{true}$. Now assume for contradiction that $\phi_A(t_i[A], t_k[A]) = \texttt{true}$. Since, $\phi_A(t_k[A], t_j[A]) = \texttt{true}$, we derive $\phi_A(t_i[A], t_j[A]) = \texttt{true}$ by transitivity of ϕ_A, a contradiction. Therefore, $\phi_A(t_i[A], t_k[A]) = \texttt{false}$. Using the fact that $\bigwedge_{B \in X} \phi_B(t_i[B], t_k[B]) = \texttt{true}$, we conclude that (t_i, t_k) is also a counterexample to $X \to A$. The transitivity of $\leq$ follows.   □

Consequently, $\leq$ is a partial order and G is indeed a comparability graph. Since MIS can be solved in polynomial time for comparability graphs [18], the result follows.

We can deduce the following corollary on total orders, that can be used for ordered dependencies.

Corollary 2. *Let (R, Φ) be a relation scheme with predicates. Then,* EVPP *can be solved in polymomial time if each predicate in Φ is a total order.*

In particular, Golab et al. [16] proposed a polynomial-time algorithm for a variant of g_3 applied to a restricted type of sequential dependencies using total orders on each attribute.

7   Conclusion and Future Work

In this work, we have studied the complexity of computing the g_3-error when equality is replaced by more general predicates. We studied four common properties of binary predicates: reflexivity, symmetry, transitivity, and antisymmetry. We have shown that when symmetry and transitivity are taken together, the g_3-error can be computed in polynomial time. Transitivity strongly impacts the structure of the conflict-graph of the counterexamples to a functional dependency in a relation. Thus, it comes as no surprise that dropping transitivity makes the g_3-error hard to compute. More surprisingly, removing symmetry instead of transitivity leads to the same conclusion. This is because deleting symmetry makes the conflict-graph directed. In this case, the orientation of the edges weakens the impact of transitivity, thus allowing the conflict-graph to be complex enough to make the g_3-error computation problem intractable.

We believe our approach sheds new light on the problem of computing the g_3-error, and that it is suitable for estimating the complexity of this problem when defining new types of FDs, by looking at the properties of predicates used to compare values.

We highlight now some research directions for future works. In a recent paper [25], Livshits et al. study the problem of computing optimal repairs in a relation with respect to a set of functional dependencies. A repair is a collection of tuples which does not violate a prescribed set of FDs. It is optimal if it is of maximal size among all possible repairs. Henceforth, there is a strong connection between the problem of computing repairs and computing the g_3-error with respect to a collection of FDs. In their work, the authors give a dichotomy between tractable and intractable cases based on the structure of FDs. In particular, they use previous results from Gribkoff et al. [19] to show that the problem is already **NP**-complete for 2 FDs in general. In the case where computing an optimal repair can be done in polynomial time, it would be interesting to use our approach and relax equality with predicates in order to study the tractability of computing the g_3-error on a collection of FDs with relaxed equality.

From a practical point of view, the exact computation of the g_3-error is extremely expensive in large datasets. Recent works [7,12] have proposed to use approximation algorithms to compute the g_3-error both for equality and predicates. It could be of interest to identify properties or classes of predicates where more efficient algorithms can be adopted. It is also possible to extend the existing algorithms calculating the classical g_3-error (see *e.g.* [21]). They use the projection to identify equivalence classes among values of A and X. However, when dropping transitivity (for instance in similarity predicates), separating the values of a relation into *"similar classes"* requires to devise a new projection operation, a seemingly tough but fascinating problem to investigate.

Acknowledgment. we thank the reviewers for their constructive feedback and the Datavalor initiative of Insavalor (subsidiary of INSA Lyon) for funding part of this work.

References

1. Bassée, R., Wijsen, J.: Neighborhood dependencies for prediction. In: Cheung, D., Williams, G.J., Li, Q. (eds.) PAKDD 2001. LNCS (LNAI), vol. 2035, pp. 562–567. Springer, Heidelberg (2001). https://doi.org/10.1007/3-540-45357-1_59
2. Berge, C.: Graphs and Hypergraphs. North-Holland Pub. Co., Amsterdam (1973)
3. Bertossi, L.: Database repairing and consistent query answering. Synth. Lect. Data Manag. **3**(5), 1–121 (2011)
4. Bertossi, L., Bravo, L., Franconi, E., Lopatenko, A.: Complexity and approximation of fixing numerical attributes in databases under integrity constraints. In: Bierman, G., Koch, C. (eds.) DBPL 2005. LNCS, vol. 3774, pp. 262–278. Springer, Heidelberg (2005). https://doi.org/10.1007/11601524_17
5. Bohannon, P., Fan, W., Geerts, F., Jia, X., Kementsietsidis, A.: Conditional functional dependencies for data cleaning. In: 2007 IEEE 23rd International Conference on Data Engineering, pp. 746–755. IEEE (2007)
6. Caruccio, L., Deufemia, V., Polese, G.: Relaxed functional dependencies-a survey of approaches. IEEE Trans. Knowl. Data Eng. **28**(1), 147–165 (2015)
7. Caruccio, L., Deufemia, V., Polese, G.: On the discovery of relaxed functional dependencies. In: Proceedings of the 20th International Database Engineering & Applications Symposium, pp. 53–61 (2016)
8. Cormode, G., Golab, L., Flip, K., McGregor, A., Srivastava, D., Zhang, X.: Estimating the confidence of conditional functional dependencies. In: Proceedings of the 2009 ACM SIGMOD International Conference on Management of Data, SIGMOD 2009, pp. 469–482. Association for Computing Machinery, New York (2009). https://doi.org/10.1145/1559845.1559895
9. Davey, B.A., Priestley, H.A.: Introduction to Lattices and Order. Cambridge University Press, Cambridge (2002)
10. Dong, J., Hull, R.: Applying approximate order dependency to reduce indexing space. In: Proceedings of the 1982 ACM SIGMOD International Conference on Management of Data, pp. 119–127 (1982)
11. Fan, W.: Dependencies revisited for improving data quality. In: Proceedings of the Twenty-Seventh ACM SIGMOD-SIGACT-SIGART Symposium on Principles of Database Systems, pp. 159–170 (2008)
12. Faure-Giovagnoli, P., Petit, J.M., Scuturici, V.M.: Assessing the existence of a function in a dataset with the g3 indicator. In: IEEE International Conference on Data Engineering (2022)
13. Garey, M.R., Johnson, D.S.: Computers and Intractability, vol. 174. Freeman, San Francisco (1979)

14. Giakoumakis, V., Roussel, F., Thuillier, H.: On p_4-tidy graphs. Disc. Math. Theor. Comput. Sci. **1**, 17–41 (1997)
15. Ginsburg, S., Hull, R.: Order dependency in the relational model. Theor. Comput. Sci. **26**(1–2), 149–195 (1983)
16. Golab, L., Karloff, H., Korn, F., Saha, A., Srivastava, D.: Sequential dependencies. Proc. VLDB Endow. **2**(1), 574–585 (2009)
17. Golab, L., Karloff, H., Korn, F., Srivastava, D., Yu, B.: On generating near-optimal tableaux for conditional functional dependencies. Proc. VLDB Endow. **1**(1), 376–390 (2008)
18. Golumbic, M.C.: Algorithmic Graph Theory and Perfect Graphs. Elsevier, Amsterdam (2004)
19. Gribkoff, E., Van den Broeck, G., Suciu, D.: The most probable database problem. In: Proceedings of the First International Workshop on Big Uncertain Data (BUDA), pp. 1–7 (2014)
20. Huhtala, Y., Karkkainen, J., Porkka, P., Toivonen, H.: Efficient discovery of functional and approximate dependencies using partitions. In: Proceedings 14th International Conference on Data Engineering, pp. 392–401. IEEE (1998)
21. Huhtala, Y., Kärkkäinen, J., Porkka, P., Toivonen, H.: Tane: an efficient algorithm for discovering functional and approximate dependencies. Comput. J. **42**(2), 100–111 (1999)
22. Kivinen, J., Mannila, H.: Approximate inference of functional dependencies from relations. Theor. Comput. Sci. **149**(1), 129–149 (1995)
23. Koudas, N., Saha, A., Srivastava, D., Venkatasubramanian, S.: Metric functional dependencies. In: 2009 IEEE 25th International Conference on Data Engineering, pp. 1275–1278. IEEE (2009)
24. Levene, M., Loizou, G.: A Guided Tour of Relational Databases and Beyond. Springer, Heidelberg (2012). https://doi.org/10.1007/978-0-85729-349-7
25. Livshits, E., Kimelfeld, B., Roy, S.: Computing optimal repairs for functional dependencies. ACM Trans. Datab. Syst. (TODS) **45**(1), 1–46 (2020)
26. Mannila, H., Räihä, K.J.: The Design of Relational Databases. Addison-Wesley Longman Publishing Co., Inc., Boston (1992)
27. Ng, W.: An extension of the relational data model to incorporate ordered domains. ACM Trans. Datab. Syst. (TODS) **26**(3), 344–383 (2001)
28. Novelli, N., Cicchetti, R.: Functional and embedded dependency inference: a data mining point of view. Inf. Syst. **26**(7), 477–506 (2001)
29. Poljak, S.: A note on stable sets and colorings of graphs. Commentationes Mathematicae Universitatis Carolinae **15**(2), 307–309 (1974)
30. Song, S.: Data dependencies in the presence of difference. Ph.D. thesis, Hong Kong University of Science and Technology (2010)
31. Song, S., Chen, L., Philip, S.Y.: Comparable dependencies over heterogeneous data. VLDB J. **22**(2), 253–274 (2013)
32. Song, S., Gao, F., Huang, R., Wang, C.: Data dependencies extended for variety and veracity: a family tree. IEEE Trans. Knowl. Data Eng. **34**, 4717–4736 (2020). https://doi.org/10.1109/TKDE.2020.3046443
33. Vilmin, S., Faure-Giovagnoli, P., Petit, J.M., Scuturici, V.M.: Functional dependencies with predicates: what makes the g_3-error easy to compute? arXiv preprint arXiv:2306.09006 (2023)

Formal Concept Analysis: Theoretical Advances

Squared Symmetric Formal Contexts and Their Connections with Correlation Matrices

Ľubomír Antoni[1(✉)] , Peter Eliaš[2] , Tomáš Horváth[1,3] ,
Stanislav Krajči[1] , Ondrej Krídlo[1] , and Csaba Török[1]

[1] Pavol Jozef Šafárik University in Košice, Faculty of Science, Institute of Computer Science, 040 01 Košice, Slovakia
{lubomir.antoni,tomas.horvath,stanislav.krajci,ondrej.kridlo,
csaba.torok}@upjs.sk

[2] Mathematical Institute, Slovak Academy of Sciences, Grešákova 6, 040 01 Košice, Slovak Republic
elias@saske.sk

[3] Faculty of Informatics, Department of Data Science and Engineering, ELTE Eötvös Loránd University, Budapest 1053, Hungary

Abstract. Formal Concept Analysis identifies hidden patterns in data that can be presented to the user or the data analyst. We propose a method for analyzing the correlation matrices based on Formal concept analysis. In particular, we define a notion of squared symmetric formal context and prove its properties. Transforming a correlation matrix into a squared symmetric formal context is feasible with the help of fuzzy logic. Thus, the concept hierarchies of squared symmetric formal contexts can be thoroughly investigated and visualized. Moreover, information hidden in such type of data can help to find some interrelations between attributes and can help to solve pending issues within enterprise or science. To illustrate our approach, we include our novel results by analyzing a correlation matrix with 36 variables computed from a real dataset.

Keywords: Formal Concept Analysis · correlation matrix · fuzzy logic

1 Introduction

The selection of appropriate data structures and mappings represents the important challenges researchers face in data analysis and machine learning. The various attempts to interpret the results of lattice theory have led to a data analysis method based on binary relations, so-called formal contexts, between sets of objects and attributes [1,2]. Since concept hierarchies play an important role here, the term Formal Concept Analysis (FCA) has been adopted for this reasoning. Briefly, FCA scrutinizes an object-attribute block of relational data. The mathematical foundations of FCA were built in [3].

Conceptual scaling [3] and pattern structures [4] offer the possibility to process many-valued formal contexts. In this direction, the researchers advocate for truth degrees from fuzzy logic in an effort to promote the representation and

© The Author(s), under exclusive license to Springer Nature Switzerland AG 2023
M. Ojeda-Aciego et al. (Eds.): ICCS 2023, LNAI 14133, pp. 19–27, 2023.
https://doi.org/10.1007/978-3-031-40960-8_2

interpretation of data in a many-valued form. An extensive overview of the various application domains, including software mining, web analytics, medicine, biology, and chemistry data, is given by [5] and [6]. L-fuzzy approaches and their one-sided versions were proposed independently in [7–14]. Recently, feasible attempts and generalizations were investigated in [15–30].

An interesting application area in which FCA could be used is correlation analysis. Data scientists often face the problem of selecting data attributes (variables) for further analysis based on their mutual correlation represented in a correlation matrix having some unique characteristics, according to which we will introduce particular symmetric formal contexts in this paper.

In this paper, we present a bridge between correlation matrices and symmetric formal contexts. To illustrate our novel approach to using FCA in correlation analysis, we present the results on a correlation matrix with 36 variables from real data of a health insurance company. We recall the preliminaries in Sect. 2. We propose a definition of squared symmetric formal contexts and study their properties with respect to the correlation matrices in Sect. 3. Finally, Sect. 4 provides the results of the case study of real data analysis from a health insurance company.

2   Formal Context and its Fuzzy Version

A formal context, illustrated in Fig. 1, can be imagined as a cross table, mostly rectangular, in which the rows represent objects and the columns their binary attributes [3,31].

R	a_1	a_2	a_3
b_1	×		
b_2	×	×	×
b_3		×	
b_4	×	×	

Fig. 1. Example of a formal context

Definition 1. *Let B and A be the nonempty sets and let $R \subseteq B \times A$ be a relation between B and A. A triple $\langle B, A, R \rangle$ is called a (crisp) formal context, the elements of set B are called objects, the elements of set A are called attributes and the relation R is called incidence relation.*

Definition 2. *Let $\langle B, A, R \rangle$ be a formal context. Let X and Y be the subsets of B and A, respectively (i. e. $X \in \mathcal{P}(B)$, $Y \in \mathcal{P}(A)$). Then the maps $g : \mathcal{P}(B) \to \mathcal{P}(A)$ and $f : \mathcal{P}(A) \to \mathcal{P}(B)$ defined by*

$$g(X) = \{y \in A : (\forall x \in X)\langle x, y \rangle \in R\}$$

and

$$f(Y) = \{x \in B : (\forall y \in Y)\langle x, y \rangle \in R\}$$

are called concept-forming operators of a given formal context. A pair $\langle X, Y \rangle$ such that $g(X) = Y$ and $f(Y) = X$ is called a formal concept of a given formal context. The set X is called extent of a formal concept and the set Y is called intent of a formal concept.

The set of all formal concepts of a formal context $\langle B, A, R \rangle$ can be ordered by a partial order in which $\langle X_1, Y_1 \rangle \preceq \langle X_2, Y_2 \rangle$ if and only if $X_1 \subseteq X_2$. This produces the hierarchy of formal concepts. A formal concept can be seen as a closed rectangle that is full of crosses (with respect to a permutation of rows and columns) as illustrated in Fig. 2.

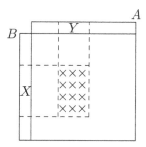

Fig. 2. Scheme of a formal concept after a permutation of rows and columns

People communicate facts about the world not only in bivalent statements. The validity of such statements is a matter of degree, rather than being only true or false. Fuzzy logic and fuzzy set theory are frameworks that extend FCA in various independent ways. Here, we recall the basic definition of fuzzy formal context [15,31].

Definition 3. *Consider two nonempty sets B a A, a set of truth degrees T and a mapping R such that $R : B \times A \longrightarrow T$. Then the triple $\langle B, A, R \rangle$ is called a (T)-fuzzy formal context, the elements of the sets B and A are called objects and attributes, respectively. The mapping R is a fuzzy incidence relation.*

In the definition of (T)-fuzzy formal context, we often take the interval $T = [0, 1]$, because it is a frequent scale of truth degrees in many applications. For such replacement, the terminology of $[0, 1]$-fuzzy formal context has been adopted. In [32], the authors reflect the transformation of the original $[0, 1]$-fuzzy formal context to a sequence of classical formal contexts (from Definition 1) using binary relations called α-cuts for $\alpha \in [0, 1]$.

Definition 4. *Let $\langle B, A, R \rangle$ be a $[0, 1]$-fuzzy formal context and let $\alpha \in [0, 1]$. Then the binary relation $R_\alpha \subseteq B \times A$ is called upper α-cut if $\langle b, a \rangle \in R_\alpha$ is equivalent to $R(b, a) \geq \alpha$ (Fig. 3).*

R	a_1	a_2	a_3
b_1	1	0.9	0.8
b_2	0.8	0.1	0.7
b_3	0.3	0.3	0.3
b_4	0.2	0.5	0.9

$R_{0.5}$	a_1	a_2	a_3
b_1	×	×	×
b_2	×		×
b_3			
b_4		×	×

Fig. 3. Example of $[0,1]$-fuzzy formal context and its 0.5-cut

It can be seen that the triple $\langle B, A, R_\alpha \rangle$ for every $\alpha \in [0,1]$ forms the formal context given by Definition 1. For each formal context, one can build the set of its formal concepts as introduced in Definition 2.

3 Evaluation of Closed Rectangles in Squared Symmetric Contexts

Squared symmetric formal context and its properties are introduced in this section on which our approach to correlation matrix analysis is based.

Definition 5. *A (crisp) formal context $\langle B, A, R \rangle$ in which $|B| = |A|$ holds will be called squared formal context. Let $\langle B, A, R \rangle$ be a squared formal context such that $B = A$ and let $A = \{a_1, a_2, \ldots, a_n\}$. Then a formal context $\langle A, A, R \rangle$ in which $\langle a_i, a_j \rangle \in R$ iff $\langle a_j, a_i \rangle \in R$ for all $i \in \{1, \ldots, n\}$ and $j \in \{1, \ldots, n\}$ will be called a squared symmetric formal context.*

We will show that the symmetricity of a formal context is transferred into the components of all formal concepts. The following lemma shows that for each formal concept exists its symmetric counterpart.

Lemma 1. *Let $\langle A, A, R \rangle$ be a squared symmetric formal context. Then $\langle X, Y \rangle$ is a formal concept of $\langle A, A, R \rangle$ if and only if $\langle Y, X \rangle$ is a formal concept of $\langle A, A, R \rangle$.*

Proof. We need to prove that $g(X) = f(X)$ and $g(Y) = f(Y)$. Consider $A = \{a_1, a_2, \ldots, a_n\}$. We have:
$a_i \in g(X)$ iff $a_i \in \{y \in A : (\forall x \in X)\langle x, y \rangle \in R\}$
iff $a_i \in \{y \in A : (\forall x \in X)\langle y, x \rangle \in R\}$
iff $a_i \in f(X)$. Similarly one can prove that $g(Y) = f(Y)$. $\qquad \square$

From Lemma 1 we can see that it is sufficient to take only the formal concepts $\langle X, Y \rangle$ in which $|X| > |Y|$ or $X = Y$, because the others are uniquely determined. Moreover, we can use three measures for evaluating the resulting formal concepts:

– A precision is the ratio of the number of common attributes $|X \cap Y|$ in a formal concept to the total number of attributes $|Y|$ in its intent.

– A recall is the ratio of the number of common attributes $|X \cap Y|$ in a formal concept to the total number of attributes $|X|$ in its extent.
– The size of a formal concept will be measured as the number of all attributes $|Y \cup X|$ retrieved in a formal concept. If both precision and recall are equal to one, then $X = Y$.

3.1   Analysis of a Correlation Matrix Using FCA

A correlation matrix is used to investigate dependencies between variables in the data and contains the correlation coefficients between each pair of variables. The correlation matrix is always symmetric since the correlation between two variables is commutative. The following procedure can be applied if we do not distinguish between positive and negative correlation (usually, data analysts are interested in the magnitude of the correlation at first).

Let A be the set of variables and $\mathrm{cor}(a_i, a_j)$ be the correlation coefficients between a_i and a_j for all $a_i \in A$ and $a_j \in A$. Let M be a correlation matrix of type $A \times A$ with elements $m_{i,j} = \mathrm{cor}(a_i, a_j)$. It holds that $\mathrm{abs}(m_{i,j}) \in [0, 1]$ for each $a_i \in A$ and $a_j \in A$. Then $\langle A, A, R \rangle$ given by $R(a_i, a_j) = \mathrm{abs}(m_{i,j})$ is a $[0, 1]$-fuzzy formal context from Definition 3. From Definition 4 and from $\alpha \in [0, 1]$, we have that $R_\alpha \subseteq A \times A$ is the upper α-cut and it holds $\langle a_i, a_j \rangle \in R_\alpha$ if and only if $\mathrm{abs}(m_{i,j}) \geq \alpha$. Finally, from the symmetricity of M and from Definition 4 we have that $\langle A, A, R_\alpha \rangle$ is a squared symmetric formal context obtained from M. We summarize it in the following definition.

Definition 6. *Let A be the set of variables and let M be a correlation matrix of type $A \times A$. Let $\alpha \in [0, 1]$ a R_α be a binary relation such that $\langle a_i, a_j \rangle \in R_\alpha$ if and only if $\mathrm{abs}(m_{i,j}) \geq \alpha$ for all $a_i, a_j \in A$. Thus, a triple $\langle A, A, R_\alpha \rangle$ is called a squared symmetric formal context obtained from M.*

Definition 6 offers the possibility to investigate a correlation matrix M in terms of formal concepts and their evaluation in the following way:

1. Setting the value of α. We propose to compute the average value of M, i. e. $\alpha = \mathrm{mean}(M)$.
2. Construction of $\langle A, A, R_\alpha \rangle$ for $\alpha = \mathrm{mean}(M)$ by Definition 6.
3. Computation of the set of formal concepts of $\langle A, A, R_\alpha \rangle$.
4. Computation of precision, recall and size of each $\langle X, Y \rangle$.
5. Visualization of the most relevant attributes[1].

We note that we can replace the average value with the median in the first step, which is the standard procedure in the data analysis. In the second and third steps, we construct the binary formal context and its formal concepts. In the fourth step, we evaluate the selected measures of each formal concept. Finally, we can visualize the concept lattice with reduced labeling based on the attributes of the formal concept with the highest values of explored measures.

---

[1] Some fruitful ideas on how to find some interrelation between attributes are included in the following section. For visualization, we use the Concept Explorer tool in version 1.3 available at http://conexp.sourceforge.net. Nevertheless, there are other software tools, for instance FcaStone, Lattice Miner, ToscanaJ, FCART, as well.

4   Case Study

Our real data source is the health insurance company. The dataset includes healthcare records based on 36 variables including the insured people's demographic, medicine, and other cost attributes.

We constructed the correlation matrix M based on 36 variables $\{a_1, \ldots, a_{36}\}$ and Spearman correlation coefficients between each pair of these variables since the variables do not have the normal distribution. In summary, we omit 5 variables ($a_7, a_{14}, a_{15}, a_{33}, a_{35}$) from M, since they contain only one or two different values and thus their correlations are statistically not relevant.

Table 1. The formal concepts with precision and recall equal to one and the size at least 5

formal concept	size
$\langle\{a_1, a_5, a_{19}, a_{20}, a_{22}, a_{24}\}, \{a_1, a_5, a_{19}, a_{20}, a_{22}, a_{24}\}\rangle$	6
$\langle\{a_1, a_5, a_{22}, a_{23}, a_{24}\}, \{a_1, a_5, a_{22}, a_{23}, a_{24}\}\rangle$	5
$\langle\{a_{19}, a_{20}, a_{21}, a_{24}, a_{26}\}, \{a_{19}, a_{20}, a_{21}, a_{24}, a_{26}\}\rangle$	5
$\langle\{a_{21}, a_{25}, a_{27}, a_{28}, a_{36}\}, \{a_{21}, a_{25}, a_{27}, a_{28}, a_{36}\}\rangle$	5

For $\alpha = \text{mean}(M) = 0.08$, we obtained 91 formal concepts (the closed rectangles full of crosses) such that only 32 of them are in the form $|X| > |Y|$. The maximal size of a formal concept is maxsize $= 11$. The number of formal concepts with $X = Y$ is 27, i.e., both their precision and recall are equal to one (they represent the closed squares of crosses). Table 1 shows those of the 27 concepts whose size is at least $\lfloor\text{maxsize}/2\rfloor$, where $\lfloor\rfloor$ expresses the floor function.

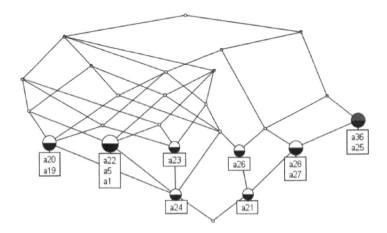

Fig. 4. The hierarchy of a set A^* of 13 selected attributes with respect to 0.08-cut

Now, we can take the union of all attributes which appear in Table 1. This set is denoted by $A^* \subseteq A$. We can reduce the formal context $\langle A, A, R_\alpha \rangle$ into $\langle A^*, A^*, R_\alpha^* \rangle$, whereby R_α^* is a sub-relation of R_α. Then we can visualize the hierarchy of attributes (as shown in Fig. 4) from which one can see that we have one triplet of attributes and the other three pairs of attributes which behave in a very similar way concerning the 0.08-cut on A^*. So there can be some interrelation between these attributes.

The second possibility is to take the formal concept with the maximal size from Table 1 (the maximal closed square of crosses). We denote its set of attributes by $A^\diamond \subseteq A$. We can visualize the hierarchy of the reduced context $\langle A^\diamond, A^\diamond, R_\beta \rangle$, where β is the average of the absolute correlation coefficients between the elements of $A^\diamond$. From Fig. 5 and $\beta = 0.39$ one can see that correlation coefficients of a_{24} is closely related with a_{19}, a_{20} and correlation coefficients of a_1 is closely related with a_5, a_{22}. It indicates that these attributes should be further analyzed based on the original data.

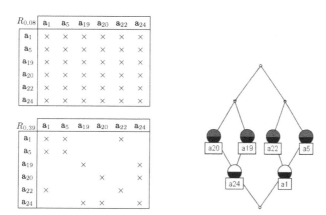

Fig. 5. The maximal closed square of crosses, its β-cut and the hierarchy of $A^\diamond$

5   Conclusion

We presented the possible application area of FCA for the analysis of correlation matrices. The proposed approach and the resulting visualizations allow the data analysts to gain deeper insight into the correlation matrix and to derive useful knowledge from the data. Such an approach is valuable when analyzing high-dimensional data such that the user can choose an appropriate level (α) of the significance of correlations which reduces the size of the resulting concept lattice to the most meaningful concepts.

In our future work, it seems interesting to explore the relationships between cliques in thresholding correlation graphs and such symmetric formal concepts here. These graphs are extensively used in recommender systems and machine learning [33]. Another interesting research direction would be to combine the proposed method of automatic completion of missing values in a non-complete correlation matrix.

Acknowledgment. This article was supported by the Scientific Grant Agency of the Ministry of Education, Science, Research and Sport of the Slovak Republic under contract VEGA 1/0645/22 (O. Krídlo, S. Krajči) entitled by Proposal of novel methods in the field of Formal concept analysis and their application. This work was supported by the Slovak Research and Development Agency under contract No. APVV-21-0468 (Ľ. Antoni). This article was partially supported by the project KEGA 012UPJŠ-4/2021 (Ľ. Antoni). P. Eliaš was supported by the Slovak Research and Development Agency under the contract no. APVV-20-0069, by the Scientific Grant Agency (VEGA) under grant no. VEGA 2/0097/20 and by the Operational Programme Integrated Infrastructure (OPII) for the project 313011BWH2: "InoCHF - Research and development in the field of innovative technologies in the management of patients with CHF", co-financed by the European Regional Development Fund.

References

1. Barbut, M., Monjardet, B.: Ordre et classification: algèbre et combinatoire. Hachette (1970)
2. Wille, R.: Restructuring lattice theory: an approach based on hierarchies of concepts. In: Ferré, S., Rudolph, S. (eds.) ICFCA 2009. LNCS (LNAI), vol. 5548, pp. 314–339. Springer, Heidelberg (2009). https://doi.org/10.1007/978-3-642-01815-2_23
3. Ganter, B., Wille, R.: Formal Concept Analysis, Mathematical Foundation. Springer, Heidelberg (1999). https://doi.org/10.1007/978-3-642-59830-2
4. Ganter, B., Kuznetsov, S.O.: Pattern structures and their projections. In: Delugach, H.S., Stumme, G. (eds.) ICCS-ConceptStruct 2001. LNCS (LNAI), vol. 2120, pp. 129–142. Springer, Heidelberg (2001). https://doi.org/10.1007/3-540-44583-8_10
5. Poelmans, J., Ignatov, D.I., Kuznetsov, S.O., Dedene, G.: Formal concept analysis in knowledge processing: a survey on applications. Expert Syst. Appl. **40**(16), 6538–6560 (2013)
6. Carpineto, C., Romano, G.: Concept Data Analysis: Theory and Applications. John Wiley, Hoboken (2004)
7. Burusco, A., Fuentes-González, R.: The study of L-fuzzy concept lattice. Mathw. Soft Comput. **3**, 209–218 (1994)
8. Bělohlávek, R.: Fuzzy concepts and conceptual structures: induced similarities. In: JCIS 1998 proceedings, International Conference on Computer Science and Informatics, pp. 179–182. Association for Intelligent Machinery (1998)
9. Bělohlávek, R.: Fuzzy Galois connections. Math. Log Q. **45**(4), 497–504 (1999)
10. Bělohlávek, R.: Concept lattices and order in fuzzy logic. Ann. Pure Appl. Logic **128**, 277–298 (2004)
11. Pollandt, S.: Datenanalyse mit Fuzzy-Begriffen. In: G. Stumme, R. Wille (eds.), Begriffliche Wissensverarbeitung. Methoden und Anwendungen, pp. 72–98. Springer, Heidelberg (2000). https://doi.org/10.1007/978-3-642-57217-3_4

12. Ben Yahia, S., Jaoua, A.: Discovering knowledge from fuzzy concept lattice. In: Kandel, A., Last, M., Bunke, H. (eds.) Data Mining and Computational Intelligence, pp. 169–190. Physica-Verlag (2001)

13. Bělohlávek, R., Sklenář, V., Zacpal, J.: Crisply generated fuzzy concepts. Lect. Notes Comput. Sci. **3403**, 268–283 (2005)

14. Krajči, S.: Cluster based efficient generation of fuzzy concepts. Neural Netw. World **13**, 521–530 (2003)

15. Bělohlávek, R.: Concept lattices and order in fuzzy logic. Ann. Pure Appl. Log. **128**(1–3), 277–298 (2004)

16. Medina, J., Ojeda-Aciego, M.: Dual multi-adjoint concept lattices. Inf. Sci. **225**, 47–54 (2013)

17. Antoni, L'., Krajči, S., Krídlo, O., Macek, B., Pisková, L.: On heterogeneous formal contexts. Fuzzy Sets Syst. **234**, 22–33 (2014)

18. Butka, P., Pócs, J., Pócsová, J.: Representation of fuzzy concept lattices in the framework of classical FCA. J. Appl. Math., Article ID 236725, 7 (2013)

19. Medina, J., Ojeda-Aciego, M., Valverde, A., Vojtáš, P.: Towards biresiduated multi-adjoint logic programming. Lect. Notes Artif. Intell. **3040**, 608–617 (2004)

20. Medina, J., Ojeda-Aciego, M., Vojtáš, P.: Multi-adjoint logic programming with continuous semantics. Lect. Notes Artif. Intell. **2173**, 351–364 (2001)

21. Medina, J., Ojeda-Aciego, M., Vojtáš, P.: Similarity-based unification: a multi-adjoint approach. Fuzzy Sets Syst. **146**, 43–62 (2004)

22. Cornejo, M.E., Medina, J., Ramírez, E.: A comparative study of adjoint triples. Fuzzy Sets Syst. **211**, 1–14 (2013)

23. Cornejo, M.E., Medina, J., Ramírez, E.: Characterizing reducts in multi-adjoint concept lattices. Inf. Sci. **422**, 364–376 (2018)

24. Madrid, N., Ojeda-Aciego, M.: Multi-adjoint lattices from adjoint triples with involutive negation. Fuzzy Sets Syst. **405**, 88–105 (2021)

25. Medina, J., Ojeda-Aciego, M.: Multi-adjoint t-concept lattices. Inf. Sci. **180**, 712–725 (2010)

26. Medina, J., Ojeda-Aciego, M.: On multi-adjoint concept lattices based on heterogeneous conjunctors. Fuzzy Sets Syst. **208**, 95–110 (2012)

27. Medina, J., Ojeda-Aciego, M., Ruiz-Calviño, J.: Formal concept analysis via multi-adjoint concept lattices. Fuzzy Sets Syst. **160**, 130–144 (2009)

28. Medina, J., Ojeda-Aciego, M., Pócs, J., Ramírez-Poussa, E.: On the Dedekind-MacNeille completion and formal concept analysis based on multilattices. Fuzzy Sets Syst. **303**, 1–20 (2016)

29. Krajči, S.: A generalized concept lattice. Logic J. IGPL **13**, 543–550 (2005)

30. Krídlo, O., Krajči, S., Antoni, L'.: Formal concept analysis of higher order. Int. J. Gen. Syst. **45**(2), 116–134 (2016)

31. Bělohlávek, R., Klir, G.J.: Concepts and Fuzzy Logic. MIT Press, Cambridge (2011)

32. Snášel, V., Duráková, D., Krajči, S., Vojtáš, P.: Merging concept lattices of α-cuts of fuzzy contexts. Contrib. Gener. Algebra **14**, 155–166 (2004D

33. Veldt, N., Wirth, A., Gleich, D. F.: Parameterized correlation clustering in hypergraphs and bipartite graphs. In: KDD 2020: Proceedings of the 26th ACM SIGKDD International Conference on Knowledge Discovery & Data Mining, pp. 1868–1876. Association for Computing Machinery, New York (2020)

Aggregation Functions and Extent Structure Preservation in Formal Concept Analysis

Carlos Bejines⑩, Domingo López-Rodríguez⑩,
and Manuel Ojeda-Hernández⁽⊠⁾ ⑩

Universidad de Málaga, Andalucía Tech, Málaga, Spain
manuojeda@uma.es

Abstract. Formal Concept Analysis (FCA) is a mathematical framework for analysing data tables that capture the relationship between objects and attributes. The concept lattice derived from such a table is a representation of the implicit knowledge about this relationship, where each concept corresponds to a bicluster of objects and attributes. FCA has been widely used for knowledge acquisition and representation, conceptual data analysis, information retrieval and other applications. In this paper, we use an extension of the classical FCA to deal with fuzzy formal contexts, where the relationship between objects and attributes is modelled by truth values indicating the degree to which an object possesses a property or attribute. Fuzzy Formal Concept Analysis (FFCA) allows us to capture vague or imprecise information and handle uncertainty or ambiguity in data analysis. Our purpose is to use aggregation functions in order to manipulate and explore fuzzy formal concepts in different ways depending on the desired properties or criteria. In this work, we will focus on the structure of the extents of the concept lattice. We define the aggregation of fuzzy extents point-wise and study how it affects its structure. We characterise the aggregation functions that preserve the fuzzy extent structure and show that they depend on the number of objects in the context. Our results contribute to a better understanding of how aggregation functions can be used to manipulate and explore fuzzy formal concepts.

Keywords: Aggregation Function · Formal Concept Analysis · Fuzzy Sets

1 Introduction

Aggregation functions have become a significant area of research in Fuzzy Set Theory and its applications. The need to combine information, typically expressed as numerical values, into a single output for decision-making has generated interest in studying functions that enable such aggregation. Aggregation functions are now widely discussed in various conferences, and a biennial

M. Ojeda-Aciego et al. (Eds.): ICCS 2023, LNAI 14133, pp. 28–35, 2023.
https://doi.org/10.1007/978-3-031-40960-8_3

congress, AGOP, is devoted to them. For further information on this topic, refer to [3,5].

Recently, there has been a considerable focus on developing a framework that concentrates on preserving the properties of fuzzy algebraic structures under aggregation functions. This framework is actively being developed and discussed, and more details can be found in [2,7,10,11].

There are some approaches to FCA that use aggregation functions but they are used in the classical setting, that is, they consider different measures on the concept lattice and aggregate these measures to a single number by using the operator [9,12]. In our approach, we focus on the concept lattice. In particular, the infimum and the supremum of the concept lattice are defined in terms of suprema and the infima of the powerset lattice [4,6]. The key point is that the supremum and the infimum are aggregation operators, and the question is whether changing these operations by another pair of aggregation operators defines a new concept lattice. Directly from the classical theory of FCA we know that we cannot interchange suprema with infima, therefore this claim will not be satisfied by some aggregation operators.

Another implication of this study would be in the study of algorithms for the computation of the concept lattice. Some of the most well-known algorithms, such as FastCbO [8] or InClose [1], use the intersection of extents to recursively find all the extents corresponding to a formal context. Since the fuzzy intersection operation is, as we will show later, a particular case of aggregation of fuzzy sets, we can expect that other aggregation functions (that preserve the extent structure) may help in accelerating the process by incorporating them into these algorithms.

The main section of this paper shows some of the properties that an aggregation operator must satisfy to be an internal operation in the set of extents, intents or formal concepts. Surprisingly, there are not many aggregation operators that preserve extents or intents. Even though this is only the first step in this line, experimentation hints that only the infimum and the projections on the components preserve these sets. In these preliminary steps, we will consider aggregation functions on the unit interval $[0,1]$ and the Gödel t-norm, which is exactly the infimum.

The remainder of this work is structured as follows: in Sect. 2, we present the preliminary ideas about aggregation functions and fuzzy FCA that will help in the understanding of the results, that will be detailed in Sect. 3. Finally, in Sect. 4, the final conclusions and future research lines are commented.

2   Preliminaries

In this section, we outline some of the concepts which will be necessary to follow the paper. This work is set in the fuzzy framework so some concepts on fuzzy structures and methods are presented.

A complete residuated lattice $\mathbb{L} = (L, \wedge, \vee, \otimes, \rightarrow, 0, 1)$ is a structure such that $(L, \wedge, \vee, 0, 1)$ is a complete lattice where 0 is the bottom element and 1 is the top one, $(L, \otimes, 1)$ is a commutative monoid, that is, $\otimes$ is an associative and commutative binary operation and 1 is the identity element; and $(\otimes, \rightarrow)$ is an adjoint pair, that is

$$x \otimes y \leq z \text{ if and only if } y \leq x \rightarrow z.$$

In this particular paper, the role of $\mathbb{L}$ will be played by the unit interval $[0, 1]$.

One of the main concepts used in this work is that of aggregation function. Here is a short description of what they are and their most important types.

Definition 1. *([5]) Let $A : [0, 1]^n \longrightarrow [0, 1]$ be a function. We say that A is an aggregation function if:*

(A1) $A(0, ..., 0) = 0$ and $A(1, ..., 1) = 1$.   *(Boundary conditions)*
(A2) $A(x_1, ..., x_n) \leq A(y_1, ..., y_n)$ whenever $x_i \leq y_i$ for each $1 \leq i \leq n$. *(Monotonicity)*

Definition 2. *Given an arbitrary set S, an aggregation function $A : [0, 1] \times [0, 1] \longrightarrow [0, 1]$ and two fuzzy subsets $X, Y : S \longrightarrow [0, 1]$, the fuzzy set $A(X, Y) : S \longrightarrow [0, 1]$ defined point-wise by*

$$A(X, Y)(t) := A(X(t), Y(t))$$

is the aggregation of X and Y using A.

We give now some brief preliminaries on Fuzzy FCA. A fuzzy formal context is a tuple $\mathbb{K} = (G, M, I)$ where G and M are the sets of objects and attributes, respectively and $I : G \times M \rightarrow [0, 1]$ is a fuzzy relation. The degree $I(g, m)$ is understood as the degree to which the object g has the attribute m. The concept-forming operators $\uparrow$ and $\downarrow$ are defined as follows, for a pair of fuzzy sets $X \in [0, 1]^G, Y \in [0, 1]^M$,

$$X^{\uparrow}(m) = \bigwedge_{g \in G} (X(g) \rightarrow I(g, m)) \qquad Y^{\downarrow}(g) = \bigwedge_{m \in M} (Y(m) \rightarrow I(g, m))$$

As in the classical case, a fuzzy formal concept is a pair $\langle X, Y \rangle \in [0, 1]^G \times [0, 1]^M$ such that $X^{\uparrow} = Y$ and $Y^{\downarrow} = X$. The set of fuzzy formal concepts, denoted by $\mathbb{B}(\mathbb{K})$ is a complete lattice with the following infima and suprema, let $\{\langle X_i, Y_i \rangle\}_{i \in I} \subseteq \mathbb{B}(\mathbb{K})$, then

$$\bigwedge \{\langle X_i, Y_i \rangle\}_{i \in I} = \left\langle \bigcap_{i \in I} X_i, \left(\bigcup_{i \in I} Y_i \right)^{\downarrow \uparrow} \right\rangle,$$

$$\bigvee \{\langle X_i, Y_i \rangle\}_{i \in I} = \left\langle \left(\bigcup_{i \in I} X_i \right)^{\uparrow \downarrow}, \bigcap_{i \in I} Y_i \right\rangle.$$

This hints at the preliminary idea of this work, the infimum operator is an aggregation function and the supremum operator is known as its dual aggregation function. Thus we wonder, assuming A is an aggregation function with dual A^*: can we ensure $\langle A(X_i), A^*(Y_i)^{\downarrow \uparrow} \rangle$ is a formal concept?

Table 1. A formal context (left) and an aggregation function (right) described as a table on the chain $\{0, 0.25, 0.5, 0.75, 1\}$.

$\mathbb{K}$	m_1	m_2	m_3
g_1	0.25	0.5	0
g_2	0.75	0.25	0
g_3	0	1	0.75

Formal context

A	0	0.25	0.5	0.75	1
0	0	0	0	0	0.5
0.25	0	0	0.25	0.5	1
0.5	0	0.5	1	1	1
0.75	0	0.75	1	1	1
1	0.5	1	1	1	1

Aggregation function

Example 1. Let L be the unit interval $[0, 1]$ and let us consider the formal context $\mathbb{K}$ and an aggregation function A whose restriction to $\{0, 0.25, 0.5, 0.75, 1\}$ are shown in Table 1. The formal concepts of the context above are the following.

$$\langle \{g_1, g_2, g_3\}, \qquad \{^{0.25}/m_2\} \rangle \qquad (1)$$
$$\langle \{g_1, {}^{0.25}/g_2, g_3\}, \qquad \{^{0.5}/m_2\} \rangle \qquad (2)$$
$$\langle \{^{0.5}/g_1, {}^{0.25}/g_2, g_3\}, \qquad \{m_2\} \rangle\rangle \qquad (3)$$
$$\langle \{g_3\}, \qquad \{m_2, {}^{0.75}/m_3\} \rangle \qquad (4)$$
$$\langle \{^{0.75}/g_3\}, \qquad \{m_2, m_3\} \rangle \qquad (5)$$
$$\langle \{g_1, g_2\}, \qquad \{^{0.25}/m_1, {}^{0.25}/m_2\} \rangle \qquad (6)$$
$$\langle \{g_1, {}^{0.25}/g_2\}, \qquad \{^{0.25}/m_1, {}^{0.5}/m_2\} \rangle \qquad (7)$$
$$\langle \{^{0.5}/g_1, {}^{0.25}/g_2\}, \qquad \{^{0.25}/m_1, m_2\} \rangle \qquad (8)$$
$$\langle \{^{0.25}/g_1, g_2\}, \qquad \{^{0.75}/m_1, {}^{0.25}/m_2\} \rangle \qquad (9)$$
$$\langle \{^{0.25}/g_1, {}^{0.75}/g_2\}, \qquad \{m_1, {}^{0.25}/m_2\} \rangle \qquad (10)$$
$$\langle \{^{0.25}/g_1, {}^{0.25}/g_2\}, \qquad \{m_1, m_2\} \rangle \qquad (11)$$
$$\langle \varnothing, \qquad \{m_1, m_2, m_3\} \rangle \qquad (12)$$

Consider for example concepts (7) and (8) above and the aggregation function A.

$$C_7 = \langle \{g_1, {}^{0.25}/g_2\}, \{^{0.25}/m_1, {}^{0.5}/m_2\} \rangle,$$
$$C_8 = \langle \{^{0.5}/g_1, {}^{0.25}/g_2\}, \{^{0.25}/m_1, m_2\} \rangle.$$

We show the aggregation of the two previous extents using A, according to Definition 2:

$$A\left(\{g_1, {}^{0.25}/g_2\}, \{^{0.5}/g_1, {}^{0.25}/g_2\}\right) = \left\{^{A(1,0.5)}/g_1, {}^{A(0.25,0.25)}/g_2\right\} =$$
$$= \{^1/g_1, {}^0/g_2\} = \{g_1\}.$$

An analogous procedure can be performed to aggregate the two intents. We should remember that we can only aggregate fuzzy sets over the same universe. Therefore, in general, we cannot aggregate extents and intents together.

As an extreme case, we can consider the top $\top$ and the bottom $\bot$ of the concept lattice:

$$\top = \left\langle \{g_1, g_2, g_3\}, \left\{ {}^{0.25}/m_2 \right\} \right\rangle,$$
$$\bot = \left\langle \{\varnothing\}, \{m_1, m_2, m_3\} \right\rangle,$$

and examine the aggregation of these concepts (defining the aggregation by parts –extents and intents–):

$$
\begin{aligned}
A(\top, \bot) &= A\left(\left\langle \{g_1, g_2, g_3\}, \left\{ {}^{0.25}/m_2 \right\} \right\rangle, \left\langle \{\varnothing\}, \{m_1, m_2, m_3\} \right\rangle\right) = \\
&= \left\langle A\left(\{g_1, g_2, g_3\}, \varnothing\right), A\left(\left\{ {}^{0.25}/m_2 \right\}, \{m_1, m_2, m_3\}\right)\right\rangle = \\
&= \left\langle \left\{ {}^{A(1,0)}/g_1, {}^{A(1,0)}/g_2, {}^{A(1,0)}/g_3 \right\}, \left\{ {}^{A(0,1)}/m_1, {}^{A(0.25,1)}/m_2, {}^{A(0,1)}/m_3 \right\} \right\rangle = \\
&= \left\langle \left\{ {}^{0.5}/g_1, {}^{0.5}/g_2, {}^{0.5}/g_3 \right\}, \left\{ {}^{0.25}/m_1, {}^{1}/m_2, {}^{0.25}/m_3 \right\} \right\rangle = \\
&= \left\langle \left\{ {}^{0.5}/g_1, {}^{0.5}/g_2, {}^{0.5}/g_3 \right\}, \left\{ {}^{0.25}/m_1, m_2, {}^{0.25}/m_3 \right\} \right\rangle.
\end{aligned}
$$

Therefore, $A(\top, \bot)$ is not a fuzzy formal concept.

The last example shows that $\langle A(X_i), A^*(Y_i)^{\downarrow\uparrow} \rangle$ is not a fuzzy formal concept in general. Nowadays, knowing the properties on aggregation functions which preserve fuzzy formal concepts is an open problem.

3   Aggregation in FCA: First Results

In this section, we wonder what conditions endow to an aggregation function in order to be closed on the set of fuzzy formal concepts. For a general aggregation function, it may be easy to find a formal context such that the aggregation of two given extents is not an extent.

Example 2. We continue our discussion using the same context and aggregation function as in Example 1. We got that the aggregation of the extents of C_1 and C_2 was the set $\{g_1\}$. We can check that it is not an extent, since

$$\{g_1\}^{\uparrow\downarrow} = \left\{ {}^{0.25}/m_1, {}^{0.5}/m_2 \right\}^{\downarrow} = \left\{ g_1, {}^{0.25}/g_2 \right\},$$

and therefore it is not a closed set of objects. The same reasoning (the computations are straightforward) can be done to deduce that the aggregation of the intents of C_1 and C_2 is not an intent of the formal context.

One can also easily check that the aggregation of the two concepts $\top$ and $\bot$ is not a concept, since:

$$\left\{ {}^{0.5}/g_1, {}^{0.5}/g_2, {}^{0.5}/g_3 \right\}^{\uparrow\downarrow} = \{g_1, g_2, g_3\},$$
$$\left\{ {}^{0.25}/m_1, m_2, {}^{0.25}/m_3 \right\}^{\downarrow\uparrow} = \{m_1, m_2, m_3\}.$$

Thus, A does not preserve the algebraic structures of extent or intent. Consequently, neither of concept.

Our aim in this work is to present a preliminary study of the conditions that allow us to determine if an aggregation function will preserve those structures.

Definition 3. *Let* $\mathbb{K} = (G, M, I)$ *be a formal context and denote by* $\text{Ext}(\mathbb{K})$, $\text{Int}(\mathbb{K})$ *and* $\mathbb{B}(\mathbb{K})$, *the sets of extents, intents and formal concepts of* $\mathbb{K}$, *respectively. An aggregation function* A *is said to be:*

- extent-consistent *with* $\mathbb{K}$ *if* $A(X_1, X_2) \in \text{Ext}(\mathbb{K})$ *for all* $X_1, X_2 \in \text{Ext}(\mathbb{K})$.
- intent-consistent *with* $\mathbb{K}$ *if* $A(Y_1, Y_2) \in \text{Int}(\mathbb{K})$ *for all* $Y_1, Y_2 \in \text{Int}(\mathbb{K})$.
- consistent *with* $\mathbb{K}$ *if* $A(C_1, C_2) \in \mathbb{B}(\mathbb{K})$ *for all concepts* C_1 *and* C_2 *of* $\mathbb{K}$.

Example 3. Continuing with the same situation as in Example 1, we can see that the aggregation function A is neither extent-consistent, intent-consistent, nor consistent at all.

However, there are aggregation functions that will always preserve the algebraic structure, e.g., the minimum operator or the projections. Let us consider the aggregation functions A_m, π_1 and π_2 given by:

$$A_m(x, y) := x \wedge y,$$
$$\pi_1(x, y) := x,$$
$$\pi_2(x, y) := y.$$

Proposition 1. *Let* $\mathbb{K} = (G, M, I)$ *be a formal context. Then:*

1. A_m, π_1 *and* π_2 *are extent- and intent-consistent with* $\mathbb{K}$.
2. π_1 *and* π_2 *are consistent with* $\mathbb{K}$.

Proof. 1. A_m is extent-consistent and intent-consistent since it is used in the definition of the intersection of fuzzy sets: let $S \in \{G, M\}$, then, given two extents or intents $X, Y \in [0, 1]^S$, we have that $(X \cap Y)(s) := X(s) \wedge Y(s) = A_m(X(s), Y(s))$ for all $s \in S$. Since the set of extents and the set of intents are closed under intersections, then $A_m(X, Y) = A \cap Y$ is also an extent or an intent, respectively. It is evident that the two projections are extent- and intent-consistent since they always return one of their inputs.
2. The projections applied to concepts return one of their inputs, as mentioned before, and therefore, projections are consistent with $\mathbb{K}$.

Notice that A_m may not be consistent with some formal context $\mathbb{K}$, as shown in the next example.

Example 4. Following our running example, let us compute:

$$A_m(\top, \bot) = A_m\left(\langle\{g_1, g_2, g_3\}, \{^{0.25}\!/m_2\}\rangle, \langle\{\varnothing\}, \{m_1, m_2, m_3\}\rangle\right) =$$
$$= \langle A_m(\{g_1, g_2, g_3\}, \varnothing), A_m(\{^{0.25}\!/m_2\}, \{m_1, m_2, m_3\})\rangle =$$
$$= \langle\{g_1, g_2, g_3\} \cap \varnothing, \{^{0.25}\!/m_2\} \cap \{m_1, m_2, m_3\}\rangle =$$
$$= \langle\varnothing, \{^{0.25}\!/m_2\}\rangle.$$

which is not a concept of the formal context, as it is easy to check.

Let us now inspect a simple formal context, as given in the next table, for $a, b \in [0, 1]$:

$$\begin{array}{c|cc} & m_1 & m_2 \\ \hline g_1 & a & b \end{array}$$

Let us suppose $a < b$. Then, the set of formal concepts (using, as we mentioned before, the Gödel logic structure) is:

$$\langle \{g_1\}, \{{}^a\!/m_1, {}^b\!/m_2\} \rangle,$$
$$\langle \{{}^b\!/g_1\}, \{{}^a\!/m_1, m_2\} \rangle,$$
$$\langle \{{}^a\!/g_1\}, \{m_1, m_2\} \rangle.$$

Note that if A is an aggregation function such that $A(a, b) \notin \{a, b, 1\}$, then A is not extent-consistent. By duality, it cannot be intent-consistent. This motivates the following:

Conjecture. If there exists $a, b \in [0, 1]$ such that $A(a, b) \notin \{a, b\}$ then there exists a formal context $\mathbb{K} = (G, M, I)$ such that A is not extent-consistent (dually, intent-consistent) with $\mathbb{K}$.

Notice that we have removed the possibility $A(a, b) = 1$ in this conjecture. Also, observe that A_m, π_1 and π_2 satisfy $A(x, y) \in \{x, y\}$ for all $x, y \in [0, 1]$. The proof of this conjecture would imply that the aggregation functions that are extent-consistent or intent-consistent belong to the average class. As a main result, fixed a formal context $\mathbb{K}$, we wish to find a total classification or identification of the aggregation functions which preserve the algebraic structure of extents and intents, that is, finding the ones which are extent-consistent with $\mathbb{K}$ and intent-consistent with $\mathbb{K}$.

4   Conclusions

In this work we have explored the properties an aggregation function must satisfy in order to preserve the structure of extents, intents or formal concepts in the setting of Fuzzy Formal Concept Analysis. We have discarded some preliminary hypotheses via a series of illustrative examples and some conjectures have arisen from experimentation. Even in the first steps in this line, we have found some interesting results.

As a prospect of near future work, we intend to study thoroughly this problem in order to prove or refute the conjectures presented. Experiments suggest that there are distinct situations depending on the size of the formal context. These results will also have an impact from the practical standpoint: the consistent aggregation functions could be incorporated into algorithms for concept lattice construction in order to reduce the computational cost of exploring and computing the set of extents, intents and concepts.

Acknowledgments. This research is partially supported by the State Agency of Research (AEI), the Spanish Ministry of Science, Innovation, and Universities (MCIU), the European Social Fund (FEDER), the Junta de Andalucía (JA), and the Universidad de Málaga (UMA) through the FPU19/01467 (MCIU) internship and the research projects with reference PID2021-127870OB-I00 and PID2022-140630NB-I00 (MCIU/AEI/FEDER, UE).

References

1. Andrews, S.: Making use of empty intersections to improve the performance of CbO-type algorithms. In: Bertet, K., Borchmann, D., Cellier, P., Ferré, S. (eds.) ICFCA 2017. LNCS (LNAI), vol. 10308, pp. 56–71. Springer, Cham (2017). https://doi.org/10.1007/978-3-319-59271-8_4

2. Bejines, C., Ardanza-Trevijano, S., Chasco, M., Elorza, J.: Aggregation of indistinguishability operators. Fuzzy Sets Syst. **446**, 53–67 (2022)

3. Beliakov, G., Pradera, A., Calvo, T., et al.: Aggregation Functions: A guide for practitioners, vol. 221. Springer, Heidelberg (2007). https://doi.org/10.1007/978-3-540-73721-6

4. Bělohlávek, R.: Fuzzy Relational Systems. Springer, Heidelberg (2002). https://doi.org/10.1007/978-1-4615-0633-1

5. Calvo, T., Kolesárová, A., Komorníková, M., Mesiar, R.: Aggregation Operators: Properties, Classes and Construction Methods, pp. 3–104. Physica-Verlag, Heidelberg (2002). http://dl.acm.org/citation.cfm?id=774556.774559

6. Ganter, B., Wille, R.: Formal Concept Analysis: Mathematical Foundation. Springer, Heidelberg (1999). https://doi.org/10.1007/978-3-642-59830-2

7. Jana, C., Pal, M., Wang, J.: A robust aggregation operator for multi-criteria decision-making method with bipolar fuzzy soft environment. Iran. J. Fuzzy Syst. **16**(6), 1–16 (2019)

8. Krajča, P., Outrata, J., Vychodil, V.: Advances in algorithms based on cbo. In: Kryszkiewicz, M., Obiedkov, S.A. (eds.) Proceedings of the 7th International Conference on Concept Lattices and Their Applications, Sevilla, Spain, 19–21 October 2010, CEUR Workshop Proceedings, vol. 672, pp. 325–337. CEUR-WS.org (2010)

9. Kuznetsov, S.O., Makhalova, T.: On interestingness measures of formal concepts. Inf. Sci. **442**, 202–219 (2018)

10. Pedraza, T., Ramos-Canós, J., Rodríguez-López, J.: Aggregation of weak fuzzy norms. Symmetry **13**(10), 1908 (2021)

11. Pedraza, T., Rodríguez-López, J., Valero, Ó.: Aggregation of fuzzy quasi-metrics. Inf. Sci. **581**, 362–389 (2021)

12. Poelmans, J., Kuznetsov, S.O., Ignatov, D.I., Dedene, G.: Formal concept analysis in knowledge processing: a survey on models and techniques. Expert Syst. Appl. **40**(16), 6601–6623 (2013). https://doi.org/10.1016/j.eswa.2013.05.007

On Pseudointents in Fuzzy Formal Concept Analysis

Manuel Ojeda-Hernández$^{(\boxtimes)}$ iD, Inma P. Cabrera iD, Pablo Cordero iD, and Emilio Muñoz-Velasco iD

Universidad de Málaga, Andalucía Tech, Málaga, Spain
manuojeda@uma.es

Abstract. Formal Concept Analysis (FCA) is a mathematical framework for analysing data tables that capture the relationship between objects and attributes. FCA deals with two main structures of knowledge, namely the concept lattice and the basis of attribute implications. There are several sets of implications in the literature, for instance minimal bases, direct bases or direct minimal bases. In this work we are interested in the concept of pseudointent in the fuzzy framework in order to define the Duquenne-Guigues basis in the fuzzy setting.

Keywords: Formal Concept Analysis · Fuzzy Sets · Pseudointents · Attribute-implications

1 Introduction

The notion of attribute-implication is fundamental in the context of FCA. Implications show implicit relationships and dependencies among the attributes of a formal context. Explicitly, if M is the set of attributes, an attribute implication is an expression $A \Rightarrow B$ where $A, B \subseteq M$. An implication is said to be valid in a formal context if all the objects that satisfy the attributes in A also satisfy all the attributes in B, which is equivalent to $B \subseteq A^{\downarrow\uparrow}$. All this terminology has been extended to the fuzzy setting where each object can have an attribute to some degree. The underlying structure of truth values is a complete residuated lattice $(L, \wedge, \vee, \otimes, \rightarrow, 0, 1)$ where $(L, \wedge, \vee, 0, 1)$ is a complete lattice, $(L, \otimes, 1)$ is a commutative monoid and $(\otimes, \rightarrow)$ is an adjoint pair, i.e.,

$$a \otimes b \leq c \text{ if and only if } a \leq b \rightarrow c.$$

A fuzzy formal context is a tuple (G, M, I) where G and M are sets of objects and attributes, respectively; and $I \colon G \times M \rightarrow L$ is the fuzzy incidence relation. The derivation operators are defined as follows for all $X \in L^G, Y \in L^M$,

$$X^{\uparrow}(m) = \bigwedge_{g \in G} (X(g) \rightarrow I(g, m))$$

$$Y^{\downarrow}(g) = \bigwedge_{m \in M} (Y(m) \rightarrow I(g, m)).$$

M. Ojeda-Aciego et al. (Eds.): ICCS 2023, LNAI 14133, pp. 36–40, 2023.
https://doi.org/10.1007/978-3-031-40960-8_4

A fuzzy attribute implication is an expression of $A \Rightarrow B$, where $A, B \in L^M$. The degree of validity of a fuzzy attribute implication in a formal context is defined as

$$\|A \Rightarrow B\|_{(G,M,I)} = \bigwedge_{g \in G} S(A, I_g) \rightarrow S(B, I_g),$$

where S is the subsethood degree relation $S(X, Y) = \bigwedge_{m \in M}(X(m) \rightarrow Y(m))$ and $I_g(m) = I(g, m)$. It has also been proved that $\|A \Rightarrow B\|_{(G,M,I)} = S(B, A^{\uparrow\downarrow})$. Consider the following example.

Example 1. Consider the formal context given by the following table.
Notice that the crisp relation gives no information on the size of Neptune, this is because Neptune is known to be a medium-sized planet which is neither large or small. The introduction of graduality in this context may look something like the following [2], where we can grasp more information on the size of Neptune, to continue with the last example, given it is somewhat large and somewhat small, but rather bigger than smaller (Tables 1 and 2).

Table 1. Formal context of planets (crisp)

	small	large	near	far
Mercury	×		×	
Venus	×		×	
Earth	×		×	
Mars	×		×	
Jupiter		×		×
Saturn		×		×
Uranus				×
Neptune				×
Pluto	×			×

Table 2. Formal context of planets (fuzzy)

	small	large	near	far
Mercury	1	0	1	0
Venus	0.75	0	1	0
Earth	0.75	0	0.75	0
Mars	1	0	0.75	0.5
Jupiter	0	1	0.5	0.75
Saturn	0	1	0.5	0.75
Uranus	0.25	0.5	1	0.25
Neptune	0.25	0.5	1	0
Pluto	1	0	1	0

2   Pseudointents

Given a formal context, the two main knowledge structures we have are the concept lattice and the set of implications. However, even a small context may have a massive number of valid attribute implications, therefore we need a subset of them from which we could derive all the others. This is what is known as a basis of implications. In the classical case, the Duquenne-Guigues basis is a complete and non-redundant set of implications, that is, every valid implication in the context can be derived from the basis, every implication in the basis provides information that cannot be retrieved from the rest. Furthermore, this basis is minimal, that is, there is no complete and non-redundant set of implications that has less implications than the Duquenne-Guigues one. This basis depends strongly on the concept of pseudointent, originally defined in [3] in a recursive manner.

Definition 1. *Let (G, M, I) be a classical formal context, then a set $P \subseteq M$ is said to be a pseudointent if*

$$Q < P \text{ implies } Q^{\downarrow\uparrow} < P, \text{ for all pseudointent } Q.$$

In the literature, there is one main approach to fuzzy pseudointents. It is the definition by Belohlavek and Vychodil, which is presented below.

Definition 2. ([6]) *Let (G, M, I) be a fuzzy formal context. A system $\mathcal{P} \subseteq L^M$ is said to be a system of pseudointents if*

$$P \in \mathcal{P} \text{ if and only if } P \neq P^{\downarrow\uparrow} \text{ and } \|Q \Rightarrow Q^{\downarrow\uparrow}\|_P = 1 \text{ for all } Q \in \mathcal{P}, Q \neq P.$$

Notice that this definition follows the first idea of pseudointents and expresses, which degrees, that whenever Q is below P then the closure of Q is also below P.

Even though this definition was a huge step forward in the search for minimal bases of implications in the fuzzy setting, neither the existence or the uniqueness of the system of pseudointents is ensured with this definition. In addition, the minimality of the basis is only ensured under the use of a restrictive "very true" operator.

Cut to the present day and we are looking for an alternative way of defining pseudointents in the fuzzy setting. Our main idea is to mimic the classical framework and study quasi-closed elements. Let us recall this definition to the reader.

Definition 3. *Let (G, M, I) be a classical formal context. An element $Q \subseteq M$ is said to be quasi-closed if for all $X \subseteq M$ we have that,*

$$X < Q \text{ implies } X^{\downarrow\uparrow} < Q \text{ or } X^{\downarrow\uparrow} = Q^{\downarrow\uparrow}.$$

These elements help define the so-called pseudo-closed elements in the classical case.

Definition 4. *Let (G, M, I) be a classical formal context. An element $P \subseteq M$ is said to be pseudo-closed if*

$$Q < P \text{ implies } Q^{\downarrow\uparrow} < P \text{ for all quasi-closed element } Q.$$

This line of work is linked to the previous one via the following theorem.

Theorem 1. *Let (G, M, I) be a classical formal context. An element $P \subseteq M$ is a pseudointent if and only if it is pseudo-closed.*

Our proposal is to present the notion of quasi-closed element to the fuzzy setting, a line of work that started in [4]. The topic of the cited paper was to discern among the extensions of the different properties that characterise quasi-closedness in the classical setting. At the end of the discussion some interesting algebraic properties are proved on the following definition.

Definition 5 (Discarded). *An element q in a fuzzy lattice is said to be quasi-closed if*

$$\rho(a, q) \otimes \neg\rho(q, a) \otimes \rho(\mathsf{c}(a), \mathsf{c}(q)) \otimes \neg\rho(\mathsf{c}(q), \mathsf{c}(a)) \le \rho(\mathsf{c}(a), q), \text{ for all } a \in A.$$

Nevertheless, this definition, while mathematically relevant, does not reflect the properties of quasi-closed elements. For instance, adding a quasi-closed element to the set of formal concepts is not a closure system.

Example 2 Consider the following fuzzy formal context with the complete residuated lattice $\{0, 0.5, 1\}$ and the Lukasiewicz t-norm and residuum.

	a	b
x	1	0.5

The intents of this formal context are

$$I_1 = \{a, b\} \text{ and } I_2 = \{^a/1, ^b/0.5\}.$$

It is only a matter of calculation to see that $Q = \{^a/0.5, ^b/1\}$ is quasi-closed in this context, however the infimum $Q \cap I_2 = \{^a/0.5, ^b/0.5\}$ is not an intent.

Here we present some sketches of the current work we are doing on quasi-closed elements.

Definition 6 (Tentative). *Let (G, M, I) be a fuzzy formal context. The degree to which an element $Q \in L^M$ is quasi-closed is defined as follows,*

$$QC(Q) = \bigwedge_{\substack{Y \in L^M \\ S(Q^{\downarrow\uparrow}, Y^{\downarrow\uparrow}) \ne 1}} \|Y \Rightarrow Y^{\downarrow\uparrow}\|_Q.$$

We say that $Q \in L^M$ is a quasi-closed element when $QC(Q) = 1$.

Notice that this definition of quasi-closedness is equivalent to the following property

$$Q \text{ is quasi-closed if } \|Y \Rightarrow Y^{\downarrow\uparrow}\|_Q = 1 \text{ or } S(Q^{\downarrow\uparrow}, Y^{\downarrow\uparrow}) = 1,$$

which is similar to the definition in the classical case.

Even though Definition 5 and Definition 6 are not similar, they are related. This is shown in the next result.

Proposition 1. *Let $q \in A$, if q is a quasi-closed as in Definition 6 then it is a quasi-closed element as per Definition 5*

Starting from Definition 6 we would like to obtain properties that resemble the classical case in some way, for example we are considering the following.

Conjecture 1. Let (G, M, I) be a fuzzy formal context and let $\mathcal{F}$ be the set of intents. An element q is quasi-closed if and only if $\mathcal{F} \cup \{q\}$ is a closure system.

The definition of closure system in this case would be the one in the fuzzy setting, we refer the reader to [1,5].

Also, the set of quasi-closed elements induces a complete set of implications in the classical case. Hence, we are also trying to prove.

Conjecture 2. The set of implications

$$\{q \Rightarrow \mathsf{c}(q) \mid q \text{ is quasi-intent}\}$$

is complete.

Acknowledgement. This research is partially supported by the State Agency of Research (AEI), the Spanish Ministry of Science, Innovation, and Universities (MCIU), the European Social Fund (FEDER), the Junta de Andalucía (JA), and the Universidad de Málaga (UMA) through the FPU19/01467 (MCIU) internship and the research projects with reference PID2021-127870OB-I00 and PID2022-140630NB-I00 (MCIU/AEI/FEDER, UE).

References

1. Bělohlávek, R.: Fuzzy closure operators. J. Math. Anal. Appl. **262**, 473–489 (2001)
2. Belohlávek, R., Outrata, J., Vychodil, V.: On factorization by similarity of fuzzy concept lattices with hedges. CLA proceedings (2006)
3. Ganter, B., Wille, R.: Formal Concept Analysis. Springer, Heidelberg (1999). https://doi.org/10.1007/978-3-642-59830-2
4. Ojeda-Hernández, M., Cabrera, I.P., Cordero, P.: Quasi-closed elements in fuzzy posets. J. Comput. Appl. Math. **404**, 113390 (2022). https://doi.org/10.1016/j.cam.2021.113390
5. Ojeda-Hernández, M., Cabrera, I.P., Cordero, P., Muñoz-Velasco, E.: On (fuzzy) closure systems in complete fuzzy lattices. In: 2021 IEEE International Conference on Fuzzy Systems (FUZZ-IEEE), pp. 1–6 (2021). https://doi.org/10.1109/FUZZ45933.2021.9494404
6. Vychodil, V., Bělohlávek, R.: Fuzzy attribute logic: Attribute implications, their validity, entailment, and non-redundant basis. Repository of the University Palacky of Olomouc, pp. 1–6

Maximal Ordinal Two-Factorizations

Dominik Dürrschnabel[1,2(✉)] ⒾⒹ and Gerd Stumme[1,2] ⒾⒹ

[1] Knowledge & Data Engineering Group, University of Kassel, Kassel, Germany
{duerrschnabel,stumme}@cs.uni-kassel.de
[2] Interdisciplinary Research Center for Information System Design,
University of Kassel, Kassel, Germany

Abstract. Given a formal context, an ordinal factor is a subset of its incidence relation that forms a chain in the concept lattice, i.e., a part of the dataset that corresponds to a linear order. To visualize the data in a formal context, Ganter and Glodeanu proposed a biplot based on two ordinal factors. For the biplot to be useful, it is important that these factors comprise as much data points as possible, i.e., that they cover a large part of the incidence relation. In this work, we investigate such ordinal two-factorizations. First, we investigate for formal contexts that omit ordinal two-factorizations the disjointness of the two factors. Then, we show that deciding on the existence of two-factorizations of a given size is an NP-complete problem which makes computing maximal factorizations computationally expensive. Finally, we provide the algorithm ORD2FACTOR that allows us to compute large ordinal two-factorizations.

Keywords: Formal concept analysis · Ordinal factor analysis · Ordinal two-factorization · Disjoint factorizations

1 Introduction

A common way to analyze datasets with binary attributes is to treat them as numerical, i.e., the value 1 is assigned to each attribute-object incidence and 0 to each missing one. Then, dimension reduction methods such as principal component analysis can be applied. Thereby, multiple attributes are merged into a few number of axes while being weighted differently. The emerging axes thus condense the presence or absence of correlated features. The objects are embedded into these axes as follows. Each object is assigned to a real-valued number in each axis to represent the best position of the object in the respective axis. Thereby, the resulting placement of an object that only has some of these attributes yields an ambiguous representation. Therefore, the main issues of this method arise. Assigning a real value to an object is not consistent with the level of measurement of the underlying binary data. It promotes the perception that an element has, compared to others, a stronger bond to some attributes, which is not possible in a formal context. A method that encourages such comparisons and results in such an inaccurate representation of the original information is, in our opinion, not valid. An example of such a principal component analysis projection is given in Fig. 1.

M. Ojeda-Aciego et al. (Eds.): ICCS 2023, LNAI 14133, pp. 41–55, 2023.
https://doi.org/10.1007/978-3-031-40960-8_5

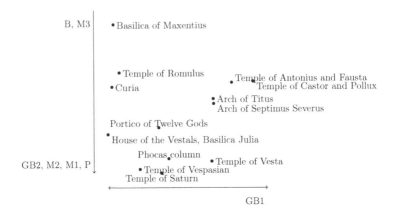

Fig. 1. A 2-dimensional projection of the objects from the dataset depicted in Fig. 3 using principal component analysis. This figure encourages the perception, that "Temple of Castor and Pollux" has a stronger bond to "GB1" than "Temple of Antonius and Fausta", which is false.

To address this problem, Ganter and Glodeanu [14] developed the method of *ordinal factor analysis*. It allows for a similar visualization technique while avoiding the problems that stem from the real-valued measurement on the binary attributes. Once again, multiple attributes are merged into a single factor. The computed projection in ordinal factor analysis thereby consists of linear orders of attributes, the so-called *ordinal factors*. Then, the method assigns each object, based on its attributes, a position in every factor. Compared to the principal component analysis approach, the positions assigned in the process are natural numbers instead of real-valued ones. Therefore, if interpreted correctly, the resulting projection does not express inaccurate and incorrect information. A desirable property of ordinal factorizations is completeness which allows the deduction of all original information. The positions of the objects are determined as follows. Each object in the two-dimensional coordinate system is placed at the last position of each axis such that it has all attributes until this position. Such a plot can be seen in Fig. 2. Reading the biplot is done as follows: Consider the "Portico of Twelve Gods" object. In the vertical factor, it is at position "GB1" which is preceded by the attributes "M1", and "P" in this factor. Thus, the object has all three of these attributes. In the horizontal factor, it is at position "M1" which has no preceding attributes. These incidences together precisely represents the incidences of the object. Deducing the same information from Fig. 1 is hardly possible.

However, Ganter and Glodeanu do not provide a method for the computation of ordinal two-factorizations. This is the point, where we step in with this work. We provide an algorithm to compute ordinal two-factorizations if they exist. We couple this algorithm with a method to compute a subset of the incidence relation of large size such that it admits an ordinal two-factorization. This enables the computation of ordinal two-factorizations of arbitrary datasets. This process combined results in the algorithm ORD2FACTOR. Furthermore, we investigate ordinal two-factorizations with respect to their disjointness.

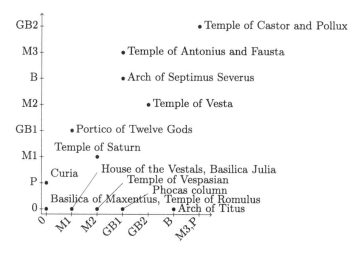

Fig. 2. A biplot of a maximal ordinal two-factorization of the data from Fig. 3. It represents all incidences from the formal context except (Temple of Romulus, GB1) and (Basilica of Maxentius, B).

2   Related Work

In this work, we consider a method that represent the objects in a low number of dimensions which condense multiple merged attributes. A commonly applied approach with the same fundamental idea is principal component analysis [26], which is a method that minimizes the average squared distances from the data points to a line. An example for a principal component analysis projection is depicted in Fig. 3. For an extensive survey on dimensional reduction methods, we refer the reader to Espadoto et al. [11]. A comparison of principal component analysis with the methods from formal concept analysis was described by Spangenberg and Wolff [27].

Our work is located in the research area formal concept analysis [15] (FCA). One well-researched way to apply dimensionality reduction in FCA is Boolean factor analysis [2–4,21,22]. Thereby, the incidence relation is represented by families of incident attribute and object subsets. This idea is highly related to the notion of a formal concept in FCA. Based on this method, Ganter and Glodeanu propose in [14] to group multiple Boolean factors into many-valued factors. One research direction that they consider to be of special interest is grouping them into ordinal factors, which is the direction we follow in this work. The same authors also demonstrate [17] that the research method is useful in application.

	B	GB1	GB2	M1	M2	M3	P
Arch of Septimus Severus	×	×		×	×		×
Arch of Titus	×	×	×	×	×		
Basilica Julia				×			
Basilica of Maxentius	×						
Curia							×
House of the Vestals				×			
Phocas column		×		×	×		
Portico of Twelve Gods		×		×			×
Temple of Antonius and Fausta	×	×		×	×	×	×
Temple of Castor and Pollux	×	×	×	×	×	×	×
Temple of Romulus		×					
Temple of Saturn				×	×		×
Temple of Vespasian				×	×		
Temple of Vesta		×	×	×	×		×

Fig. 3. Running example: This dataset compares attributes of different social media platforms.

The theory was also lifted to the triadic case [16] and graded data [18]. In our previous work [10], we propose an algorithm to greedily compute ordinal factors in large formal contexts. In a broader sense, the discovery of substructures, such as induced contranominal scales [9] or ordinal motifs [20] is an often-considered problem in the context of structural investigations in formal concept analysis.

The methods developed in this paper can be considered dual to the DIM-DRAW-algorithm [7]. In both approaches, two linear orders are sought-after to represent the dataset which is done using a connection to a bipartite subgraph.

3   Foundations of Ordinal Factor Analysis

In this section we briefly recap the definitions and notions from graph theory, formal concept analysis and ordinal factor analysis that are necessary to understand this paper. A graph is a tuple (V, E) with $E \subseteq \binom{V}{2}$. The set V is called the set of *vertices* and E the set of *edges*. A path between two vertices v_1 and v_n is a sequence of vertices $v_1 \dots v_n$ with $\{v_i, v_{i+1}\} \in E$. A (connected) component is a maximal subset of the vertices of a graph, such that between every pair of vertices in the component there is a path. An *ordered set* is a tuple $(B, \leq)$ where $\leq$ is a binary relation on $B \times B$ that is reflexive, antisymmetric and transitive. The cocomparability graph of the ordered set $(B, \leq)$ is the graph (B, E) where $\{a, b\} \in E$ if $a \not\leq b$ and $b \not\leq a$. A *formal context* is a triple (G, M, I), where G is called the set of *objects*, M is called the set of *attributes* and $I \subseteq G \times M$ is called the incidence relation. The two *derivation operators* between the power sets of attributes and objects are given by $A' = \{m \in M \mid \forall g \in A : (g, m) \in I\}$ and $B' = \{g \in G \mid \forall m \in B : (g, m) \in I\}$. A formal concept is a tuple (A, B) with $A \subseteq G$ and $B \subseteq M$ such that $A' = B$ and $B' = A$. The set of all formal concepts with is denoted by $\mathfrak{B}$ and forms together with the order relation $\leq$ for which $(A_1, B_1) \leq (A_2, B_2)$ if and only if $A_1 \subseteq A_2$, the concept lattice $\underline{\mathfrak{B}} = (\mathfrak{B}, \leq)$.

From here on we introduce the notions that are important for the present work. A *Ferrers relation* is a binary relation $F \subseteq G \times M$ with the property that if $(g, m) \in F$ and $(h, n) \in F$, either $(g, n) \in F$ or $(h, m) \in F$. An *ordinal two-factorization* of a formal context (G, M, I) is a set of two Ferrers relations F_1 and F_2 such that $F_1 \cup F_2 = I$. The *incompatibility graph* of a formal context (G, M, I) is the graph (I, E) with $\{(g, m), (h, n)\} \in E$ if and only if $(g, n) \notin I$ and $(h, m) \notin I$. We also say that (g, n) and (h, m) are *incompatible*. It is known, that a formal context admits an ordinal two-factorization, if and only if the incompatibility graph is bipartite [6, Sec.2, Prop.2]. Also note, that it is possible to extend an ordinal factor, i.e., a Ferrers relation, to a chain of formal concepts [14, Prop.7].

4   Disjointness of Ordinal Two-Factorizations

It is of interest wether the computed two ordinal factors are disjoint, i.e., if there is no information that is represented by both factors. Otherwise, the ordinal factorization contains redundant information as the two Ferrers relations share pairs of the incidence relation. However, as the formal context in Fig. 4 shows, achieving two disjoint ordinal factors is not always possible. The example is due to Das et al. [5], where they characterize the formal contexts that are factorizable into two disjoint ordinal factors as interval digraphs. The incompatibility graph of the example consists of two connected components, one consists of the single vertex $(6, f)$ and the other the vertices $I \setminus \{(6, f)\}$. We can assign the bipartition classes of this second component to factor 1 and 2 without loss of generality as shown on the right side of the Figure 4. But then the incidence pair then $(6, f)$ has to be in both factors, in factor 1 because as $(6, e) \in I$ and $(2, f) \in I$ but $(2, e) \notin I$ and in factor 2 because of $(5, f) \in I$, $(6, b) \in I$, and $(5, b) \notin I$.

We know that a formal context admits a two-factorization if its incompatibility graph is bipartite, and we can deduce from its incompatibility graph incidence pairs that cannot appear in the same ordinal factor. Still, we note that even in cases where disjoint two-factorizations do exist, the bipartition classes of the

	a	b	c	d	e	f	g
1				×	×	×	×
2						×	×
3							×
4	×						
5	×					×	
6	×	×			×	×	×
7	×	×	×			×	

	a	b	c	d	e	f	g
1				1	1	1	1
2						1	1
3							1
4	2						
5	2					2	
6	2	2			1	×	1
7	2	2	2			2	

Fig. 4. Example of a context with a maximal bipartite subgraph that does not give rise to an ordinal two-factorization. This example is due to Das et al. [5].

Fig. 5. *Left:* The formal context of a contranominal scale. *Middle:* its comparability graph. *Right:* A bipartition of the transitive comparability graph that does not give rise to an ordinal two-factorization.

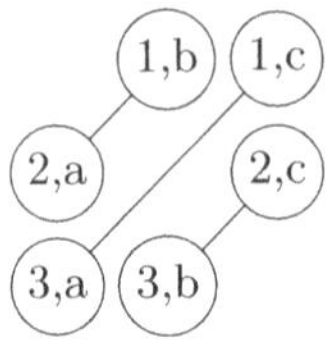

incompatibility graph do not necessarily give rise to an ordinal two-factorization. To see this, refer to Fig. 5. The incompatibility graph (middle) of the formal context (left) consists of three components. An assignment of the incompatibility graph to bipartition classes can be seen on the right, however the elements $(2, a)$ and $(3, b)$ of factor 2 would imply, that the element $(3, a)$ also has to be in factor 2. However, this element is incompatible to element $(3, c)$, which is also in factor 2 by the assignment of the incompatibility graph. Thus, such an assignment does not always result in a valid ordinal two-factorization.

On the other hand, if the incompatibility graph is connected and bipartite, any assignment of the elements to bipartition classes of the incompatibility graph generates a valid ordinal two-factorization, as the following shows.

Proposition 1. *Let $\mathbb{K}$ be a formal context with a connected and bipartite incompatibility graph. Then there are two unique disjoint factors F_1 and F_2 that factorize $\mathbb{K}$. The sets F_1 and F_2 correspond to the bipartition classes of the incompatibility graph.*

Proof. As the cocomparability graph is bipartite, $\mathbb{K}$ admits an ordinal two-factorization. As the incompatibility graph is connected, it has unique bipartition classes. Finally, two elements in the same bipartition class cannot appear in the same ordinal factor.

On the other hand, if the incompatibility graph is not connected, it is of interest to further investigate the incidence pairs that can appear in both ordinal factors. We do so in the following.

Lemma 1. *Let $\mathbb{K} = (G, M, I)$ be a formal context with bipartite incompatibility graph (I, E). Let F_1, F_2 be an ordinal two-factorization of $\mathbb{K}$. For all elements $(g, m) \in F_1 \cap F_2$ it holds that $\{(g, m)\}$ is a connected component in (I, E).*

Proof. Assume not, i.e., there is an element $(g, m) \in F_1 \cap F_2$ that is not its own component. Then, there has to be some element $(h, n) \in I$ that is incompatible to (g, m), i.e., $(g, n) \notin I$ and $(h, m) \notin I$. But then (h, n) can be in neither F_1 nor F_2 which contradicts the definition of a Ferrers relation.

Thus, only the elements of the incompatibility graph that are not connected to another element can be in both ordinal factors. In the following, we further characterize these isolated elements, as we show that for these elements it is always possible that they are in both factors, which then fully characterizes the intersection of the two ordinal factors.

Lemma 2. *Let $\mathbb{K} = (G, M, I)$ be a formal context with a two-factorization F_1, F_2. Let C be the set of all elements of I that are incompatible to no other element. Then $F_1 \cup C$, $F_2 \cup C$ is also an ordinal two-factorization.*

Proof. Let $G_i = F_i \setminus C$ and $\tilde{F}_i = F_i \cup C$ for $i \in \{1, 2\}$ Assume the statement is not true, i.e., either $\tilde{F}_1$ or $\tilde{F}_2$ is no ordinal factor. Without loss of generality, let $\tilde{F}_1 = F_1 \cup C$ be no ordinal factor. Then, there are two elements $(g, m), (h, n) \in \tilde{F}_1$ such that $(g, n) \notin \tilde{F}_1$ and $(h, m) \notin \tilde{F}_1$. As F_1 is an ordinal factor, at least one of the two elements has to be in C, let without loss of generality $(g, m) \in C$. We now do a case distinction whether one or both of them are in C.

Case 1. Let first $(g, m) \in C$ and $(h, n) \notin C$. One of the elements (g, n) or (h, m) has to be in I, otherwise (g, m) and (h, n) are incompatible, without loss of generality, let $(h, m) \in I$. As $(h, m) \notin C$, it has to hold that $(h, m) \in G_2$ and there has to be some $(x, y) \in G_1$ with $(h, y) \notin I$ and $(x, m) \notin I$. As $(x, y) \in G_1$, $(h, n) \in G_1$, and $(h, y) \notin I$ and F_1 is an ordinal factor, $(x, n) \in F_1$. As $(g, m) \in C$ it is incompatible with no element and thus not incompatible with (x, n) in particular, but $(x, m) \notin I$, it holds that $(g, n) \in I$. The element (g, n) has to be in G_2, as otherwise (g, m) and (h, n) are not incompatible. Thus, there also has to be some element in $(a, b) \in G_1$ with $(a, n) \notin I$ and $(g, b) \notin I$. As F_1 is an ordinal factor and $(x, n) \in F_1, (a, b) \in F_1$ and $(a, n) \notin F_1$, the element $(x, b) \in F_1$. But then (x, b) is incompatible to (g, m) which is a contradiction to (g, m) being in C.

Case 2. Let $(g, m) \in C$ and $(h, n) \in C$. Either $(g, n) \in I$ or $(h, m) \in I$, let without loss of generality $(g, n) \in I$. Then it has to be hold more specifically that in $(g, n) \in G_2$. Thus, there is some element $(x, y) \in G_1$ with $(h, y) \notin I$ and $(x, m) \notin I$. Because (x, y) has to be compatible with (h, n), it has to hold that $(x, n) \in I$. On the other hand, (x, n) has to be compatible with (g, m), thus $(g, n) \in I$. It then has to hold that $(g, n) \in G_2$ and thus some element $(a, b) \in G_1$ has to exist with $(g, b) \notin I$ and $(a, n) \notin I$. As $(x, y) \in F_1$ and $(a, b) \in F_1$ and F_1 is an ordinal factor, either $(a, y) \in F_1$ or $(x, b) \in F_1$. If $(a, y) \in F_1$, it would be incompatible to (g, m), if $(x, b) \in F_1$ it would be incompatible to (h, n). Both would be a contradiction to the respective element being in C.

This theorem finishes a complete characterization of the non-disjoint part of ordinal factors. Therefore, a partition of the incidence as follows always exists, if the context is ordinal two-factorizable.

Theorem 1. *Let $\mathbb{K} = (G, M, I)$ be a two-factorizable formal context with (I, E) its incompatibility graph. Then there is a partition of I into F_1, F_2, C with $C = \{D \mid D$ connected component of $(I, E), |D| = 1\}$ and $F_1 \cup C$ and $F_2 \cup C$ are Ferrers relations.*

Proof. This theorem directly follows from the previous lemma. Let $\tilde{F}_1, \tilde{F}_2$ be a two-factorization and $C = \{D \mid D$ connected component of $(I, E), |D| = 1\}$. Then the partition is given by $\tilde{F}_1 \setminus C$, $\tilde{F}_2 \setminus C$, and C.

5   An Algorithm for Ordinal Two-Factorizations

Now, we propose an algorithm to compute ordinal two-factorizations if they exist. As we saw in the last section, the bipartition classes of the incompatibility graph do not directly give rise to an ordinal two-factorizations. An important observation [15, Thm.46] is that a formal context can be described by the intersection of two Ferrers relations, if and only if its corresponding concept lattice can be described as the intersection of two linear orders, i.e., if it has order dimension two. As the complement of a Ferrers relation is once again a Ferrers relation, a formal context is two-factorizable if and only if the concept lattice of its complement context has order dimension two. We leverage this relationship with the following theorem, to explicitly compute the ordinal two-factorization.

Theorem 2. *Let* $\mathbb{K} = (G, M, I)$ *be a formal context. Let* $(B, \leq) = \underline{\mathfrak{B}}(\mathbb{K}^c)$*. If* $\mathbb{K}$ *is two-factorizable, then* $\leq$ *is two-dimensional and there is a conjugate order* $\leq_c$*. The sets*

$$F_1 = \{(g, m) \in G \times M \mid \nexists (A, B), (C, D) \in \mathfrak{B}(\mathbb{K}^c), g \in A, m \in D,$$
$$((A, B), (C, D)) \in (\leq \cup \leq_c)\}$$

and

$$F_2 = \{(g, m) \in G \times M \mid \nexists (A, B), (C, D) \in \mathfrak{B}(\mathbb{K}^c), g \in A, m \in D,$$
$$((A, B), (C, D)) \in (\leq \cup \geq_c)\}$$

give rise to an ordinal factorization of $\mathbb{K}$*.*

Proof. We have to show that F_1 and F_2 are Ferrers relations and $F_1 \cup F_2 = I$. We first show that F_1 is a Ferrers relation. By definition $\lessdot := \leq \cup \leq_c$ is a chain ordering all formal concepts of $\mathfrak{B}(K^c)$. Let (g, m) and (h, n) be two pairs in F_1. Assume that $(g, n) \notin F_1$ and $(h, m) \notin F_1$. Then there have to be two concept (A_1, B_1) and (A_2, B_2) with $g \in A_1$, $n \in B_2$ such that $(A_1, B_1) \lessdot (A_2, B_2)$. Similarly, there have to be two concepts (A_3, B_3) and (A_4, B_4) with $h \in A_3$, $m \in B_4$ such that $(A_3, B_3) \lessdot (A_4, B_4)$. For the concepts (A_2, B_2) and (A_3, B_3) it holds that $(A_2, B_2) \lessdot (A_3, B_3)$, as $(A_2, B_2) \neq (A_3, B_3)$ and $(A_3, B_3) \not\lessdot (A_2, B_2)$ because $(g, m) \notin F_1$. By the same argument, $(A_4, B_4) \lessdot (A_1, B_1)$. Thus, $(A_1, B_1) \lessdot (A_2, B_2) \lessdot (A_3, B_3) \lessdot (A_4, B_4) \lessdot (A_1, B_1)$, which would imply that these three concepts are equal and is thus a contradiction. This proves that F_1 is a Ferrers relation. The argument to shows that F_2 is a Ferrers relation is dual. We now show that $F_1 \cup F_2 = I$. Let $(g, m) \in F_1 \cup F_2$, without loss of generality let it be an element of F_1. Then there are no two concepts $(A, B), (C, D) \in \mathfrak{B}(\mathbb{K}^c)$, with $g \in A$, $m \in D$ and $((A, B), (C, D)) \in (\leq \cup \leq_c)$. Consider the concept (g'', g') with the derivation from the complement context. By definition $((g'', g'), (g'', g')) \in (\leq \cup \leq_c)$ and thus $m \notin g'$ when using the derivation from the complement context, i.e., $(g, m) \notin I^c$. But then, $(g, m) \in I$. Now, let $(g, m) \in I$ and assume that $(g, m) \notin F_1$. Let (A, B) and (C, D) be arbitrary concepts of $\mathfrak{B}(\mathbb{K}^c)$ with $g \in A$ and $m \in D$. As $(g, m) \in I$, it is not in the incidence of

---

Algorithm 1. Compute Ordinal Two-Factorization

Input: Ordinal Two-Factorizable Formal Context $\mathbb{K} = (G, M, I)$
Output: Ordinal Two-Factorization F_1, F_2

```
def two_factor(G, M, I):
    (𝔅, ≤) = 𝔅(𝕂ᶜ)
    (𝔅, E) = co_comparability_graph(𝔅, ≤)
    ≤c = transitive_orientation(𝔅, E)
    ≺₁ = ≤ ∪ ≤c
    ≺₂ = ≤ ∪ ≥c
    for i in {1, 2}:
        Lᵢ = {}
        Ã = {}
        for (A, B) in 𝔅 ordered by ≺ᵢ:
            Ã = Ã ∪ A
            Lᵢ = Lᵢ ∪ (Ã × B)
        Fᵢ = (G × M) \ Lᵢ
    return F₁, F₂
```

$\mathbb{K}^c$ and thus (A, B) and (C, D) are not comparable with $\leq$. As $(g, m) \notin F_1$ it holds $(A, B) \not\leq_c (C, D)$ and as they are incomparable with $\leq$ it has to hold that $(A, B) \geq_c (C, D)$. Thus, $(g, m) \in F_2$. This shows that $F_1 \cup F_2 = I$ and thus concludes the proof.

This proof gives rise to the routine in Algorithm 1 where this information is used to compute an ordinal two-factorization of the formal context. It computes the two sets F_1 and F_2 from the previous theorem. To do so, it has to be paired with an algorithm to compute the concept lattice. An algorithm that is suitable is due to Lindig [24], as it computes the covering relation together with the concept lattice. Furthermore, an algorithm for transitive orientations [19] is required to compute the conjugate order. As we will discuss later, for both these algorithms the runtime is not critical, as we are interested in ordinal two-factorizations of small formal contexts. Modern computers are easily able to deal with such contexts. Still, if suitable supporting algorithms are chosen, this procedure results in a polynomial-time algorithm that computes ordinal two-factorizations.

6 Maximal Ordinal Two-Factorizations

In this section, we propose an algorithm to compute an ordinal two-factorizations of a formal context that covers a large part of the incidence relation.

Definition 1 (Maximal Ordinal Two-Factorizations). *For a formal context* $\mathbb{K} = (G, M, I)$ *a maximal ordinal two-factorization is a pair of Ferrers relations* $F_1, F_2 \subseteq I$ *such that there are no Ferrers relations* $\tilde{F}_1, \tilde{F}_2 \subseteq I$ *with* $|\tilde{F}_1 \cup \tilde{F}_2| \geq |F_1 \cup F_2|$.

While there are various thinkable ways, how to define maximal ordinal two-factorizations, we have chosen to do so by minimizing the size of not-covered incidence, as each element in the incidence can be viewed as a data point that would thus be lost. This definition also aligns with Ganter's suggestion in his textbook to maximize the size of the union [13]. Note, that a maximal two-factorization always exists, as a single element in the incidences is a Ferrers relation by itself.

6.1   Maximal Ordinal Two-Factorizations Are Hard

First, we investigate the computational complexity of the MAXIMAL ORDINAL TWO-FACTORIZATION PROBLEM. To do so, we perform a reduction from the TWO-DIMENSION EXTENSION PROBLEM. The problem requires finding the minimum number of pairs that need to be added to an order relation to make it two-dimensional. Formally, given an ordered set $(X, \leq)$ and a $k \in \mathbb{N}$ requests the decision whether there is a set $\tilde{\leq} \supset \leq$ such that is an order and $(X, \tilde{\leq})$ has order dimension two and $|\tilde{\leq}| - |\leq| = k$. Felsner and Reuter [12] showed that deciding this problem is NP-complete.

The decision problem, that is linked to the minimum number of pairs that we need to add to a relation to make it two-dimensional is the ORDINAL TWO-FACTORIZATION PROBLEM. For it, a formal context (G, M, I) and a $k \in \mathbb{N}$ are given. It is requested to decide the existance of a formal context $(G, M, \tilde{I})$ with $\tilde{I} \subseteq I$ and $|I| - |\tilde{I}| = k$ that has an ordinal two-factorization.

The relation between these two problems gives rise to the computational complexity of computing a two-factorization.

Lemma 3. *There is a polynomial-time reduction from the* TWO-DIMENSION EXTENSION PROBLEM *to the* ORDINAL TWO-FACTORIZATION PROBLEM.

Proof. Let $(X, \leq)$ and $k \in \mathbb{N}$ be an instance of the TWO-DIMENSION EXTENSION PROBLEM. We claim, that the problem has a solution if and only if ORDINAL TWO-FACTORIZATION PROBLEM $(X, X, \nleq)$ with k has a solution.

Let $(X, \leq)$ be an ordered set with a two-dimension-extension C of size k. Let L_1, L_2 be a realizer, i.e., two linear extensions of $\leq \cup C$ with $L_1 \cap L_2 = \leq \cup C$. Then the relations $F_1 := (X \times X) \setminus L_1$ and $F_2 := (X \times X) \setminus L_2$ are Ferrers relations. Furthermore, $F_1 \subseteq \nleq$ and $F_2 \subseteq \nleq$ by definition. Assume that $F_1 \cup F_2 \cup C \neq \nleq$. Then there has to be a pair $a, b \in X$ with $a \nleq b$ and $(a, b) \notin C$. Then $(b, a) \in L_1$, or $(b, a) \in L_2$, or both, without loss of generality let $(b, a) \in L_1$. But this implies that $(a, b) \in L_1$ which is a contradiction.

Now, let for the formal context $(X, X, \nleq)$ be C a set of cardinality k such that there are two Ferrers relations F_1, F_2 with $|F_1 \cup F_2 \cup C| = |\nleq|$. Now, let $L_1 = (X \times X) \setminus F_1$ and $L_2 = (X \times X) \setminus F_2$. Then it holds that $L_1 \cap L_2 = \leq \cup C$. L_1 and L_2 are supersets of $\leq$ and Ferrers relations, thus they are transitive, reflexive and for all elements $a, b \in X$ it holds that $a, b \in L_i$ or $b, a \in L_i$. By definition for both $i \in \{1, 2\}$ there is a $\tilde{L}_i \subseteq L_i$ that has all these properties and is also antisymmetric. The existence of $\tilde{L}_i$ follows from placing a linear order on each of the equivalence classes of L_i. Both $\tilde{L}_1$ and $\tilde{L}_2$ are linear extensions of $\leq$ and $|\tilde{L}_1 \cap \tilde{L}_2| \leq |L_1 \cap L_2| = |\leq| + k$.

Therefore, the claim is proven. and we reduced the TWO-DIMENSION EXTENSION PROBLEM to the ORDINAL TWO-FACTORIZATION PROBLEM. $\square$

Lemma 4. *Validation of a solution of the* ORDINAL TWO-FACTORIZATION *can be done in polynomial time.*

Proof. Given a formal context (G, M, I) and a set $C \subseteq I$ of size k, to check whether $(G, M, I \setminus C)$ admits an ordinal two-factorization is equivalent to the check whether the incompatibility graph of $(G, M, I \setminus C)$ is bipartite. $\square$

Thus, the ORDINAL TWO-FACTORIZATION PROBLEM is in the same complexity class as the TWO-DIMENSION EXTENSION PROBLEM.

Theorem 3. *The* ORDINAL TWO-FACTORIZATION PROBLEM *is* NP-*complete.*

Proof. Follows from Lemmas 3 and 4. $\square$

6.2 Maximal Bipartite Subgraphs Are Not Sufficient

	a	b	c	d	e	f	g	h	i	j	k	l	m	n	o	p	q	r
1		×	×	×		×		×		×	×	×	×	×	×	×		
2	×		×	×	×	×	×	×	×	×	×	×	×	×	×		×	
3	×	×		×	×	×	×	×	×	×	×	×	×	×	×			×
4	×	×	×		×	×		×	×		×		×			×	×	×
5	×	×	×	×		×		×		×	×	×	×	×	×	×	×	×
6	×	×	×	×	×		×		×		×		×			×	×	×
7	×	×	×	×	×	×		×	×	×	×	×	×	×	×	×	×	×
8	×	×	×	×	×	×	×		×	×		×		×		×	×	×
9	×	×	×	×	×	×	×	×		×	×	×	×	×	×	×	×	×
10	×	×	×	×	×	×	×	×	×		×	×		×		×	×	
11	×	×	×	×	×	×	×	×	×		×		×			×	×	×
12	×	×	×	×	×	×	×	×	×	×	×		×			×	×	
13	×	×	×	×	×	×	×	×	×	×	×	×		×	×	×	×	×
14	×	×	×	×	×	×	×	×	×	×	×	×	×		×		×	×
15	×	×	×	×	×	×	×	×	×	×	×	×	×	×		×	×	×
16	×	×	×	×	×	×	×	×	×	×	×	×	×	×	×		×	×
17	×	×	×	×		×	×		×	×	×	×	×	×	×	×		×
18	×	×	×	×	×	×	×	×	×	×	×	×	×	×	×	×	×	

Fig. 6. Example of a context with a maximal bipartite subgraph that does not give rise to an ordinal two-factorization.

The structure of the incompatibility graph provides an interesting foundation to compute ordinal two-factorizations. It seems to be a tempting idea to compute

---

Algorithm 2. ORD2FACTOR to Compute Large Ordinal Two-Factorization

---

Input: Formal Context (G, M, I)
Output: Ordinal Factors F_1 and F_2

```
def Ord2Factor(G, M, I):
    (I, E) = incompatibility_graph(G, M, I)
    while (I, E) not bipartite:
        I = maximal_bipartite_inducing_vertex_set(I, E)
        (I, E) = incompatibility_graph(G, M, I)
    return two_factor(G, M, I)
```

---

the maximal induced bipartite subgraph of a formal context. The vertex set that induces such a maximal bipartite subgraph could than be used for the ordinal two-factorization. However, it turns out a bipartite subgraph does not always give rise to an ordinal two-factorization as Fig. 6 demonstrates. Its incompatibility graph has an odd cycle, and it is thus not bipartite. This fact makes the formal context not two-factorizable. An inclusion-minimal set that can be removed to make it bipartite is given by

$$C = \{(6, j), (4, n), (7, p), (18, p), (6, p), (6, n), (12, k), (10, g), (6, g), (5, p), (2, i),$$
$$(4, p), (12, m), (3, i), (12, h), (1, p), (2, q)\}.$$

However, the formal context $(G, M, I \setminus C)$ is again not two-factorizable as its incompatibility graph contains once again an odd cycle. This is possible as new incompatibilities can arise with the removal of incidences.

6.3   Computing Maximal Ordinal Two-Factorizations

In the last sections, we did structural investigations on ordinal two-factorizations and provided an algorithm to compute them. We now use this algorithm to compute a large ordinal two-factorization. To this end, we propose the algorithm ORD2FACTOR in Algorithm 2. Thereby, the induced bipartite subgraph of the incompatibility graph is computed. As new incompatibilities can arise by the removal of crosses, as noted previous section, we might have to repeat this procedure.

The induced bipartite subgraph can be computed using the methods proposed by Dürrschnabel et al. [8]. We are not aware of a formal context where the SAT-sovler approach described in this paper requires a second repetition of the algorithm which motivates the following open question.

OPEN QUESTION 1. Is there a formal context (G, M, I), such that the maximal set $\tilde{I}$ that induces a bipartite subgraph on the incompatibility graph does not give rise to a two-factorizable formal context?

This open problem is of special interest, because it would allow our approach to compute globally maximal two-factorization, as the following shows.

Theorem 4. *Let* $\mathbb{K} = (G, M, I)$ *be a formal context and* $\tilde{I}$ *the subset of* I *that induces a maximal bipartite subgraph on the incompatibility graph. If the formal context* $\tilde{\mathbb{K}} = (G, M, \tilde{I})$ *admits an ordinal two-factorization, its factors are the maximal ordinal factors of* $\mathbb{K}$.

Proof. Assume there are two ordinal factors F_1 and F_2 of $\mathbb{K}$ and $|F_1 \cup F_2| > |\tilde{I}|$. But then the context $(G, M, F_1 \cup F_2)$ is a two-factorizable and thus the graph induced by $F_1 \cup F_2$ on the incompatibility graph is bipartite, a contradiction.

7   Runtime Discussion

If a formal context has order dimension two, it cannot contain a contranominal of dimension three as an induced subcontext. From a result by Albano [1], it follows that a context without a contranominal scale of dimension three and thus especially for all two-dimensional formal contexts, the number of concepts is bounded from above by $\frac{3}{2}|G|^2$ or dually $\frac{3}{2}|M|^2$. There are algorithms that compute the set of all concept of a formal context with polynomial delay [23] and the computation of a conjugate order can be performed in quadratic time [25]. Thus, the algorithm to compute ordinal two-factorizations has polynomial runtime if it paired with the these algorithms.

For the computation of large ordinal factorizations of formal contexts that do not omit ordinal two-factorizations by their structure, the runtime-obstacle is the computation of the large induced bipartite subgraph. If the exact problem is solved, the algorithm thus has exponential runtime. Our previous work [8] also discusses three heuristics for the computation of bipartite subgraphs which can be plugged to achieve an algorithm that has polynomial runtime. Usually, we are interested in two-factorizations of formal context with limited size, as a human can otherwise not grasp the connections encoded in the dataset. Thus, the runtime of these algorithms are usually not the critical limitation and thus a method that is computationally expensive can be employed.

8   Conclusion

In this paper, we expanded on the work done on ordinal two-factorizations in the realm of ordinal factor analysis. First, we performed some structural investigations about the disjointness of the two ordinal factors. Thereby, we were able to characterize the incidence pairs that can appear in both ordinal factors as the isolated elements of the incompatibility graph. Then, we proposed an algorithm for the computation of maximal ordinal two-factorizations. To this end, we developed a polynomial time algorithm to compute a two-factorization of a formal context that has a bipartite incompatibility graph. We showed, that the problem to compute maximal ordinal two-factorizations is NP-complete and proposed our approach ORD2FACTOR to compute large ordinal two-factorizations. As we demonstrated that the problem entails an NP-complete problem, the resulting algorithm is exponential.

Datasets often consist not only of binary but also already ordinal data. The ordinal factor analysis in its current form can only deal with this data by interpreting it as binary. While scaling in formal concept analysis is a tool to deal with this data, factors will not necessarily respect the order encapsulated in the data. In our opinion, the next step should be to extend this method to deal with this kind of non-binary data directly.

References

1. Albano, A., Chornomaz, B.: Why concept lattices are large: extremal theory for generators, concepts, and vc-dimension. Int. J. Gen Syst. **46**(5), 440–457 (2017). https://doi.org/10.1080/03081079.2017.1354798
2. Belohlávek, R., Vychodil, V.: Formal concepts as optimal factors in boolean factor analysis: Implications and experiments. In: Eklund, P.W., Diatta, J., Liquiere, M. (eds.) Proceedings of the Fifth International Conference on Concept Lattices and Their Applications, CLA 2007, Montpellier, France, October 24–26, 2007. CEUR Workshop Proceedings, vol. 331. CEUR-WS.org (2007)
3. Belohlávek, R., Vychodil, V.: Discovery of optimal factors in binary data via a novel method of matrix decomposition. J. Comput. Syst. Sci. **76**(1), 3–20 (2010). https://doi.org/10.1016/j.jcss.2009.05.002
4. Boeck, P.D., Rosenberg, S.: Hierarchical classes: model and data analysis. Psychometrika **53**(3), 361–381 (1988). https://doi.org/10.1007/BF02294218
5. Das, S., Sen, M.K., Roy, A.B., West, D.B.: Interval digraphs: an analogue of interval graphs. J. Graph Theor. **13**(2), 189–202 (1989). https://doi.org/10.1002/jgt.3190130206
6. Doignon, J.P., Ducamp, A., Falmagne, J.C.: On realizable biorders and the biorder dimension of a relation. J. Math. Psychol. **28**(1), 73–109 (1984). https://doi.org/10.1016/0022-2496(84)90020-8
7. Dürrschnabel, D., Hanika, T., Stumme, G.: Drawing order diagrams through two-dimension extension. CoRR abs/1906.06208 (2019), arxiv.org/abs/1906.06208
8. Dürrschnabel, D., Hanika, T., Stumme, G.: Discovering locally maximal bipartite subgraphs. CoRR abs/2211.10446 (2022). 10.48550/arXiv. 2211.10446, https://doi.org/10.48550/arXiv.2211.10446
9. Dürrschnabel, D., Koyda, M., Stumme, G.: Attribute selection using contranominal scales. In: Braun, T., Gehrke, M., Hanika, T., Hernandez, N. (eds.) Graph-Based Representation and Reasoning - 26th International Conference on Conceptual Structures, ICCS 2021, Virtual Event, September 20–22, 2021, Proceedings. Lecture Notes in Computer Science, vol. 12879, pp. 127–141. Springer (2021). https://doi.org/10.1007/978-3-030-86982-3_10
10. Dürrschnabel, D., Stumme, G.: Greedy discovery of ordinal factors. CoRR abs/2302.11554 (2023). https://doi.org/10.48550/arXiv.2302.11554
11. Espadoto, M., Martins, R.M., Kerren, A., Hirata, N.S.T., Telea, A.C.: Toward a quantitative survey of dimension reduction techniques. IEEE Trans. Vis. Comput. Graph. **27**(3), 2153–2173 (2021). https://doi.org/10.1109/TVCG.2019.2944182
12. Felsner, S., Reuter, K.: The linear extension diameter of a poset. SIAM J. Discret. Math. **12**(3), 360–373 (1999). https://doi.org/10.1137/S0895480197326139
13. Ganter, B.: Diskrete Mathematik: Geordnete Mengen. Springer-Lehrbuch, Springer Spektrum Berlin, Heidelberg, 1 edn. (2013). https://doi.org/10.1007/978-3-642-37500-2

14. Ganter, B., Glodeanu, C.V.: Ordinal Factor Analysis. In: Domenach, F., Ignatov, D.I., Poelmans, J. (eds.) ICFCA 2012. LNCS (LNAI), vol. 7278, pp. 128–139. Springer, Heidelberg (2012). https://doi.org/10.1007/978-3-642-29892-9_15

15. Ganter, B., Wille, R.: Formal Concept Analysis. Springer, Heidelberg (1999). https://doi.org/10.1007/978-3-642-59830-2

16. Glodeanu, C.V.: Tri-ordinal factor analysis. In: Cellier, P., Distel, F., Ganter, B. (eds.) Formal Concept Analysis, 11th International Conference, ICFCA 2013, Dresden, Germany, May 21–24, 2013. Proceedings. Lecture Notes in Computer Science, vol. 7880, pp. 125–140. Springer (2013). https://doi.org/10.1007/978-3-642-38317-5_8

17. Glodeanu, C.V., Ganter, B.: Applications of ordinal factor analysis. In: Cellier, P., Distel, F., Ganter, B. (eds.) Formal Concept Analysis, 11th International Conference, ICFCA 2013, Dresden, Germany, May 21–24, 2013. In: Proceedings. Lecture Notes in Computer Science, vol. 7880, pp. 109–124. Springer (2013). https://doi.org/10.1007/978-3-642-38317-5_7

18. Glodeanu, C.V., Konecny, J.: Ordinal factor analysis of graded data. In: Glodeanu, C.V., Kaytoue, M., Sacarea, C. (eds.) ICFCA 2014. LNCS (LNAI), vol. 8478, pp. 128–140. Springer, Cham (2014). https://doi.org/10.1007/978-3-319-07248-7_10

19. Golumbic, M.C.: The complexity of comparability graph recognition and coloring. Computing **18**(3), 199–208 (1977). https://doi.org/10.1007/BF02253207

20. Hirth, J., Horn, V., Stumme, G., Hanika, T.: Ordinal motifs in lattices. CoRR abs/2304.04827 (2023). arXiv:2304.04827

21. Keprt, A.: Algorithms for Binary Factor Analysis. Ph.D. thesis (2006)

22. Keprt, A., Snásel, V.: Binary factor analysis with help of formal concepts. In: Snásel, V., Belohlávek, R. (eds.) Proceedings of the CLA 2004 International Workshop on Concept Lattices and their Applications, Ostrava, Czech Republic, September 23–24, 2004. CEUR Workshop Proceedings, vol. 110. CEUR-WS.org (2004)

23. Kuznetsov, S.O., Obiedkov, S.A.: Comparing performance of algorithms for generating concept lattices. J. Exp. Theor. Artif. Intell. **14**(2–3), 189–216 (2002). https://doi.org/10.1080/09528130210164170

24. Lindig, C.: Fast concept analysis. Work. Conceptual Struct.-Contrib. ICCS **2000**, 152–161 (2000)

25. McConnell, R.M., Spinrad, J.P.: Linear-time transitive orientation. In: Saks, M.E. (ed.) Proceedings of the Eighth Annual ACM-SIAM Symposium on Discrete Algorithms, 5–7 January 1997, New Orleans, Louisiana, USA, pp. 19–25. ACM/SIAM (1997)

26. Pearson, K.: LIII. on lines and planes of closest fit to systems of points in space. London, Edinburgh, Dublin Philosophical Mag. J. Sci. **2**(11), 559–572 (1901). https://doi.org/10.1080/14786440109462720

27. Spangenberg, N., Wolff, K.E.: Comparison of biplot analysis and formal concept analysis in the case of a repertory grid. In: Bock, H.H., Ihm, P. (eds.) Classification, Data Analysis, and Knowledge Organization, pp. 104–112. Springer, Berlin Heidelberg, Berlin, Heidelberg (1991)

A Note on the Number of (Maximal) Antichains in the Lattice of Set Partitions

Dmitry I. Ignatov$^{(\boxtimes)}$ ⓘ

School of Data Analysis and Artificial Intelligence, Laboratory for Models and
Methods of Computational Pragmatics, National Research University Higher School
of Economics, Moscow, Russia
dignatov@hse.ru
http://www.hse.ru

Abstract. Set partitions and partition lattices are well-known objects
in combinatorics and play an important role as a search space in many
applied problems including ensemble clustering. Searching for antichains
in such lattices is similar to that of in Boolean lattices. Counting the number of antichains in Boolean lattices is known as the Dedekind problem.
In spite of the known asymptotic for the latter problem, the behaviour
of the number of antichains in partition lattices has been paid less attention. In this short paper, we show how to obtain a few first numbers
of antichains and maximal antichains in the partition lattices with the
help of concept lattices and provide the reader with some related heuristic bounds. The results of our computational experiments confirm the
known values and are also recorded in the Online Encyclopaedia of Inte-
ger Sequences (see https://oeis.org/A358041).

Keywords: Formal Concept Analysis · partition lattice · maximal
antichains · concept lattices · enumerative combinatorics

1 Introduction

Partitions and their lattices are among the basic combinatorial structures [1] and
have various applications, for example, blocks of a partition of objects are known
as clusters in data analysis [2,3], while in social network analysis the partition
blocks of graph vertices (actors) are known as social communities [4,5]. As the
Boolean lattice of an n-element set, the lattice of all partitions of this set plays
a fundamental role as an ordered search space when we need to find a partition
with certain properties, e.g. when we search for partitions with a concrete number
of blocks with no two specific elements in one block (cf. constrained clustering [6]
or granular computing [7]) or generate functional dependencies over a relational
database (cf. partition pattern structures [8]). In Formal Concept Analysis, there
are also interesting attempts to employ the idea of independence for data analysis
via partitions of objects w.r.t. their attributes where a special variant of Galois
connection appears [9–11].

The original version of this chapter was revised: this chapter contains errors and
typos. This has been corrected. The correction to this chapter is available at
https://doi.org/10.1007/978-3-031-40960-8_19

M. Ojeda-Aciego et al. (Eds.): ICCS 2023, LNAI 14133, pp. 56–69, 2023.
https://doi.org/10.1007/978-3-031-40959-2_6

In combinatorics, special attention is paid to the number of antichains in Boolean lattices, that is to the number of all possible families of mutually incomparable sets. This problem is known as the Dedekind problem [12] and its asymptotic is well studied [13,14]. However, an analogous problem for antichains of partitions has been paid less attention. For example, we know a few values for the number of antichains in the partition lattice for n up to 5^1. Another interesting question, for which there is the famous Sperner theorem, is about the size of the maximum antichain in the Boolean lattice (actually, its width) [15]. R.L. Graham overviewed the results on maximum antichains of the partition lattice [16]. Also, the number of maximal antichains (w.r.t. their extensibility) in the Boolean lattice [17], a sibling of the Dedekind problem, was algorithmically attacked and we know these numbers up to $n = 7^2$ [18]. The lattices of maximal antichains for event sets play an important role in parallel programming [19].

In this paper, we not only confirm the results on the number of antichains in the partition lattice, but also share our recent results on the number of maximal antichains in the partition lattice up to $n = 5$, show recent progress for $n = 6$, and provide some useful bounds for this number. All these results were obtained with the help of concept lattices isomorphic to the partition lattice and parallel versions of classic algorithms designed for that purpose.

2 Basic Definitions

Formal Concept Analysis is an applied branch of modern lattice theory aimed at data analysis, knowledge representation and processing with the help of (formal) concepts and their hierarchies. Here we reproduce basic definitions from [1,20] and our related tutorial [21].

First, we recall several notions related to lattices and partitions.

Definition 1. *A partition of a nonempty set A is a set of its nonempty subsets $\sigma = \{B \mid B \subseteq A\}$ such that $\bigcup_{B \in \sigma} B = A$ and $B \cap C = \emptyset$ for all $B, C \in \sigma$. Every element of σ is called* block.

Definition 2. *A poset $\mathbf{L} = (L, \leq)$ is a* **lattice**, *if for any two elements a and b in L the supremum $a \vee b$ and the infimum $a \wedge b$ always exist. $\mathbf{L}$ is called a* **complete lattice**, *if the supremum $\bigvee X$ and the infimum $\bigwedge X$ exist for any subset A of L. For every complete lattice $\mathbf{L}$ there exists its largest element, $\bigvee L$, called the* **unit element** *of the lattice, denoted by $\mathbf{1}_L$. Dually, the smallest element $\mathbf{0}_L$ is called the* **zero element**.

Definition 3. *A partition lattice of set A is an ordered set $(Part(A), \vee, \wedge)$ where $Part(A)$ is a set of all possible partitions of A and for all partitions σ and ρ supremum and infimum are defined as follows:*

$$\sigma \vee \rho = \left\{ \bigcup conn_{\sigma,\rho}(B) \mid \forall B \in \sigma \right\},$$

---

[1] https://oeis.org/A302250.
[2] https://oeis.org/A326358.

$$\sigma \wedge \rho = \{B \cap C \mid \exists B \in \sigma, \exists C \in \rho : B \cap C \neq \emptyset\}, \text{ where}$$

$conn_{\sigma,\rho}(B)$ *is the connected component to which* B *belongs to in the bipartite graph* (σ, ρ, E) *such that* $(B, C) \in E$ *iff* $C \cap B \neq \emptyset$.

Definition 4. *Let* A *be a set and let* $\rho, \sigma \in Part(A)$. *The partition* ρ *is finer than the partition* σ *if every block* B *of* σ *is a union of blocks of* ρ, *that is* $\rho \leq \sigma$.

Equivalently one can use the traditional connection between supremum, infimum and partial order in the lattice: $\rho \leq \sigma$ iff $\rho \vee \sigma = \sigma$ $(\rho \wedge \sigma = \rho)$.

Definition 5. *A* **formal context** $\mathbb{K} = (G, M, I)$ *consists of two sets* G *and* M *and a relation* I *between* G *and* M. *The elements of* G *are called the* **objects** *and the elements of* M *are called the* **attributes** *of the context. The notation* gIm *or* $(g, m) \in I$ *means that the object* g *has attribute* m.

Definition 6. *For* $A \subseteq G$, *let*

$$A' := \{m \in M \mid (g, m) \in I \text{ for all } g \in A\}$$

and, for $B \subseteq M$, *let*

$$B' := \{g \in G \mid (g, m) \in I \text{ for all } m \in B\}.$$

These operators are called **derivation operators** *or* **concept-forming operators** *for* $\mathbb{K} = (G, M, I)$.

Let (G, M, I) be a context, one can prove that operators

$$(\cdot)'' : 2^G \to 2^G, \ (\cdot)'' : 2^M \to 2^M$$

are closure operators (i.e. idempotent, extensive, and monotone).

Definition 7. *A* **formal concept** *of a formal context* $\mathbb{K} = (G, M, I)$ *is a pair* (A, B) *with* $A \subseteq G$, $B \subseteq M$, $A' = B$ *and* $B' = A$. *The sets* A *and* B *are called the extent and the intent of the formal concept* (A, B), *respectively. The* **subconcept-superconcept relation** *is given by* $(A_1, B_1) \leq (A_2, B_2)$ *iff* $A_1 \subseteq A_2$ $(B_2 \subseteq B_1)$.

This definition implies that every formal concept has two constituent parts, namely, its extent and intent.

Definition 8. *The set of all formal concepts of a context* $\mathbb{K}$ *together with the order relation* $\leq$ *forms a complete lattice, called the* **concept lattice** *of* $\mathbb{K}$ *and denoted by* $\underline{\mathfrak{B}}(\mathbb{K})$.

Definition 9. *For every two formal concepts* (A_1, B_1) *and* (A_2, B_2) *of a certain formal context their* **greatest common subconcept** *is defined as follows:*

$$(A_1, B_1) \wedge (A_2, B_2) = (A_1 \cap A_2, (B_1 \cup B_2)'').$$

The **least common superconcept** *of* (A_1, B_1) *and* (A_2, B_2) *is given as*

$$(A_1, B_1) \vee (A_2, B_2) = ((A_1 \cup A_2)'', B_1 \cap B_2).$$

We say supremum instead of "least common superconcept", and instead of "greatest common subconcept" we use the term infimum.

In Fig. 1, one can see the context whose concept lattice is isomorphic to the partition lattice of a four-element set and the line (or Hasse) diagram of its concept lattice.

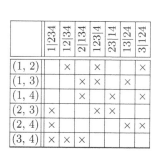
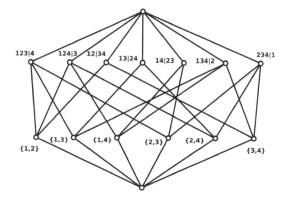

Fig. 1. The formal context (left) and the line diagram of the concept lattice (right) which is isomorphic to $\mathcal{P}_4$.

Theorem 1 *(Ganter & Wille [20]). For a given partially ordered set $\mathfrak{P} = (P, \leq)$ the concept lattice of the formal context $\mathbb{K} = (J(P), M(P), \leq)$ is isomorphic to the Dedekind–MacNeille completion of $\mathfrak{P}$, where $J(P)$ and $M(P)$ are sets of join-irreducible and meet-irreducible elements of $\mathfrak{P}$, respectively.*

A join-irreducible[3] lattice element cannot be represented as the supremum of strictly smaller elements; dually, for meet-irreducible elements. If $(P, \leq)$ is a lattice, then $\mathbb{K} = (J(P), M(P), \leq)$ is called its **standard context**.

Theorem 2 *(Bocharov et al. [2]). For a given partition lattice $\mathfrak{L} = (Part(A), \vee, \wedge)$ there exist a formal context $\mathbb{K} = (P_2, A_2, I)$, where $P_2 = \{\{a, b\} \mid a, b \in A \text{ and } a \neq b\}$, $A_2 = \{\sigma \mid \sigma \in Part(A) \text{ and } |\sigma| = 2\}$ and $\{a, b\}I\sigma$ when a and b belong to the same block of σ. The concept lattice $\underline{\mathfrak{B}}(P_2, A_2, I)$ is isomorphic to the initial lattice $(Part(A), \vee, \wedge)$.*

There is a natural bijection between elements of $\mathfrak{L} = (Part(A), \vee, \wedge)$ and formal concepts of $\underline{\mathfrak{B}}(P_2, A_2, I)$. Every $(A, B) \in \underline{\mathfrak{B}}(P_2, A_2, I)$ corresponds to $\sigma = \bigwedge B$ and every pair $\{i, j\}$ from A is in one of σ blocks, where $\sigma \in Part(A)$. Every $(A, B) \in \underline{\mathfrak{B}}(J(\mathfrak{L}), M(\mathfrak{L}), \leq)$ corresponds to $\sigma = \bigwedge B = \bigvee A$.

---

[3] join- and meet-irreducible elements are also called supremum- and infimum-irreducible elements, respectively.

3   Problem Statement

Let us denote the partition lattice of set $[n] = \{1, \ldots, n\}$ by $\mathcal{P}_n = (Part([n]), \leq)$, where $Part([n])$ is the set of all partitions of $[n]$.

Two related problems, which we are going to consider are as follows.

Problem 1 (#ACP). *Count the number of antichains of $\mathcal{P}_n = (Part([n]), \leq)$ for a given $n \in \mathbb{N}$.*

Problem 2 (#MaxACP). *Count the number of maximal antichains of $\mathcal{P}_n = (Part([n]), \leq)$ for a given $n \in \mathbb{N}$.*

4   Proposed Approach

Our approach to computing maximal antichains of the considered lattice is a direct consequence of the Dedekind-MacNeille completion and the basic theorem of FCA. The first one allows building the minimal extension of a partial order such that this extension forms a lattice. From the second theorem, we know that every complete lattice can be represented by a formal context built on the supremum- and infimum-irreducible elements of the lattice.

When Klaus Reuter was studying jump numbers of partial orders $(P, \leq)$, he found their connection with the number of maximal antichains and reported about it as follows [22]: "Originally we have discovered a connection of the concept lattice of $(P, P, \not\geq)$ to the jump number of P. Later on, we learned from Wille that this lattice is isomorphic to the lattice of maximal antichains of P. Thus with speaking about $MA(P)$ it is now quite hidden that we have gained most of our results by knowledge of Formal Concept Analysis." Here, $MA(P)$ denotes the set of maximal antichains of $(P, \leq)$.

An order ideal $\downarrow X$ of $X \subseteq P$ is a set $\{y \in P \mid \exists x \in X : y \leq x\}$, while $\uparrow X$ denotes the order filter generated by X (dually defined).

The lattice of maximal antichains of P, $(MA(P), \leq)$ is defined by $A_1 \leq A_2$ iff $\downarrow A_1 \subseteq \downarrow A_2$ for $A_1, A_2 \in MA(P)$.

It is known that two fundamental lattices related to orders, the distributive lattice of order ideals and the lattice of the Dedekind-MacNeille completion can be naturally described by FCA means [22]: $\mathfrak{B}(P, P, \leq)$ represents the Dedekind-MacNeille completion (completion by cuts) of $(P, \leq)$, while $\mathfrak{B}(P, P, \not\geq)$ represents the lattice of order ideals of $(P, \leq)$ (which is isomorphic to the lattice of all antichains of $(P, \leq)$).

The observation made by Wille makes it possible to fit the lattice of maximal antichains in this framework: $\mathfrak{B}(P, P, \not\geq)$ represents the lattice of maximal antichains of $(P, \leq)$.

Proposition 1 ([22], Proposition 2.1). $(MA(P), \leq)$ *is isomorphic to* $\mathfrak{B}(P, P, \not\geq)$.

Corollary 1. #MAxACP *(Problem 2) is equivalent to determining the number of formal concepts of* $\mathfrak{B}(Part([n]), Part([n]), \not\geq)$.

So, our approach has two steps:

- 1. Generate the formal context $\mathbb{K} = (Part([n]), Part([n]), \not\geq)$ for a given n.
- 2. Count the cardinality of $\mathbf{L}_n = \mathfrak{B}(Part([n]), Part([n]), \not\geq)$.

$\mathbb{K}(\mathcal{P}_3)$	1|23	12|3	2|13
$(1, 2)$		×	
$(1, 3)$			×
$(2, 3)$	×		

$\not\geq$	0	4	2	1	7
0		×	×	×	×
4			×	×	×
2		×		×	×
1		×	×		×
7					

$\not>$	0	4	2	1	7
0	×	×	×	×	×
4		×	×	×	×
2		×	×	×	×
1		×	×	×	×
7					×

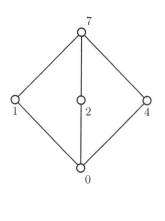 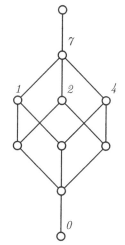 

Fig. 2. The formal contexts $\mathbb{K}(\mathcal{P}_3) = (J(\mathcal{P}_3), M(\mathcal{P}_3), \leq)$ (left), $(Part([3]), Part([3]), \not\geq)$ (centre), and $(Part([3]), Part([3]), \not>)$ (right) along with the line diagrams of their concept lattices [20] (bottom line), respectively.

The line diagram of $\mathfrak{B}(Part([3]), Part([3]), \not>)$, which is isomorphic to the lattice of maximal antichains $(MA(\mathcal{P}_3), \leq)$, and its formal context are given in Fig. 2, the right column. The context for the lattice isomorphic to the lattice of ideals of $\mathcal{P}_3$ is in the centre, while the original context for the lattice isomorphic to $\mathcal{P}_3$ is shown on the right. The nodes of $\mathfrak{B}(J(\mathcal{P}_3), M(\mathcal{P}_3), \leq)$ are labelled with integers, whose binary codes correspond to concept extents. For example, label 4 encodes the extent of concept $((2, 3), 1|23)$ since $4_{10} = 100_2$. The orders $\not\geq$ and $\not>$ are taken with respect to hierarchical order on concepts of $\mathfrak{B}(J(\mathcal{P}_3), M(\mathcal{P}_3), \leq)$. The labels of the two remaining lattices are given with reduced attribute labelling.

Note that some rows and columns of the third context can be removed without affecting the lattice structure. For example, duplicated rows 2 and 4.

Columns and rows obtained as an intersection of other columns and rows, respectively, can also be removed without affecting the concept lattice structure. This procedure is called reducing the context [20]. Thus, for moderately large n we use the so-called standard contexts of concept lattices, $\mathbb{K}(\mathbf{L}) = (J(\mathbf{L}), M(\mathbf{L}), \leq)$, where $\mathbf{L} = (L, \leq)$ is a finite lattice, and $J(\mathbf{L})$ and $M(\mathbf{L})$ are join- and meet-irreducible elements of $\mathbf{L}$ [20].

The first step is trivial, while for the second step, we have plenty of algorithms both in FCA [23] and Frequent Closed Itemset mining [24] communities. However, having in mind the combinatorial nature of the problem, and the almost doubly-exponential growth of the sequence, we cannot use a fast algorithm which relies on recursion or (execution tree will be humongous) sophisticated structures like FP-trees due to memory constraints. We rather need a parallelisable solution which does not require the memory size of $O(|L|)$ and can be easily resumed, for example, after the break of computation for monthly routine maintenance. So, we set our eye on Ganter's Next Closure algorithm [25,26], which does not refer to the list of generated concepts and uses little storage space.

Since the extent of a concept uniquely defines its intent, to obtain the set of all formal concepts, it is enough to find closures either of subsets of objects or subsets of attributes.

We assume that there is a linear order $(<)$ on G. The algorithm starts by examining the set consisting of the object maximal with respect to $< (max(G))$ and finishes when the canonically generated closure is equal to G. Let A be a currently examined subset of G. The generation of A'' is considered canonical if $A'' \setminus A$ does not contain $g < max(A)$. If the generation of A'' is canonical (and A'' is not equal to G), the next set to be examined is obtained from A'' as follows:

$$A'' \cup \{g\} \setminus \{h | h \in A'' \text{ and } g < h\}, \text{ where } g = max(\{h | h \in G \setminus A''\}).$$

Otherwise, the set examined at the next step is obtained from A in a similar way, but the added object must be less (w.r.t. $<$) than the maximal object in A:

$$A'' \cup \{g\} \setminus \{h | h \in A \text{ and } g < h\}, \text{ where } g = max(\{h | h \in G \setminus A \text{ and } h < max(A)\}).$$

The pseudocode of NEXTCLOSURE is given in Algorithm 1.

The NEXTCLOSURE algorithm is enumerative and produces the set of all concepts in time $O(|G|^2|M||L|)$ and also has polynomial delay $O(|G|^2|M|)$. For our counting purposes, Step 5 of the algorithm should be replaced with $|L| := |L| + 1$, while Step 12 should return $|L|$.

Our modification of the algorithm features parallel computing, saving of intermediate results as pairs $(A'', |L|)$, and representation of sets as binary vectors with integers as well as usage of bit operations on them.

Algorithm 1. NextClosure

Input: $\mathbb{K} = (G, M, I)$ is a context
Output: L is the concept set
1: $L := \emptyset, A := \emptyset, g := max(G)$
2: **while** $A \neq G$ **do**
3:   $A := A'' \cup \{g\} \setminus \{h | h \in A \text{ and } g < h\}$
4:   **if** $\{h | h \in A \text{ and } g \leq h\} = \emptyset$ **then**
5:     $L := L \cup \{(A'', A')\}$
6:     $g := max(\{h | h \in G \setminus A''\})$
7:     $A := A''$
8:   **else**
9:     $g := max(\{h | h \in G \setminus A \text{ and } h < g\})$
10:   **end if**
11: **end while**
12: **return** L

5   Results and Recent Progress

The results for #ACP problem were published in OEIS by John Machacek on Apr 04 2018. We have validated them with the used approach. While our results on #MAXACP were obtained by Oct 29 2022. They are summarised for n up to 5 in Table 1.

Table 1. The confirmed (the first row) and the obtained (the last row) results

n	1	2	3	4	5
#ACP, OEIS A302250		2	3	10	347	79814832
#MAXACP, OEIS A358041	1	2	3	32	14094

All the contexts and codes are available on GitHub: https://github.com/dimachine/SetPartAnti. We used IPython for its ease of implementation and speeded it up with Cython and multiprocess(ing) libraries. To compute all the known values for #MAXACP it took about 357 ms, while similar experiments for #ACP took 26 min 44 s on a laptop with 2.9 GHz 6-core processor, Intel Core i9.

To compute #MAXACP for $n = 6$, we used Intel Core i9-12900KS with 24 threads (at maximum capacity) and 3.4 GHz of base processor frequency. Sixty branches of computation have been completed with 250201481250 maximal antichains, while twelve branches are still in progress (see Fig. 3) with the preliminary sum 1320200000000 obtained during more than one month of computations.

As for the lower and upper bounds and asymptotic analysis on the number of (maximal) antichains of set partitions, it is more complex than that of set subsets.

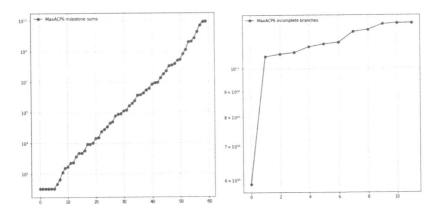

Fig. 3. Completed (left) and incomplete branches (right) for our current $ma(\mathcal{P}_6)$ computation

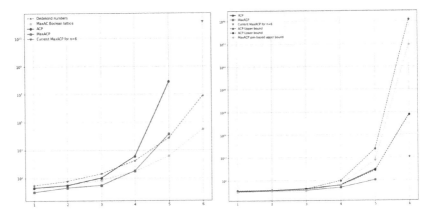

Fig. 4. Comparison with D_n and $ma(\mathcal{B}_n)$ (left) and with the lower and upper bounds of $acp(\mathcal{P}_n)$ (right) for our current $macp(\mathcal{P}_6)$ computation

The size of the level sets of the partition lattice is given by Stirling numbers of the second kind, while the sizes of the level sets of the Boolean lattice are given by binomial coefficients. The lower bound and the asymptotic for the Boolean lattice are based on the size of its largest level set(s) (maximal antichain), so we could use similar logic for the partition lattice. However, the maximal value of the Stirling number of the second kind, $\max_{k \leq n} \left\{{n \atop k}\right\}$, is not always equal to the size of the maximum antichain in $\mathcal{P}_n$ and the connection between these numbers is non-linear with unknown constants [27][4].

Thus, from [27], we know that

---

[4] The question on the equality was posed by G.C. Rota [16].

$$d(\mathcal{P}_n) = \max_{k \leq n} \left\{ {n \atop k} \right\} \Theta(n^a (\ln n)^{-a-1/4}), \text{ where}$$

$d(\mathcal{P}_n)$ is is the size of the maximal antichain in $\mathcal{P}_n$ and $a = \frac{2-e\ln 2}{4} \approx 0.02895765$.

Luckily, according to [16], it was first shown that a maximal antichain has at most $\max_{k \leq n} \left\{ {n \atop k} \right\}$ elements for $n \leq 20$, while later it was obtained that the discrepancy arises when $n \geq 3.4 \cdot 10^6$ [28,29]. Thus, a simple lower bound for #ACP problem is given by $2^{\max_{k \leq n} \left\{ {n \atop k} \right\}} \leq 2^{d(\mathcal{P}_n)}$, and can be further improved by considering not only the partition lattice level for $\max_{k \leq n} \left\{ {n \atop k} \right\}$.

Proposition 2. $acp(\mathcal{P}_n) \geq \sum_{k=1}^{n} 2^{\left\{ {n \atop k} \right\}} - n + 1$ for $n \geq 1$.

Proof. Each partition lattice level contains partitions in k blocks for a given $1 \leq k \leq n$. These partitions form a maximal antichain and each of its subsets forms an antichain. The number of unique antichains by each level is given by $2^{\left\{ {n \atop k} \right\}} - 1$ since the empty set should be counted only once.

For the upper bounds, we can use knowledge of FCA, where the largest number of concepts of a context with n objects and m attributes is given by $2^{\min(n,m)}$. Since the Bell numbers B_n count the size of the Partition lattice on n elements, the number of objects (and attributes) in $\mathbb{K} = (Part([n]), Part([n]), \not>)$ and $\mathbb{K} = (Part([n]), Part([n]), \not\geq)$ is given by B_n. Thus, the trivial upper bound is given by 2^{B_n} but it is equivalent to the powerset of all partitions. We can notice the $\mathbf{0}$ and $\mathbf{1}$ of the set partition lattice are represented by empty column and empty row in the context inducing the order ideals lattice, while for the context inducing the lattice of maximal antichains, they are represented by full row and column, respectively. This implies slightly better upper bounds $2^{B_n-1} + 2$ with $n > 1$ (although, it is still valid for $n = 1$ giving $3 > acp(1) = 2^{B_1} = 2$) for #ACP and 2^{B_n-1} for #MAXACP.

Remark 1. Since we deal with lattices, which are partial orders (reflexive, anti-symmetric, and transitive), their incidence relations can be represented with formal contexts with identical sets of objects and attributes where each object-attribute pair on the main diagonal belongs to the incidence relation (the main diagonal is full) while all the pairs below the diagonal do not.

Proposition 3. Let $\mathbf{L} = (L, \leq)$ be a finite lattice, then $|\mathfrak{B}(L, L, \not\geq)| \leq 2^{|L|-2} + 2$.

Proof. 1) Let $|L| = 1$, then $|\mathfrak{B}(L, L, \not\geq)| = 2$ which is less than $2\frac{1}{2}$. 2) Let $|L| = 2$, then $|\mathfrak{B}(L, L, \not\geq)| = 3$ which is equal to the right-hand side of the inequality. 3) For $|L| \geq 3$, let us consider the subcontext $(L \setminus \mathbf{1}, L \setminus \mathbf{0}, \not\geq)$. Recalling the structure of the incidence table for a partial order with all empty pairs below the main diagonal, we obtain that one of the context objects, $\mathbf{0}$, and one of its attributes, $\mathbf{1}$, are represented by a full row and a full column, respectively, while the main diagonal is full and the pairs above the main diagonal belong to $\not\geq$. It is so, since for every pair (a, b) above the main diagonal of the original context $|(L, L, \leq)|$ only one of the cases fulfils 1) $a < b$ or 2) $a \not< b$ (which implies $a \not> b$, i.e. a and b incomparable). Either case implies $a \not\geq b$.

At the same time, the first subdiagonal is empty since $\not\geq$ is antireflexive. It implies that the number of concepts $|\mathfrak{B}(L \setminus \mathbf{1}, L \setminus \mathbf{0}, \not\geq)| \leq 2^{\min(|L \setminus \mathbf{1}|-1, |L \setminus \mathbf{0}|-1)} = 2^{|L|-2}$. Going back to the original context, we obtain two more concepts for the deleted object $\mathbf{1}$, $(\mathbf{1}'', \mathbf{1}') = (L, \emptyset)$ and for the deleted attribute $\mathbf{0}$, $(\mathbf{0}', \mathbf{0}'') = (\emptyset, L)$, respectively.

Unfortunately, even these slightly better upper bounds are overly high, but at least we can do better by providing an upper bound for $macp(n)$, which can be also estimated via the sizes of the standard context for $MA(\mathcal{P}_n)$. Thus, for $MA(\mathcal{P}_n)$ the upper bound is as follows:

$$2^{\min(|J(MA(\mathcal{P}_6))|, |M(MA(\mathcal{P}_6))|)} = 2^{\min(172, 188)} \approx 5.986 \cdot 10^{51} .$$

Table 2. The sizes of standard context for $MA(\mathcal{P}_n)$ compared to Bell numbers for n up 7

n	1	2	3	4	5	6	7
Bell numbers	1	2	5	15	52	203	877
$J(MA(\mathcal{P}_n))$	0	1	2	8	37	172	814
$M(MA(\mathcal{P}_n))$	0	1	2	9	42	188	856

The size of the standard context for the lattice of antichains on partitions for a fixed n is given by Bell numbers both for join- and meet-irreducible elements (see Table 2).

Since we know $macp(\mathcal{P}_n) \leq acp(\mathcal{P}_n)$, we can try to further sharpen this inequality by discarding some of those antichains that are not maximal.

Proposition 4. $macp(\mathcal{P}_n) \leq acp(\mathcal{P}_n) - \sum_{k=1}^{n} 2^{\{^n_k\}} + 2n - 1$ for $n \geq 1$.

Proof. We subtract from $acp(\mathcal{P}_n)$ the number of all non-maximal antichains obtained by each level of the partition lattice, which gives us a decrement $2^{\{^n_k\}} - 2$ for each k (the empty set is counted only once).

Let us use $\Delta(n)$ for $acp(n) - macp(n)$ and $D_l(n)$ for the decrement by levels $\sum_{k=1}^{n} 2^{\{^n_k\}} - 2n + 1$. In Table 3, it is shown that for the first three values $\Delta(n)$ and $D_l(n)$ coincide, but later the antichains different from the level antichain's subsets appear.

Proposition 4 gives us a tool to establish an improved upper bound for $macp(\mathcal{P}_n)$.

Table 3. The signed relative error $\frac{\Delta(n) - D_l(n)}{\Delta(n)}$

n	1	2	3	4	5
$\Delta(n)$	1	1	7	315	79800738
$D_l(n)$	1	1	7	189	33588219
Relative error	0	0	0	0.4	≈ 0.5791

Proposition 5. $macp(\mathcal{P}_n) \leq 2^{B_n - 2} - \sum_{k=1}^{n} 2\left\{{n \atop k}\right\} + 2n + 1$ *for* $n \geq 1$.

Proof. We directly plug in $2^{B_n-2} + 2$ in the previous inequality. Note that for $n = 1$, $macp(\mathcal{P}_n) = 1 < 2^{1-2} - 2\left\{{1 \atop 1}\right\} + 2 + 1 = 1\frac{1}{2}$.

Since $\binom{n}{k} \leq \left\{{n \atop k}\right\}$, we could expect that the Dedekind numbers D_n and the number of maximal antichains of the Boolean lattice, $ma(\mathcal{B}_n)$, are good candidates for heuristic lower bounds. As we can see from Fig. 4, they become lower than their counterparts for the set partition lattice already at $n = 4$.

It is known that $B_n < \left(\frac{0.792n}{\ln(n+1)}\right)^n$ for all positive integers n [30]. So, $\log B_n$ is bounded by a superlinear function in n^5. Thus, we can try a linear approximation for the logarithms of the number of maximal antichains, $macp(\mathcal{P}_6)$, and that of antichains, $acp(\mathcal{P}_6)$, respectively, by a tangential line passing through the line segments $[\log macp(\mathcal{P}_4), \log macp(\mathcal{P}_5)]$ and $[\log acp(\mathcal{P}_4), \log acp(\mathcal{P}_5)]$, respectively. Let us consider the natural logarithm, ln. Thus, these heuristic lower bounds are as follows:

$$e^{\ln^2 acp(5)/\ln acp(4)} \approx 1.25 \cdot 10^{26} \text{ and } e^{\ln^2 macp(5)/\ln macp(4)} \approx 273562462667.8.$$

The latter heuristic lower bound is already about 5.74 times smaller than the currently precomputed estimate of $macp(6)$, i.e. 1570401481250.

6   Conclusion

We hope that this paper will stimulate the interest of the conceptual structures community in computational combinatorics, both from algorithmic and theoretic points of view. Recent progress in computing such numbers as the Dedekind number for $n = 9$ due to high-performance computing and FCA-based algorithms can be relevant here [31].

Acknowledgements. This study was implemented in the Basic Research Program's framework at HSE University. This research was also supported in part through computational resources of HPC facilities at HSE University. We would like to thank all the OEIS editors, especially Joerg Arndt, Michel Marcus, and N. J. A. Sloane. We also would like to thank anonymous reviewers and Jaume Baixeries for relevant suggestions, and Lev P. Shibasov and Valentina A. Goloubeva for the lasting flame of inspiration.

---

[5] We use log when the logarithm base is not specified.

References

1. Aigner, M.: Combinatorial Theory. Springer, Heidelberg (2012). https://doi.org/10.1007/978-3-642-59101-3
2. Bocharov, A., Gnatyshak, D., Ignatov, D.I., Mirkin, B.G., Shestakov, A.: A lattice-based consensus clustering algorithm. In: Huchard, M., Kuznetsov, S.O. (eds.) Proceedings of the 13th International Conference on Concept Lattices and Their Applications, Moscow, Russia, 18–22 July 2016, Volume 1624 of CEUR Workshop Proceedings, pp. 45–56. CEUR-WS.org (2016)
3. Brabant, Q., Mouakher, A., Bertaux, A.: Preventing overlaps in agglomerative hierarchical conceptual clustering. In: Alam, M., Braun, T., Yun, B. (eds.) ICCS 2020. LNCS (LNAI), vol. 12277, pp. 74–89. Springer, Cham (2020). https://doi.org/10.1007/978-3-030-57855-8_6
4. Doreian, P., Batagelj, V., Ferligoj, A.: Generalized blockmodeling of two-mode network data. Soc. Netw. **26**(1), 29–53 (2004)
5. Missaoui, R., Kuznetsov, S.O., Obiedkov, S.A. (eds.): Formal Concept Analysis of Social Networks. Lecture Notes in Social Networks (LNSN). Springer, Cham (2017). https://doi.org/10.1007/978-3-319-64167-6
6. de Amorim, R.C.: Constrained clustering with Minkowski Weighted K-Means. In: 2012 IEEE 13th International Symposium on Computational Intelligence and Informatics (CINTI), pp. 13–17 (2012)
7. Chiaselotti, G., Ciucci, D., Gentile, T., Infusino, F.G.: The granular partition lattice of an information table. Inf. Sci. **373**, 57–78 (2016)
8. Baixeries, J., Kaytoue, M., Napoli, A.: Characterizing functional dependencies in formal concept analysis with pattern structures. Ann. Math. Artif. Intell. **72**(1), 129–149 (2014)
9. Valverde-Albacete, F.J., Peláez-Moreno, C., Cabrera, I.P., Cordero, P., Ojeda-Aciego, M.: Formal independence analysis. In: Medina, J., et al. (eds.) IPMU 2018. CCIS, vol. 853, pp. 596–608. Springer, Cham (2018). https://doi.org/10.1007/978-3-319-91473-2_51
10. Valverde-Albacete, F.J., Peláez-Moreno, C., Cabrera, I.P., Cordero, P., Ojeda-Aciego, M.: A data analysis application of formal independence analysis. In: CLA, pp. 117–128 (2018)
11. Albacete, F.J.V., Peláez-Moreno, C., Cordero, P., Ojeda-Aciego, M.: Formal equivalence analysis. In: Proceedings of the 11th Conference of the European Society for Fuzzy Logic and Technology, EUSFLAT 2019, September 2019, pp. 797–804. Atlantis Press (2019)
12. Dedekind, R.: Über zerlegung von zahlen durch ihre grössten gemeinsamen theiler. In: Gesammelte Werke, vol. 2, pp. 103–148. Vieweg, Braunschweig (1897)
13. Kleitman, D., Markowsky, G.: On Dedekind's problem: the number of isotone Boolean functions. II. Trans. Am. Math. Soc. **213**, 373–390 (1975)
14. Korshunov, A.D.: On the number of monotone Boolean functions. Probl. Kibern. **38**, 5–108 (1981)
15. Sperner, E.: Ein Satz über Untermengen einer endlichen Menge. Math. Z. **27**, 544–548 (1928). https://doi.org/10.1007/BF01171114
16. Graham, R.L.: Maximum antichains in the partition lattice. Math. Intelligencer **1**(2), 84–86 (1978). https://doi.org/10.1007/BF03023067
17. Ilinca, L., Kahn, J.: Counting maximal antichains and independent sets. Order **30**(2), 427–435 (2013). https://doi.org/10.1007/s11083-012-9253-5

18. Ignatov, D.I.: On the number of maximal antichains in Boolean lattices for n up to 7. Lobachevskii J. Math. **44**(1), 137–146 (2023). https://doi.org/10.1134/S1995080223010158

19. Garg, V.K.: Lattice of maximal antichains. In: Introduction to Lattice Theory with Computer Science Applications, pp. 175–192. Wiley (2015). https://doi.org/10.1002/9781119069706

20. Ganter, B., Wille, R.: Formal Concept Analysis. Mathematical Foundations, 1st edn. Springer, Heidelberg (1999). https://doi.org/10.1007/978-3-642-59830-2

21. Ignatov, D.I.: Introduction to formal concept analysis and its applications in information retrieval and related fields. In: Braslavski, P., Karpov, N., Worring, M., Volkovich, Y., Ignatov, D.I. (eds.) RuSSIR 2014. CCIS, vol. 505, pp. 42–141. Springer, Cham (2015). https://doi.org/10.1007/978-3-319-25485-2_3

22. Reuter, K.: The jump number and the lattice of maximal antichains. Discret. Math. **88**(2), 289–307 (1991)

23. Kuznetsov, S.O., Obiedkov, S.A.: Comparing performance of algorithms for generating concept lattices. J. Exp. Theor. Artif. Intell. **14**(2–3), 189–216 (2002)

24. Zaki, M.J., Hsiao, C.: Efficient algorithms for mining closed itemsets and their lattice structure. IEEE Trans. Knowl. Data Eng. **17**(4), 462–478 (2005)

25. Ganter, B., Reuter, K.: Finding all closed sets: a general approach. Order **8**(3), 283–290 (1991)

26. Ganter, B.: Two basic algorithms in concept analysis. In: Kwuida, L., Sertkaya, B. (eds.) ICFCA 2010. LNCS (LNAI), vol. 5986, pp. 312–340. Springer, Heidelberg (2010). https://doi.org/10.1007/978-3-642-11928-6_22

27. Canfield, E.R.: The size of the largest antichain in the partition lattice. J. Comb. Theor. Ser. A **83**(2), 188–201 (1998)

28. Jichang, S., Kleitman, D.J.: Superantichains in the lattice of partitions of a set. Stud. Appl. Math. **71**(3), 207–241 (1984)

29. Canfield, E.R., Harper, L.H.: Large antichains in the partition lattice. Random Struct. Algorithms **6**(1), 89–104 (1995)

30. Berend, D., Tassa, T.: Improved bounds on Bell numbers and on moments of sums of random variables. Probab. Math. Stat. **30**(2), 185–205 (2010)

31. Jäkel, C.: A computation of the ninth Dedekind Number (2023)

Formal Concept Analysis: Applications

Formal Concept Analysis for Trace Clustering in Process Mining

Salah Eddine Boukhetta$^{(\boxtimes)}$ and Marwa Trabelsi$^{(\boxtimes)}$

L3i Laboratory, University of La Rochelle, La Rochelle, France
{salah.boukhetta,marwa.trabelsi}@univ-lr.fr

Abstract. Modeling user interaction in information systems (IS) using Process Mining techniques is an intriguing requirement for designers looking to optimize the use of various IS functionalities and make stored resources more accessible. Discovered models can thus be used in future work to present a set of recommendations to IS users. However, the large number of generated logs or user's traces result in complex models. To address this problem, in this paper, we propose a new methodology for grouping user traces prior to modeling using Formal Concept Analysis. The clustering method relies on the GALACTIC framework to generate relevant concepts, which are then used to select a specific concept for each trace using a distance measure. Considering a trace as a sequence, the proposed method generate concepts based on maximal common subsequences. The experimental part shows that our method successfully found the original clusters on a simulated dataset.

Keywords: Formal Concept Analysis · Trace clustering · Process mining · GALACTIC

1 Introduction

The practical need to investigate how users interact with information systems by examining their digital traces is growing significantly. Indeed, companies' business processes through these systems are fragmented, leaving users to determine their own path to achieve their objectives. In such a context, the user's journey to perform a task (purchase of a product on a website, search for a document in a digital library, etc.) corresponds to an "unstructured process". The meaning, structure and results depend on the user's skills.

In this work, we focus on the case of digital libraries in particular. Digital libraries (DLs) are complex and advanced information systems that attract a multitude of users for various information retrieval tasks. They store and manage a large amount of digital documents and objects. They provide many services to their users, such as the information retrieval system, personalization, etc. [25].

To model the different paths leading DLs users to the resolution of their information retrieval task, we chose to use process mining techniques. Process mining proposes a suite of methods for discovering and modeling human behavior from digital traces generated during the interaction with information systems [1].

M. Ojeda-Aciego et al. (Eds.): ICCS 2023, LNAI 14133, pp. 73–88, 2023.
https://doi.org/10.1007/978-3-031-40960-8_7

The main advantage of these techniques is their ability to handle the whole information retrieval process (the sequence of activities carried out by users from the beginning to the end of their navigation). Therefore, a model depicting the users' interactions can help system designers to answer users' practical requirements, on the one hand, and to present a set of recommendations to them, on the other hand. Moreover, modeling user's interactions could be helpful to optimize systems' design and improve the most used features.

However, due to the increasing use of DLs, very large and complex event logs are produced. These complex event logs pose additional challenges for process mining techniques. The large number of generated logs leads to complex models, commonly referred to as spaghetti models. These models can be challenging to interpret and may not fulfill all users' objectives [1,28]. Trace clustering techniques are recommended to address this issue [8]. These techniques group event logs based on similarities in executed activity sequences. Clustering approaches, on the other hand, face many challenges. When applied to user interactions in DLs, for example, numerous DLs users may have comparable sub-processes in their navigation despite conducting a different type of research or pursuing the same goal. Furthermore, despite the number of target clusters being uncertain, created process models based on clustering must present disjoint models to identify users' journeys.

In this paper, we propose a new trace clustering method for grouping user interactions prior to modeling using Formal Concept Analysis (FCA for short), a new FCA application. FCA is a data analysis method that focuses on the relationship between a set of objects and a set of attributes in data. A concept lattice, which is the main structure of FCA, gives us valuable insights from a dual viewpoint based on the objects and the attributes. In this work, FCA can be a solution to comprehend the users' navigations, group them, and extract the characteristics shared by this type of navigation. One limitation of the FCA framework is the generation of a large number of concepts, which makes extracting information from data more complex at times. To overcome this limitation, we attempt to combine the FCA framework with traditional clustering methods, beginning with generating a concept lattice and then extracting clusters based on the generated concepts.

The rest of the paper is structured as follows. After introducing FCA and process mining basics in Sect. 2 and 3 respectively, we discuss the related work in Sect. 4. Section 5 describes the proposed approach. Then, Sect. 6 describes experiments on the synthetic dataset. We consecutively present the event data and the experimental results. Finally, Sect. 7 concludes the paper and offers directions for future work.

2   Formal Concept Analysis

Formal Concept Analysis (FCA) is a field of data analysis for identifying relationships in the data set. It appears in 1982 [27], then in the Ganter and Wille's 1999 work [12], it is issued from a branch of applied lattice theory that first appeared in the book of Barbut and Monjardet in 1970 [4]. The lattice property guarantees both a hierarchy of clusters, and a complete and consistent navigation structure for interactive approaches [9]. FCA is classically designed to deal with data described by sets of attributes, thus binary data. The formalism of pattern structures [11,16] and abstract conceptual navigation [9] extend FCA to deal with non-binary data such as sequences, where patterns describe data. Inspired by pattern structures, the NEXTPRIORITYCONCEPT algorithm [7] proposes a pattern mining approach for heterogeneous and complex data. The GALACTIC platform implements the NEXTPRIORITYCONCEPT algorithm and offers an ecosystem of extensions for data processing. In a recent work, sequence data analysis was proposed and implemented in the GALACTIC platform [6].

2.1 Definitions

We present some definitions related to FCA elements here, and then we briefly present the NEXTPRIORITYCONCEPT algorithm.

Let $\langle G, M, I \rangle$ be a *formal context* where G is a non-empty set of objects, M is a non-empty set of attributes and $I \subseteq G \times M$ is a binary relation between the set of objects and the set of attributes. Let $(2^G, \subseteq) \xleftrightarrow[\alpha]{\beta} (2^M, \subseteq)$ be the corresponding *Galois connection* where:

- $\alpha : 2^G \to 2^M$ is an application which associates a subset $B \subseteq M$ to every subset $A \subseteq G$ such that $\alpha(A) = \{b : b \in M \land \forall a \in A, aIb\}$;
- $\beta : 2^M \to 2^G$ is an application which associates a subset $A \subseteq G$ to every subset $B \subseteq M$ such that $\beta(B) = \{a : a \in G \land \forall b \in B, aIb\}$.

A concept is a pair (A, B) such that $A \subseteq G$, $B \subseteq M$, $B = \alpha(A)$ and $A = \beta(B)$. The set A is called the *extent*, whereas B is called the *intent* of the concept (A, B). There is a natural hierarchical ordering relation between the concepts of a given context which is called the subconcept-superconcept relation:

$$(A_1, B_1) \leq (A_2, B_2) \iff A_1 \subseteq A_2 (\iff B_2 \subseteq B_1)$$

The ordered set of all concepts makes a complete lattice called the *concept lattice* of the context, that is, every subset of concepts has an infimum (meet) and a supremum (join).

2.2 The NEXTPRIORITYCONCEPT Algorithm

The NEXTPRIORITYCONCEPT algorithm [7] computes concepts for heterogeneous and complex data for a set of objects G. It is inspired by Bordat's algorithm [5], also found in Linding's work [20], that recursively computes the immediate predecessors of a concept, starting with the top concept $(G, \alpha(G))$ containing the whole set of objects, until no more concepts can be generated.

Descriptions as an Application Generating Predicates. The algorithm introduces the notion of *description* δ as an application to provide predicates describing a set of objects $A \subseteq G$. Each concept $(A, \delta(A))$ is composed of a subset of objects A and a set of predicates $\delta(A)$ describing them, corresponding to their pattern. Such generic use of predicates makes it possible to consider heterogeneous data as input, i.e., numerical, discrete or more complex data. A concept $(A, \delta(A))$ can be interpreted as a generalized convex hull, where each border of the hull corresponds to a predicate, and the elements inside the hull correspond to the objects A that verify all the predicates. Unlike classical pattern structures, predicates are not globally computed in a preprocessing step, but locally for each concept as the border lines of a convex hull.

Strategies as an Application Generating Selectors. The algorithm introduces the notion of *strategy* σ to provide predicates called *selectors* describing candidates for an object reduction of a concept $(A, \delta(A))$ i.e., for predecessors of $(A, \delta(A))$ in the pattern lattice. A selector proposes a way to select a reduced set $A' \subset A$ of objects and the concept $(A', \delta(A'))$ is candidate to be a predecessor of $(A, \delta(A))$. Several strategies can generate predecessors of a concept, going from the naive strategy classically used in FCA that considers all the possible predecessors, to strategies allowing to obtain few predecessors and smaller lattices. Selectors are only used for the predecessors' generation, they are not kept either in the description or in the final set of predicates. Therefore, choosing or testing several strategies at each iteration in a user-driven pattern discovery approach would be interesting.

The main result in [7] states that the NEXTPRIORITYCONCEPT algorithm computes the formal context $\langle G, P, I_P \rangle$ and its concept lattice (where P is the set of predicates describing the objects in G, and $I_P = \{(a, p), \ a \in G, p \in P \ : \ p(a)\}$ is the relation between objects and predicates) if description δ verifies $\delta(A) \sqsubseteq \delta(A')$ for $A' \subseteq A$.

2.3   GALACTIC

GALACTIC is a new platform for computing patterns from heterogeneous and complex data that extend the approach of pattern structures [11] and logical concept analysis [10]. It's a development platform for a generic implementation of the NEXTPRIORITYCONCEPT [7] algorithm allowing easy integration of new plugins for characteristics, descriptions, strategies and meta-strategies.

The GALACTIC platform allows the analysis of binary, numerical and categorical data. Sequences handling have been added to the platform recently [6] and multiple descriptions and strategies are available for simple, temporal, and interval sequences. Simple Sequences have three descriptions: Maximal Common Subsequences, Prefixed Common Subsequences and K-Common Subsequences. Simple Sequences also have two strategies: Naive Strategy and Augmented Strategy. They aim to extract subsequences from a sequence in various ways.

Meta-strategies act as filters for other strategies. The *LimitFilter* meta-strategy selects predecessors whose measure is above/below a threshold. It is possible for example to use confidence, support and cardinality measures to limit the generation of concepts to those who respect a threshold of these measures.

3   Process Mining

The idea of process mining was introduced by Aalst in 2004 [2]. Process mining is a data analytics technique that extracts knowledge from execution traces in today's information systems. These techniques provide novel methods for discovering (**Process discovery**), evaluating (**Conformance checking**), and improving processes (**Process enhancement**) in a wide range of application domains [1]. The growing interest in process mining is justified, on the one hand, by the large number of recorded traces that provide detailed information about the process history and, on the other hand, by the ability of these techniques to deal with the entire process (a complete process having a start activity and an end activity).

Table 1. Sample of DL event logs

CaseId	User	Date	Activity label
1	$user_1$	2016-01-12T10:34:25	home index
2	$user_2$	2016-01-12T10:36:25	home index
1	$user_1$	2016-01-12T10:34:26	home languages
1	$user_1$	2016-01-12T10:34:28	language selection
3	$user_3$	2016-01-12T10:36:26	home index
3	$user_3$	2016-01-12T10:36:27	catalog show

Event logs and process models are two fundamental artifacts used in process mining [1]. An event log corresponds to the set of execution traces (*i.e.* process instances) that delivers a specific service or product. For example, to make an online purchase, a user has to subscribe, select a product and proceed to payment. All of these activities are a specific trace of the main process (online purchase). For example, as shown in Table 1, for DLs, each user could be a case that follows a research process. The sequence of events related to a particular case is called a trace. Each row records an executed event, which contains information such as the identifier of each event (**CaseId**), the userId, the **activity label**, the **timestamp** (i.e. day, hour, minute and second) and some additional attributes regarding the event. Formally, an **event logs** $L = \{t_1, t_2, ..., t_k\}$ is a set of k **traces** where each trace t_i ($1 \leq i \leq k$) is a set of n_i consecutive events $t_i =< e_{i1}, e_{i2}, ...e_{in_i} >$ made by the same CaseID [1].

Process models are destined to represent the whole of event logs. They depict the sequence of activities, decision points, and flow of information or resources within the process. Process models can be created using various notations, such as BPMN (Business Process Model and Notation), Petri nets or Directly follows graphs [1].

Many process discovery methods have been proposed to generate process models in the literature. For digital library users' interactions, *Trabelsi et al.* [26] studied the contribution of Process Mining techniques to analyze the digital library users' behaviors and to thus generate effective models from such unstructured processes. The authors executed the most-known process discovery techniques through two sets of event logs produced by users researching documents in a digital library. Then, they presented and evaluated the models generated by best performing Process Mining techniques. Results showed that the Inductive Miner algorithm [17] achieves the best scores for both datasets. To evaluate the quality of the resulting process models of each method, authors used four typical metrics [3]: **Fitness**, which indicates the accordance of the model with the event log. An existing way to calculate the Fitness, is to determine how well the event log aligns with the model when replaying the traces on it [3]. **Precision** corresponds to the rate of activities in the event logs compared to the total of activities enabled in the process model. **Generalization**: it is related to the unseen behavior. This criterion aims to measure the ability of the model to generalize the behavior seen in the logs. A suitable model has to find a balance between these metrics [1]. Finally, **Simplicity** is related to a process model's complexity by capturing the simplicity dimension.

However, many other process mining works showed that discovering a single process model for an entire log is unsuitable, especially over a large dataset. Discovery algorithms usually lead to complex and/or overfitted models such as the well-known spaghetti or flower model [1]. Furthermore, various types of users behaviors can be included in the overall event logs. To tackle this issue, existing works proposed trace clustering methods prior to modeling [8].

Trace clustering in process mining is a collection of techniques for grouping sequences with similar characteristics to extract a model for each. Four approaches have been developed: trace-based clustering groups similar traces based on their syntax similarity; Feature-based clustering converts each trace into a vector of features based on its characteristics; Model-based clustering uses the process model's properties as input for clustering; and hybrid-based clustering combines previous methods [24,25,28]. Our work in this article, belongs to the trace-based approach since we consider the syntax similarity of traces for the clustering.

4   Related Works

This section introduces and discusses related works on the application of FCA in clustering and the enhancement of process models.

In the context of **clustering**, authors in [23] demonstrated how FCA techniques could be used for clustering categorical data. A global support value was used to specify which concepts can be candidate clusters. The best cluster for each object was then determined using a score function. Furthermore, to assist museum researchers in analyzing and evaluating item placement and visiting styles, authors in [15] proposed an FCA approach comprised of two independent steps: clustering and trajectory mining. A specific dataset was concerned with the trajectories of visitors. Each trajectory is made up of a series of visited items. Given that the trajectory dataset can be regarded as a sequential dataset, a proper sequence clustering method is used where the distance between any two sequences is obtained from the number of their common subsequences. On the other hand, the mining of trajectory patterns is performed by two methods based on FCA. These patterns are then used to find the characteristic behavior of each cluster.

In the context of **process model enhancement** in process mining, authors in [13], proposed to apply the FCA to process enhancement which is one of the main goals of process mining. Process enhancement consists of analyzing a discovered process from an event log, and improving its efficiency based on the analysis. For process enhancement, by FCA, authors defined subsequences of events whose stops are fatal to the execution of a process as weak points to be removed. In their method, the extent of every concept is a set of event types, and the intent is a set of resources for events in the extent, and then, for each extent, its weakness is calculated by taking into account event frequency. They also proposed some ideas to remove the weakest points. In this line, authors in [22], demonstrated that FCA can provide additional insights in situations closely related to potential value leaks in processes.

A few amounts of works focused on the analysis of digital traces. For instance, authors in [14], proposed a new method for automatically extracting smartphone users' contextual behaviors from the digital traces collected during their inter-actions with their devices. Their goal was to understand the impact of users' context (e.g., location, time, environment, etc.) on the applications they run on their smartphones. Based on the presented works, it is clear that FCA techniques can extract relevant information from event logs, allowing analysts to gain insights into the process and formulate and validate its hypotheses. Trace clustering using FCA can help process mining and allows detecting profiles to have more explainable user behaviors. In this work, we propose a new trace clustering method for grouping execution traces before process modeling.

5   Proposed Method: Trace Clustering Using FCA

The proposed approach can be divided into two parts. The first part consists of generating a concept lattice using the NEXTPRIORITYCONCEPT algorithm. Then, in the second part, trace clustering is performed based on the generated clusters in the lattice. The main idea is to use the knowledge carried by the traces to construct a concept lattice. Each concept (cluster) then contains a set of traces with their description.

For this purpose, we use the GALACTIC platform described above. The description of a set of traces can be of different forms. For event logs, we use Maximal Common Subsequence description (MCS), where traces are transformed into sequences of activities and then described by their maximal common subsequences. Moreover, the Numerical description describes a set of traces by their maximal and minimal size. Table 2 shows an example of three traces, with their description. As we mentioned in Sect. 3, a trace is a sequence of activities (or events) and a description is a set of predicates. For example, in this table, we have a sequential predicate that represents the common subsequence of the three traces and two numerical predicates defining the maximal and minimal length of the traces.

Therefore, we use these two descriptions and the naive strategies to generate the concept lattice. We also use the *LimitFilter* as meta-strategy that limits the number of generated predecessors to those of cardinality greater than a given

Table 2. Example of description of three traces

Trace id	Trace	Description
t1	⟨home_index, home_topics, home_show_topic_selection, catalog_show⟩	chain match ('home_index', 'catalog_show') and 'nb_activities' >= 3 and 'nb_activities' <= 5
t2	⟨home_index, home_topics, catalog_show⟩	
t3	⟨home_index, catalog_index_query, catalog_show, catalog_index_filter, catalog_show⟩	

threshold. Our problem here is that a trace may be present in many concepts as FCA generates overlapping clusters. As it seems to be a drawback for FCA-based clustering, it may lead to better results. First, clustering methods are based on the distance between traces which is a kind of distance calculation, whereas using FCA, the concepts/clusters discovery is based on sequences and their common subsequences (symbolic approach). Second, existing clustering methods may be robust, but they generate a local minimum for each execution. Last, the lattice generated by FCA contains by default all the clusters, using FCA will certainly generate the exact clusters we are seeking alongside with other clusters, we just have to find the right ones from the lattice.

One solution to get a disjoint clustering is to assign a score function that evaluates the distance between a trace and all its concepts, and then select the best concept for this trace. The score function was introduced firstly by [23]. The data used by the authors was binary data, and the score function uses the frequency of the attributes. In this work, we propose a score function that uses the distance between a trace and the concept description.

Let $A = \{t_1, t_2, ...t_k\}$ be a set of traces where each trace t_i is a set of events $t_i = \langle e_{i1}, e_{i2}, ...e_{in_i}\rangle$, and $c = (A, \delta(A))$ be a concept, where the description $\delta(A)$ is defined by:

$$\delta(A) = \delta^{Seq}(A) \cup \delta^{Num}(A)$$

Where $\delta^{Seq}(A)$ is a set of predicates of sequential data, and $\delta^{Num}(A)$ is a set of predicates of numerical data. We define *Score* as a function that gives a distance value between a trace t and a concept c where $t \in A$ by:

$$Score(t, c) = \frac{d^{Seq}(t, \delta^{Seq}(A)) + d^{Num}(t, \delta^{Num}(A)))}{2} \text{ , where:}$$

- $d^{Seq}(t, \delta^{Seq}(A))$ is the *edit distance* between two sequences: the trace sequence, and the predicate sequence of $\delta^{Seq}(A)$ that is a subsequence of t. The edit distance is the minimum number of insertions, deletions, and substitutions required to transform one sequence to another [19].
- $d^{Num}(t, \delta^{Num}(A))$ is simply the mean of absolute values of the difference between the size of t and the numeric values of the predicates in $\delta^{Num}(A)$.

Algorithm 1 introduces the Lattice-Based Trace Clustering approach, which accepts a lattice L and a list of traces T as input and produces a list of disjoint concepts that represent a set of clusters for the traces given as input.

The algorithm starts by calculating each couple's scores (trace, concept) (lines 1, 2). Then it selects one concept with the highest score value for each trace (lines 3, 4). In the case of score equality between a trace and many concepts, the selection is then made by selecting the concept with the highest cardinality. Finally, we create the clusters with the selected concepts and their traces (lines 5–15).

Algorithm 1. Lattice Based Trace Clustering

    Input: A concept lattice L and a list of traces T
    Output: A set of clusters

1: *// Calculate the scores for each couple (trace, concepts)*
2: $TC \leftarrow$ triples of (Trace, Concept, Score)
3: *// Select the best concept for each trace*
4: $TC \leftarrow$ couples of (Trace, Concept) where the score is the highest
5: *// calculate the clusters*
6: $Clusters \leftarrow \emptyset$ *// (Concept, $\emptyset$) list of clusters*
7: **for** $tc \in TC$ **do**
8:     $Trace, Concept \leftarrow tc$
9:     **if** $Concept \in Clusters$ **then**:
10:         $Clusters[Concept].add(Trace)$
11:     **else**
12:         $Clusters.add(Concept, \{Trace\})$
13:     **end if**
14: **end for**
15: **Return** $Clusters$

---

6 Experiments

6.1 Datasets

As mentioned in the introduction, we chose information systems conceived for Digital Libraries (DLs) as a case study. To validate our new trace clustering method based on the FCA, we simulated DLs users' search behaviors[1] by reproducing the characteristics of the main categories described by Marchionini [21]. This experimental strategy is simplified compared to the use of real data. Our objective is the validity of the approach. Its main goal is to assess the ability of the proposed approach to model users' behaviors. By leveraging a simulated dataset, the study benefits from the controlled environment and the availability of ground truth information, enabling a comprehensive evaluation of the FCA-based clustering method's performance.

The simulated dataset distinguishes three types of traces. **Lookup** traces where users can access precisely identified documents with few manipulations via the search engine or by browsing through the various document categories. **Borderline** traces where users can access documents within a well-defined subject area, using multiple searching methods and filtering results. Finally,

---

[1] Based on https://projectblacklight.org/.

Exploratory traces, where users can access a wide range of documents in various fields and types, using more advanced search and filtering functions [21].

The simulated dataset contains quantitatively 100 traces distributed as 40 lookup traces, 30 borderline traces and 30 exploratory traces. Each trace is related to a user. Obviously, exploratory traces which are the most complex cover more than 10 types of events for a total of events (310). The borderline traces are made from 6 types of events (170 events) and the lookup traces are limited to 5 types of events for a total of 140 events.

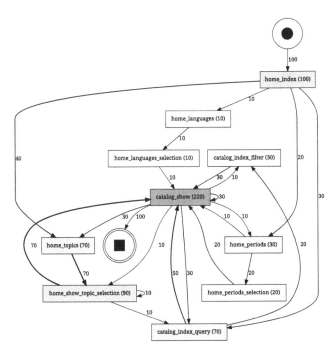

Fig. 1. Discovered Directly Follows Graph for the whole simulated event logs

The process model in Fig. 1 is a Directly-Follows Graph (DFG)[2] discovered on the simulated dataset. The process discovery method utilized considers the events and their frequency in the event logs and the frequency of direct succession between events [18]. The event logs will be mapped to a DFG whose vertices are events and edges are the direct relations. However, as previously said, understanding a DFG incorporating many sorts of research is far from simple for designers. It is usually easier to find each kind in a distinct graph rather than from the entire graph (cf. Fig. 1).

---

[2] Along this paper, we use Directly-Follows Graph to show our models instead of Petri Net for simplicity.

6.2   Clustering Results Using FCA

In this part, we provide the experimental results related to the clustering on the simulated DL event logs. Our aim is to retrieve the three desired DL users' groups described in the simulated data using the proposed clustering method based on FCA. Figure 2 shows the Hasse diagram of the generated lattice using the MCS and the Numerical descriptions and their respective Naive strategies. We use a *Cardinality* measure to limit the generation of concepts to those where the number of traces didn't exceed a given cardinality parameter (here 25). The generated lattice contains 20 concepts. In this figure, the \$ symbol represents the *id* of the concept and the # symbol represents the number of traces of this concept. Each concept comprises two parts, the upper part, where we can see the description represented by a set of predicates, and the lower part where we can identify traces by their ids. The concept \$14 here contains 30 traces described by two predicates:

- Chain predicates δ^{Seq}: *chain match ('home_index', 'catalog_show', 'catalog_show', 'catalog_show', 'catalog_show')*
- Numerical predicates δ^{Num}: *'nb_activities'$\geq$ 11*

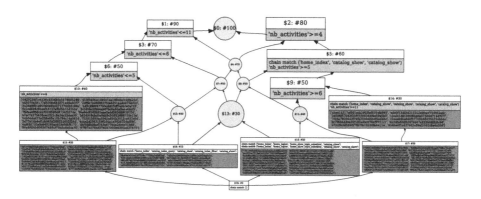

Fig. 2. Hasse diagram of the concept lattice generated by the MCS and Numerical descriptions and their respective Naive strategies with cardinality 25, with a zoom of concept \$14

Remember that in this lattice, a trace may be present in different concepts. To perform a disjoint clustering, we use our method to select one concept for each trace. Table 3 shows the selected concepts, their description, and the number of traces in each class. We clearly can conclude that this is a perfect clustering as each concept represents the exact initial class.

Table 3. The selected concepts with their description and the number of traces in each class

Cluster	1	2	3
Description	chain match ('home_index', 'catalog_show') and 'nb_activities' $>= 3$ and 'nb_activities' $<= 12$	chain match ('home_index', 'catalog_show', 'catalog_show') and 'nb_activities' $>= 5$ and 'nb_activities' $<= 12$	chain match ('home_index', 'catalog_show', 'catalog_show', 'catalog_show', 'catalog_show') and 'nb_activities' $>= 11$ and 'nb_activities' $<= 12$
Lookup	40	0	0
Borderline	0	30	0
Exploratory	0	0	30

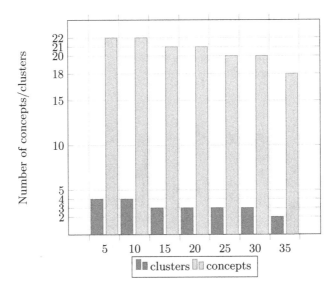

Fig. 3. The number of concepts and clusters according to cardinality change

However, this method only sometimes finds the exact number of classes we are looking for; if we change the cardinality parameter, we may have more/fewer concepts in the lattice and thus more/fewer resulting clusters. Figure 3 shows the number of clusters found according to the cardinality parameter.

6.3 Process Modeling Results

In this part, we provide the experimental results related to the process modeling step using the process discovery algorithm (the Inductive Miner algorithm). After discovering the Petri nets using the process discovery algorithm, we used the four metrics, that we mentioned previously in Sect. 3, to evaluate the models: the Fitness criteria, the Precision, the Generalization and the Simplicity.

Table 4 compares the process models discovered for each event log cluster (three clusters) and the process model mined from the complete simulated dataset. The results indicate that the FCA-based method consistently achieves the highest Precision scores for each discovered process model, demonstrating its effectiveness in accurately identifying process patterns compared to the discovered process models from the complete real logs. Additionally, this method shows a superior balance between Precision and Generalization, suggesting its ability to capture both specific and generalized process behaviors effectively in a more balanced manner. Moreover, the FCA clustering method outperforms others in terms of Simplicity, highlighting its capability to provide straightforward and easily understandable process representations.

Table 4. Process models comparison metrics for the simulated DL event logs

	Real logs	Cluster 1	Cluster 2	Cluster 3
Fitness	1	1	1	1
Precision	0,406	**1**	**0,496**	**0,414**
Generalization	0.853	0.734	0.760	0.800
Simplicity	0.696	**0.779**	**0.700**	**0.739**

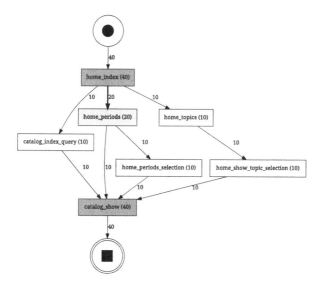

Fig. 4. Discovered DFG from the first cluster: lookup event logs

In addition to the aforementioned findings, Fig. 4 provides visual evidence supporting the effectiveness of the proposed FCA clustering method in generating the expected event log clusters, namely Lookup, Borderline, and Exploratory traces. These clusters align with the outcomes mentioned in Sect. 6.2.

For example, the process model derived from the first cluster exhibits the capability to gather users who can access specific documents with minimal manipulation, indicating its suitability for lookup-based activities. This confirms the ability of the FCA clustering method to identify and group similar traces based on their underlying characteristics, leading to the discovery of process models that align with the expected behavior and requirements.

7   Conclusion

This work focuses on extracting similar users' journeys in information systems with unstructured business processes. In this paper, we propose a new method to cluster traces (users interactions) in process mining using FCA. To the best of our knowledge, this work is the first process mining study processing users traces and generating models for users and tasks using FCA techniques. The FCA clustering method generates a lattice based on user traces and then uses a score function to select one concept for each trace. Results showed the effectiveness of our method for clustering users' traces and modeling their journeys. The generated models allow for the improvement of DL design by identifying unused features that may require more documentation and improving useful ones related to frequent events. Furthermore, based on the paths in models, designers can make practical recommendations to help new users achieve their goals by following the event sequences created by advanced users. For future work, it is desirable to work with a large and real dataset that covers the whole journeys of DLs uses. Also, we plan to explore more trace clustering algorithms to compare the obtained results. Furthermore, considering the temporal information in generating the lattice using the temporal sequence plugins of GALACTIC may be a promising approach.

Acknowledgment. This article is supported by the ANR SmartFCA project Grant ANR-21-CE23-0023 of the French National Research Agency.

References

1. Van der Aalst, W.: Process Mining: Data Science in Action. Springer, Heidelberg (2016). https://doi.org/10.1007/978-3-662-49851-4
2. Van der Aalst, W.M., Weijters, A.J.: Process mining: a research agenda. Comput. Ind. **53**(3), 231–244 (2004)
3. Adriansyah, A.: Aligning observed and modeled behavior. Ph.D. thesis, Technische Universiteit Eindhoven (2014)
4. Barbut, M., Monjardet, B.: Ordres et classifications: Algèbre et combinatoire. Hachette, Paris (1970). 2 tomes
5. Bordat, J.P.: Calcul pratique du treillis de Galois d'une correspondance. Mathématiques et Sciences Humaines **96**, 31–47 (1986)
6. Boukhetta, S.E., Demko, Ch., Richard, J., Bertet, K.: Sequence mining using FCA and the NextPriorityConcept algorithm. In: Concept Lattices and Their Applications 2020. vol. 2668, pp. 209–222 (2020)
7. Demko, Ch., Bertet, K., Faucher, C., Viaud, J.F., Kuznetsov, S.O.: NextPriorityConcept: a new and generic algorithm computing concepts from complex and heterogeneous data. Theoret. Comput. Sci. **845**, 1–20 (2020)

8. Diamantini, C., Genga, L., Potena, D.: Behavioral process mining for unstructured processes. J. Intell. Inf. Syst. **47**(1), 5–32 (2016)
9. Ferré, S.: Reconciling expressivity and usability in information access from file systems to the semantic web (2014)
10. Ferré, S., Ridoux, O.: A logical generalization of formal concept analysis. In: Ganter, B., Mineau, G.W. (eds.) ICCS-ConceptStruct 2000. LNCS (LNAI), vol. 1867, pp. 371–384. Springer, Heidelberg (2000). https://doi.org/10.1007/10722280_26
11. Ganter, B., Kuznetsov, S.O.: Pattern structures and their projections. In: Delugach, H.S., Stumme, G. (eds.) ICCS-ConceptStruct 2001. LNCS (LNAI), vol. 2120, pp. 129–142. Springer, Heidelberg (2001). https://doi.org/10.1007/3-540-44583-8_10
12. Ganter, B., Wille, R.: Formal Concept Analysis. Springer, Heidelberg (1999). https://doi.org/10.1007/978-3-642-59830-2
13. Ikeda, M., Otaki, K., Yamamoto, A.: Formal concept analysis for process enhancement based on a pair of perspectives. In: CLA, pp. 59–70 (2014)
14. Jaffal, A., Le Grand, B.: Towards an automatic extraction of smartphone users' contextual behaviors. In: 2016 IEEE 10th International Conference on Research Challenges in Information Science (RCIS), pp. 1–6. IEEE (2016)
15. Juniarta, N.: Mining complex data and biclustering using formal concept analysis. Ph.D. thesis, Université de Lorraine (2019)
16. Kaytoue, M., Codocedo, V., Buzmakov, A., Baixeries, J., Kuznetsov, S.O., Napoli, A.: Pattern structures and concept lattices for data mining and knowledge processing. In: In Proceedings of ECML-PKDDl (2015)
17. Leemans, S.J.J., Fahland, D., van der Aalst, W.M.P.: Discovering block-structured process models from incomplete event logs. In: Ciardo, G., Kindler, E. (eds.) PETRI NETS 2014. LNCS, vol. 8489, pp. 91–110. Springer, Cham (2014). https://doi.org/10.1007/978-3-319-07734-5_6
18. Leemans, S.J., Poppe, E., Wynn, M.T.: Directly follows-based process mining: exploration & a case study. In: 2019 International Conference on Process Mining, pp. 25–32. IEEE (2019)
19. Levenshtein, V.I., et al.: Binary codes capable of correcting deletions, insertions, and reversals. Soviet Physics Doklady **10**, 707–710 (1966)
20. Troy, A.D., Zhang, G.-Q., Tian, Y.: Faster concept analysis. In: Priss, U., Polovina, S., Hill, R. (eds.) ICCS-ConceptStruct 2007. LNCS (LNAI), vol. 4604, pp. 206–219. Springer, Heidelberg (2007). https://doi.org/10.1007/978-3-540-73681-3_16
21. Marchionini, G.: Exploratory search: from finding to understanding. Commun. ACM **49**(4), 41–46 (2006)
22. Peters, E.M., Dedene, G., Poelmans, J.: Empirical discovery of potential value leaks in processes by means of formal concept analysis. In: 2013 IEEE 13th International Conference on Data Mining Workshops, pp. 433–439. IEEE (2013)
23. Saquer, J.M.: Formal concept analysis based clustering. In: Encyclopedia of Data Warehousing and Mining, pp. 514–518. IGI Global (2005)
24. Song, M., Günther, C.W., van der Aalst, W.M.P.: Trace clustering in process mining. In: Ardagna, D., Mecella, M., Yang, J. (eds.) BPM 2008. LNBIP, vol. 17, pp. 109–120. Springer, Heidelberg (2009). https://doi.org/10.1007/978-3-642-00328-8_11
25. Trabelsi, M., Suire, C., Morcos, J., Champagnat, R.: A new methodology to bring out typical users interactions in digital libraries. In: 2021 ACM/IEEE Joint Conference on Digital Libraries (JCDL), pp. 11–20. IEEE (2021)

26. Trabelsi, M., Suire, C., Morcos, J., Champagnat, R.: User's behavior in digital libraries: process mining exploration. In: Doucet, A., Isaac, A., Golub, K., Aalberg, T., Jatowt, A. (eds.) TPDL 2019. LNCS, vol. 11799, pp. 388–392. Springer, Cham (2019). https://doi.org/10.1007/978-3-030-30760-8_40

27. Wille, R.: Restructuring Lattice theory: an approach based on hierarchies of concepts. In: Rival, I. (eds.) Ordered Sets. NATO Advanced Study Institutes Series, vol. 83, pp. 445–470. Springer, Dordrecht (1982). https://doi.org/10.1007/978-94-009-7798-3_15

28. Zandkarimi, F., Rehse, J.R., Soudmand, P., Hoehle, H.: A generic framework for trace clustering in process mining. In: 2020 2nd International Conference on Process Mining (ICPM), pp. 177–184 (2020). https://doi.org/10.1109/ICPM49681.2020.00034

Summarization of Massive RDF Graphs Using Identifier Classification

André Fernandes dos Santos$^{(\boxtimes)}$ and José Paulo Leal

CRACS & INESC Tec LA/Faculty of Sciences, University of Porto, Porto, Portugal
`afs@inesctec.pt, jpleal@fc.up.pt`

Abstract. The size of massive knowledge graphs (KGs) and the lack of prior information regarding the schemas, ontologies and vocabularies they use frequently makes them hard to understand and visualize. Graph summarization techniques can help by abstracting details of the original graph to produce a reduced summary that can more easily be explored. Identifiers often carry latent information which could be used for classification of the entities they represent. Particularly, IRI namespaces can be used to classify RDF resources. Namespaces, used in some RDF serialization formats as a shortening mechanism for resource IRIs, have no role in the semantics of RDF. Nevertheless, there is often a hidden meaning behind the decision of grouping resources under a common prefix and assigning an alias to it. We improved on previous work on a namespace-based approach to KG summarization that classifies resources using their namespaces. Producing the summary graph is fast, light on computing resources and requires no previous domain knowledge. The summary graph can be used to analyze the namespace interdependencies of the original graph. We also present `chilon`, a tool for calculating namespace-based KG summaries. Namespaces are gathered from explicit declarations in the graph serialization, community contributions or resource IRI prefix analysis. We applied `chilon` to publicly available KGs, used it to generate interactive visualizations of the summaries, and discuss the results obtained.

Keywords: knowledge graphs · graph summarization · namespaces · RDF

1 Introduction

Knowledge graphs (KGs) are data modeling structures used to represent the knowledge of a given domain. KGs are commonly described using RDF, a standard where knowledge is represented through semantic triple statements. Each triple represents an edge (a relationship) connecting two nodes (a subject and an object). Consequently, a set of triples forms a directed multigraph. In some cases RDF graphs comprise thousands of millions of triples, and occupy tens of gigabytes of disk space when serialized and compressed. This makes them hard to process, explore, query and visualize. Abstracting details from the original

© The Author(s), under exclusive license to Springer Nature Switzerland AG 2023
M. Ojeda-Aciego et al. (Eds.): ICCS 2023, LNAI 14133, pp. 89–103, 2023.
https://doi.org/10.1007/978-3-031-40960-8_8

graph makes it easier to focus on the relevant features and graph summarization techniques can be used to achieve the desired level of abstraction.

RDF graphs can be serialized using several formats, most of which support namespaces, a shortening mechanism which is not actually part of the RDF semantics. Nevertheless, these IRI namespaces also carry additional implicit information: the creator of the KG deemed these prefixes relevant or frequent enough to merit an explicit alias declaration. By looking into these prefix declarations (and their use in the triples of the graph) one gathers valuable insights regarding the interactions between the original KG and other linked KGs or ontologies. Additional namespaces can be inferred by finding common prefixes in resource IRIs even when not explicitly using aliases.

In this paper, we describe an approach for KG summarization based on the classification of RDF component identifiers. This work was mainly motivated by needs related to the creation of semantic measures based on massive semantic graphs, but the same approach can be used for query result size estimation or for comparing KGs for other use cases.

Additionally, we present chilon[1], a command line application to process RDF files and produce namespace-based RDF summary graphs. chilon is a complete rewrite of our previous system [9,10]. Written with a focus on performance and interactivity, chilon is capable of processing *massive* (in the order of thousands of millions of triples) RDF graphs. We processed several publicly available knowledge graphs and present and analyze the results.

This paper is structured as follows. Section 2 provides an overview on KGs, graph summarization and namespaces. Section 3 presents our approach and main algorithms. Section 4 details the architecture and implementation decisions for our tool, chilon. Sections 5 and 6, respectively, describe the validation of chilon using several general purpose KGs and present and discuss the results obtained. Section 7 presents the conclusions and possible future work.

2   Background and Related Work

In this section, we cover background and related work on the topics of KGs and their summarization, and the use of namespaces in RDF and linked data.

2.1   Knowledge Graphs

A graph is a data type structure composed of nodes, connected between them by edges. On a digraph, these edges have a direction (Definition 1).

Definition 1 (Directed graph). *A directed graph (or digraph) G is a tuple (V, E) where:*

- *V is the set of nodes,*

---

[1] Named after Chilon of Sparta, one of the Seven Sages of Greece, who coined the ancient proverb *"less is more"* or *"brevity is a way of philosophy"*.

    – *E is the set of edges, ordered pairs such that $E \subseteq \{(v,w) : v \in V \wedge w \in V\}$*

When the digraph has multiple edges connecting the same source and target nodes it is called a directed multigraph.

A semantic graph is an abstract data modeling structure where semantic concepts (and instances of those concepts) are represented as nodes of a graph, and the relationships between them are represented as edges. While the term *knowledge graph* has been used for decades, it gained traction in more recent years with multiple companies announcing the development of their own internal KGs [14,21,28], as well as public, non-commercial and/or community-led efforts [22,27,30].

Knowledge graphs can be defined using RDF [11], a standard where knowledge is represented as triple statements. Each triple is composed of a subject node S, an object node O and a predicate edge P, representing the statement *"S is related to O through P"*. Nodes in an RDF graph can be named nodes (resources identified by IRIs), blank nodes (anonymous resources), and literals (property values with an associated datatype). Edges are resources identified by IRIs. RDF triple statements, when composed together, form a directed multigraph. A formal definition of an RDF graph can be found in Definition 2.

Definition 2 (RDF graph). *An RDF graph G is a tuple (V, D_L, P, E, I_R, i_R) where:*

- *V is the set of nodes, defined as the union of sets $N \cup B \cup L$ such that:*
  - *N is the set of named nodes,*
  - *B is the set of blank nodes,*
  - *L is the set of literals,*
- *D_L is the set of datatypes associated with literals,*
- *P is the set of predicates (resources) associated with the edges of G,*
- *E is the set of edges such that $E \subseteq \{(v,w,p) : v \in V \wedge w \in V \wedge p \in P\}$,*
- *I_R is the set of IRIs associated with the named nodes, edge predicates and literal datatypes,*
- *i_R is a function mapping between named nodes, edges and literal datatypes, and their IRIs: $N \cup P \cup D_L \mapsto I_R$.*

The reuse of resources in multiple KGs allows them to represent knowledge using shared vocabularies or taxonomies, or to independently assert (redundant, complementary or even conflicting) predicates about the same resources. This pattern of interconnection between KGs, which relies on a set of basic principles [5], has been known as *linked data* [6]. The web of KGs and ontologies linked this way and publicly accessible forms the linked open data (LOD) cloud [12].

2.2 Graph Summarization

Graphs are data modeling structures widely used in a variety of different fields, such as social networks, protein interaction, neural networks and GPS data. Frequently, graphs are very large, with sizes in the order of millions or thousands of millions of nodes and edges. We call the latter *massive* graphs.

Understanding the information encoded in such graphs is a challenge. The graphs cannot easily fit into memory. Algorithms with exponential complexity become impractical. Visual representations of the whole graph are convoluted and confusing. Graph summarization can help either by providing a higher level overview of the graph structure, or by reducing the graph to a manageable size while preserving the relevant information. RDF graph summarization can take advantage of: RDF specific features, such as class inheritance and instantiation, labels, literals, and datatypes; OWL concepts, such as equivalences between properties or classes; or even more specific knowledge obtained from the custom ontologies used by each KG.

General graph summarization techniques have been described by Bonifati et al. [7] and Liu et al. [24]. Existing semantic (RDF) graph summarization approaches have been surveyed and categorized by Cebiric et al. [8] and Kondylakis et al. [20]. The latter classifies techniques according to their *purpose* (e.g. query answering, schema discovery, visualization), *method* (structural, pattern mining, statistical, hybrid), *input* (dataset features and additional parameters), *output* (graph or another type of object, instance data vs schema, or both) and *availability* (abstract algorithm vs implementation, open vs closed source).

Structural summarization methods can be further divided in *quotient* and *non-quotient* methods. Quotient methods rely on the definition of an *equivalence relation* between the nodes of the graph (Definition 3). This relation allows partitioning the nodes of the graph into subsets where all elements are equivalent between them.

Definition 3 (Equivalence relation). *An equivalence relation $\equiv$ on a set S is a reflexive, symmetric and transitive binary relation between elements of S. For two elements a and b from S, if $\equiv (a, b)$ then a and b are said to be $\equiv$-equivalent. A subset of elements all $\equiv$-equivalent forms an $\equiv$-equivalence class.*

A quotient graph is obtained by defining a node for each class of equivalence, and an edge connecting classes of equivalence if there was at least one edge connecting a node from each class in the original graph. Definition 4 provides a more formal description of a quotient graph adapted from Čebirić, Š. et al. [8].

Definition 4 (Quotient graph). *Let $G = (V, E)$ be a digraph defined according to Definition 1. Let $\equiv$ be an equivalence relation over the nodes of V such that $\equiv \subseteq V \times V$. The quotient graph of G with respect to $\equiv$, represented as $G/_{\equiv}$ is a directed graph defined as a tuple $([V], [E])$ such that:*

- *$[V]$ is the set of $\equiv$-equivalent classes in V,*
- *$[E]$ is the set of edges such that:*

$$([v], [w]) \in [E] \implies [v] \in [V] \wedge [w] \in [V] \wedge \exists v \in [v], w \in [w] : (v, w) \in E.$$

2.3   Namespaces

RDF graphs can be serialized to several different formats, e.g. RDF/XML, Turtle, N-Triples, which use different syntax to represent RDF triples. N-Triples [2] has a simple grammar and structure, making its files easy to parse and process. In contrast, Turtle [3] has a more sophisticated grammar that results in smaller files but also makes them harder to parse. Despite some small differences in the expressiveness of these languages, most RDF graphs can be represented and converted easily between the different formats.

One feature common to most RDF serialization formats is the definition of namespace aliases. Whenever many of the IRIs referenced on an RDF graph share the same namespace (IRI prefix), it is possible to define and reuse an alias for it. This makes the resulting file smaller and easier for humans to read, as all the repetitions of long IRIs are shortened using the prefix alias. This feature is supported in Turtle, N3, JSON-LD, RDF/XML, and unsupported in N-Triples.

Prefix aliasing is a feature of these serialization formats and not a part of RDF semantics. In fact, the RDF specification explicitly states that *"Namespace IRIs and namespace prefixes are not a formal part of the RDF data model. They are merely a syntactic convenience for abbreviating IRIs."* [11]. The prefix definitions are actually internal to each RDF file. Formally there is no meaning attributed to them other than a local rewrite rule. Two files can use different alias for the same namespace prefix, or use the same alias for different prefixes.

The serialization of an RDF graph might contain many references to resources from another graph or ontology without ever explicitly defining a namespace alias. Because they are an optional feature, aliases are not always declared. Or they might be declared for some namespaces but not for others, depending on the authors or the tools used to serialize the graph. Given the lack of special meaning assigned by RDF, the decision of whether to declare namespace aliases is in most cases simply motivated by the gains obtained in storage and data transfer due to the reduction in file sizes.

Nevertheless, some consistency can be observed in alias definition. The RDF specification itself refers to `rdf`, `rdfs` and `xsd` [11]. Other aliases, such as `owl` and `foaf`, are also consistently used to refer to their namespaces.

Some efforts have been made to organize and potentiate namespace use in the linked data field. prefix.cc is a web service building a crowdsourced list with mappings between namespaces and aliases. Mappings are submitted and voted by the community, but no additional curation is performed, resulting in cases of conflicting mappings and others of questionable quality. `prefixmaps` is a Python module which allows programatically retrieving prefix mappings from a variety of sources, including prefix.cc. The different mappings are normalized, collisions identified and the integrated results are available in its GitHub repository[2].

Other projects have been created to allow surfacing semantically the namespaces definitions which are currently encoded at the syntactical level. The VoID vocabulary [1] allows expressing RDF dataset metadata, including defining vocabulary namespaces using `void:uriSpace` and `void:vocabulary`. More complex relations between vocabularies can be expressed using VOAF. Janowicz et al. propose *Five Stars of Linked Data Vocabulary Use* to improve vocabulary

---

[2] https://github.com/linkml/prefixmaps/blob/main/src/prefixmaps/data/merged. csv.

re-use [19], and Haller et al. discuss the challenges of defining namespaces in the context of RDF [16].

3   Conceptual Architecture

The goal of this work is to create an efficient summarization method for RDF graphs in which the output provides insights on how the graph connects and relates to other graphs. The summarization process should be linear on the number of IRIs of the graph, and should require no domain-specific knowledge.

Next we describe the main algorithms in our approach for namespace-based RDF graph summarization.

3.1   Classifying Identifiers

An identifier is generally a string of characters or symbols that labels the identity of an object. They enable referring to objects without using descriptive terms, e.g. *the busiest airport in Europe* (descriptive terms) is *Heathrow* or *LHR* (identifiers). Identifiers are usually unique, that is, an identifier refers to a single object. Identifiers can be arbitrary (i.e. randomly attributed to objects), but most frequently they follow some sort of pattern or encoding. Identifiers are often viewed as blackboxes; however, through their encoding, they carry latent information regarding the objects they identify.

Sequential identifiers (such as a country's citizenship number) will provide precedence data, allowing to infer that a given entity is older than another. From identifiers containing date information (e.g. university student IDs) we can extract a notion of temporal distance. Other identifiers contain categorical information, e.g. *department* or *type of product*.

In datasets where data points consist of tuples of resources, assigning classes to the identifiers can be used to obtain an overview of how the classes are interconnected. For example, on a phone call log, classifying source and target phone numbers according to their country or area code (inferred from the phone number prefix) will provide a high-level overview of how the different geographical locations interact with each other.

In RDF, named nodes, predicates and literal datatypes are identified by IRIs [13]. IRIs can be classified according to their namespaces (a prefix common to several IRIs, see Sect. 2.3), which usually include information regarding the scheme (protocol used to retrieve the resource content), host (domain, subdomains and top-level domain) and path. RDF blank nodes, which are by definition anonymous, cannot be classified in this way.

3.2   Namespace-Based RDF Graph Summarization

Our approach for graph summarization is based on the definition of quotient graphs. However, Definition 4 is insufficient for RDF graphs. It needs to be extended to allow both the original graph and the quotient graphs to have multiple edges between the same pair of nodes. Additionally, we want the resulting summary graph to be a valid RDF graph. This means that the triples in the summary graph must obey RDF and RDFS restrictions (e.g. those imposed by predicates such as `rdfs:range` or `rdfs:domain`). Lastly, we need to define how edges in the original graph are mapped into a smaller subset of superedges on the summary graph.

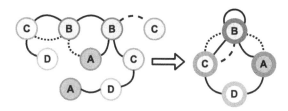

Fig. 1. Example of a multigraph quotient of a multigraph.

First we define a mapping function for the components of the graph, which will assign each one a group (namespace) based on their identifier. Based on the namespaces we can define an equivalence relationship $\equiv_{NS}$ in which two nodes of the graph are equivalent if their IRIs share the same namespace. This partitions the original graph into equivalence classes of nodes corresponding to the identifier namespaces.

We also apply the same equivalence relationship to the parallel edges of the original graph: two edges are considered equivalent if they share the same identifier class, and the same happens both for their source nodes and their target nodes. Each node in the summary graph corresponds to a class of node identifiers on the original graph. In the summary graph, two namespace nodes A_{NS} and B_{NS} are connected by a namespace edge E_{NS} if there was, in the original graph, one or more edges from the namespace E_{NS} connecting nodes from A_{NS} with nodes from B_{NS}.

Definition 5 presents a formal definition of the summary graph. Figure 1 provides a graphical representation of this process, with nodes and edges in the original graph painted according to their equivalence classes.

Definition 5 (Namespace-based summary quotient graph). *Let* $G = (V, D_L, P, E, I_R, i_R)$ *be an RDF graph defined according to Definition 2. Let* ns *be a function which maps an IRI to its namespace. Let* $\equiv$ *be an equivalence relation over the IRIs of resources of* G. *The RDF summary graph* S_G *of* G *is a directed multigraph defined as a tuple* $([V], D'_L, [P], [E], I'_R, i'_R)$ *such that:*

- $[V]$ *is the set of* $\equiv$-*equivalent classes in* V,
- $[P]$ *is the set of* $\equiv$-*equivalent classes in* P,
- $[E]$ *is the set of edges such that:*

$$([s], [o], [p]) \in [E] \implies [s] \in [V] \wedge [o] \in [V] \wedge [p] \in [P] \wedge$$
$$\exists \; s \in [s], o \in [o], p \in [p] : (s, o, p) \in E$$

4   System Overview

chilon is a multi-threaded application developed in Rust. It processes RDF
graph files in parallel, classifying its resources and generating an RDF summary
graph, which is then turned into an interactive visualization. According to the
classification framework proposed by Kondylakis et al. [20], chilon is a structural quotient graph summarizer which takes as input an RDF graph and several
optional parameters, and outputs an RDF graph summary. It is made available
both as an abstract algorithm (described in this paper) and an open source tool.
It can be used for tasks such as visualization, source selection and query result
size estimation.

In this section we present the workflow of chilon (visually represented in
Fig. 2) and describe implementation details and decisions.

Fig. 2. chilon workflow.

4.1   Namespace Discovery

Namespace mappings, i.e. a list pairs of namespace prefixes and alias, are necessary for our resource classification process. These can be obtained from external
or internal sources. External sources are objects external to the RDF graph,
and include additional JSON or RDF files with namespace mappings provided
by the user, or community sourced mappings obtained from the prefixmaps
project (see Sect. 2.3). Mappings from internal sources can be gathered by iterating once over the RDF graph files, and include extracting explicit prefix declarations (from @prefix statements) and namespaces automatically inferred by
detecting frequent prefix patterns in the IRIs of the graph.

Namespace mappings have different priorities according to their source.
User provided mappings have the highest priority, as they are the most clearly
aligned with user intentions. Then we have community sourced mappings, which
arguably have some degree of consensus behind them. Explicit namespace declarations in the graph files are next, as the author or the tools used to generate
the graph deemed them relevant to be declared. Lastly, namespaces are also
automatically inferred from IRI prefix patterns.

The algorithm for inferring namespaces from the RDF graph IRIs takes as
input the set NS of namespaces gathered from the other sources, the set R
of RDF graph files, and a set of additional parameters (maximum number of
namespaces $maxNS$, minimum namespace size $minSize$). Then:

1. The files in R are iterated in parallel. Each IRI for which a matching names-pace is not found in NS is truncated to 200 characters and added to a prefix tree T. Each node in T keeps information regarding the number of descen-dants, that is, the number of IRIs with that prefix added to T.
2. The prefix tree T is pruned, dropping prefixes corresponding to host names with less than $minSize$ IRIs.
3. Then a set C with namespace candidates is created. Each prefix corresponding to a different host name in T is added to C.
4. While the size of C is inferior to $maxNS$:
   4.1 The namespace candidate nc with the most IRIs is removed from C.
   4.2 The location l_{nc} of nc in the T tree is found. Then the set of children namespace candidates is found by walking down T starting at l_{nc}, and until a '/' or a '#' or the string end is found[3]. Each namespace candidate is added to C if it has at least $minSize$ IRIs.
5. An alias is generated for each namespace, and the pairs *(namespace, alias)* are returned.

For large RDF graphs (size threshold is configurable), steps 2 to 4 are performed periodically in parallel with step 1. This enables the use of the inferred names-paces to preemptively prune the prefix tree, which is kept in memory during the whole process. This helps keeping it small, which results in lower memory requirements for `chilon`.

4.2   Resource Classification

After gathering all the namespace mappings, resource classification is performed by iterating again over all the RDF graph files. IRIs are converted to their namespace aliases. However, triples can also be composed of blank nodes and literals. `chilon` converts all blank nodes (which, by definition, are anonymous and as such have no externally meaningful identifier) to a special class `BLANK`. Nodes with unknown namespaces are also converted to a single custom class `UNKNOWN`. Finally, RDF literals are associated with datatypes represented by IRIs. They can be associated either implicitly to the default datatype (`xsd:string`), or explicitly to a custom one (e.g. `"4.2E9"^^xsd:double`). `chilon` uses the same namespace-based classification but applied to the literal datatype. For example, the triple `dbr:Einstein ex:birthDate "1879-03-14"^^xsd:date .` would become the triple `dbr ex xsd`.

4.3   Summary Graph Generation

The data resulting from resource classification is then aggregated, counting the frequency of each reduced version of the original triples. A custom ontology is then used to represent that data as an RDF summary graph[4] Figure 3 provides

---

[3] For example, http://example.org/ → (`http://example.org/foo/`, `http://example.org/bar/`).

[4] Ontology available at https://andrefs.github.io/chilon_rs/ns-graph-summ.ttl.

a simple example of a RDF graph and the corresponding summary graph and visualization obtained with `chilon`.

```
1  dbr:Einstein dbp:birthDate "1879-03-14"^^xsd:date ;
2               ex:livedIn yago:Berlin .
3  dbr:Hawking ex:bornIn yago:Oxford .
```

```
1  @base <https://a52c.github.io/chilon/ns-graph-summ.ttl> .
2  <#t0001> a <#DatatypeLink>, rdf:Statement ;
3      rdf:subject <#dbr> ; rdf:predicate <#dbp> ; rdf:object <#xsd> ;
4      <#occurrences> "1"^^xsd:integer .
5  <#t0002> a <#NamespaceLink>, rdf:Statement ;
6      rdf:subject <#dbr> ; rdf:predicate <#ex> ; rdf:object <#yago> ;
7      <#occurrences> "2"^^xsd:integer .
```

Fig. 3. Example of RDF graph, its summary and corresponding visualization.

4.4   Visualization

The RDF summary graph can then be used to generate an interactive visualization. This visualization is an HTML page using D3.js to render the graph. The size of the nodes and the thickness of the edges in the graph are correlated to the corresponding namespace frequency in the original graph. A simple example of a summary graph and its visualization can be found in Fig. 3. Examples of visualizations for commonly used KGs can be found in Fig. 4.

The user can move around and zoom in or out using the mouse. Placing the cursor over a node or edge will highlight it and provide information regarding the namespace prefix and alias, and some metrics about its frequency. A sidebar with options allows further configuration, such as hiding loop edges, show node sizes in a logarithmic proportion, hide datatype links, among others.

5   Validation

The validation of our approach and its implementation `chilon` was performed by summarizing 11 publicly available knowledge graphs, listed in Table 1. These graphs have different sizes, from a few megabytes or less then one million triples, to over 90 gigabytes and thousands of millions of triples. They are available in different formats (N-Triples or Turtle), and compressed using different formats (Gzip or Bzip2). Most are available as one single file, but a few are split into several files.

We benchmarked `chilon` using these KGs, measuring how much time it took to process and the maximum amount of memory used for each graph. The results allowed us to make a quantitative evaluation of the summarization process. We also generated the visualization for all the graphs, and analyzed them to obtain high level information regarding the structure of the graphs and how namespaces are interlinked in each one. This allowed us to obtain a qualitative evaluation of our tool. Additionally, we performed verification checks on the correctness of our results by manually querying the original graph for resources with specific prefixes and checking whether the results would match the corresponding summary data.

6   Results and Discussion

In this section we will present and discuss the summaries obtained for two of the 11 graphs, DBpedia and ClaimsKG, by analyzing details of the visualization obtained for each one. Then we will analyze the performance of `chilon` by discussing the performance results obtained for all 11 KGs. The summaries and interactive visualizations obtained for all the other graphs have also been published at https://andrefs.github.io/chilon_rs. The code for `chilon` can be viewed and downloaded at https://github.com/andrefs/chilon_rs.

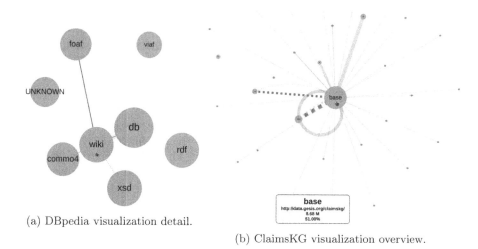

(a) DBpedia visualization detail.

(b) ClaimsKG visualization overview.

Fig. 4. Graph summary visualization for DBpedia and ClaimsKG.

6.1   Graph Summary Visualizations

Figure 4 presents cropped views of the visualizations generated from the summaries of DBpedia and ClaimsKG. In Fig. 4a we can see how DBpedia's core namespace, represented by the node **db**, connects to Wikipedia's namespace **wiki**. Hovering with the mouse over the connecting edges would reveal these to be **rdf** and **prov**. Highlighted are also other namespaces connected to **wiki**: **foaf** and **commo4**. There is also a dotted line connecting **wiki** to **xsd**, representing

Table 1. chilon performance with reference knowledge graphs.

KG	Files	Total size (GiB)	Triples (millions)	IRIs (millions)	Name-spaces	Time (s)	IRI/s	Max memory (GiB)
WordNet [26]	1	0.015	2.6	6.5	11	67.9	96 049	0.7
KBpedia [4]	1	0.009	0.5	3.0	34	28.8	106 645	0.3
LinkedMDB [17]	1	0.012	3.6	8.8	18	63.9	138 124	1.1
OpenCyc [25]	1	0.023	0.3	6.2	26	51.4	121 505	3.7
ClaimsKG [29]	1	0.121	1.0	21.6	72	250.1	86 433	11.0
DBLP [23]	1	1.464	9.7	736.8	193	4 628.1	159 195	3.4
CrunchBase [15]	1	1.111	83.5	138.3	77	1 765	78 385	10.1
DBKwik [18]	17	5.864	126.7	319.0	15	2 752.5	115 924	0.8
DBpedia [22]	153	15.641	915.9	2 527.1	878	15 738	160 575	17.9
Yago [27]	8	59.110	2 539.6	5 717.9	15	48 183	118 671	22.3
Wikidata [30]	1	92.000	3 428.0	45 923.5	2 356	367 707	124 892	8.9

elements from **wiki** connected via the namespace **dc** to literals whose datatypes belong to **xsd**. The IRI prefixes corresponding to the nodes displayed are available on the interactive visualization. Also visible in the same figure are other nodes, visually disabled because they are not directly connected to **wiki**. In this figure, node sizes are logarithmically related to the corresponding namespace frequency.

In the ClaimsKG visualization (Fig. 4b) it is possible to observe a common pattern in these summary graphs: the summary takes a radial structure, with the graph's main namespace occupying a central role (in this case, **base**), surrounded by and connected to much smaller nodes with few connections between them. In this figure node sizes are linearly correlated with their frequency.

Both figures represent a limited view of the kind of information gatherable from the web-based visualizations, which were designed specifically to be explored interactively. Dragging, scrolling and hovering with the mouse allows to pan, zoom in or out or view information regarding the namespaces, their aliases and the frequency of their occurrences in the summarized graph. Additionally, the visualization interface includes a menu which allows setting additional options, such switching between linear or logarithmic node sizes or hiding loops, blanks nodes or datatype links, among others.

6.2   Performance

Table 1 presents the performance results obtained summarizing the knowledge graphs on a laptop with an Intel i7-1165G7 CPU and 32 GB LDDR4 4266 Mhz of RAM. The largest graph, Wikidata, with a size of 92 GiB, took a little over 100 h to process using a single core. Yago required the highest maximum memory, 22.3 GiB. These values prove how even for the largest graphs, a common laptop was enough to produce results in a reasonable amount of time.

Figure 5 presents the reference graphs distributed according to their size and total processing time. The chart uses a logarithmic scale on both axes. A regression over the points on the chart (green line) demonstrates that the processing time of a graph varies linearly with the number of IRIs in that graph. Most summarizing approaches for semantic graphs described in the literature are not capable of producing summaries in linear time [8]. However, the summaries they produce present substantially different contents and properties. We could not find approaches similar enough to our own (in methodology or type of summary produced) that a meaningful comparison of algorithmic complexity was possible. More so, most if not all of these approaches do not report performance results (e.g. triples per second or total time of execution for reference graphs) which we could compare to our own.

Our previous implementation required loading the whole graph into memory to summarize it. For that reason, it was only validated using graphs which would easily fit into the memory of a normal laptop. We used Wordnet, KBpedia and LinkedMDB. `chilon` does not load the full graph into memory, allowing it to process massive KGs. To keep its memory usage as low as possible, `chilon` reads each file twice (once to extract prefixes and a second time to produce the summary). Even with two file reads, contrasting the performance results obtained previously [9, Table 5.3] with the ones from `chilon`, we can see speedups in the execution time of 500% to 800%.

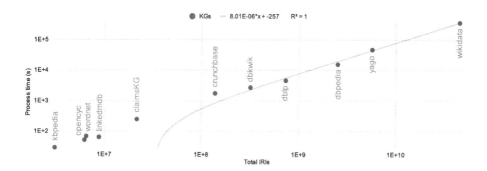

Fig. 5. Size and total processing time for reference knowledge graphs.

7 Conclusions and Future Work

The increasing size of KGs renders them difficult to process and visualize. Graph summarization techniques are a standard approach for handling this issue, but RDF graphs with hundreds of millions of triples are still challenging. Massive KGs requires summarization algorithms that are linear on the number of triples and parallelizable.

Several graph summarization techniques assemble nodes into super nodes using an equivalence relation. In such techniques, a graph summary is a quotient graph where nodes are equivalence classes. We propose a similar approach for

RDF graphs with two main features. Firstly, we use namespaces related to the IRIs to classify resources, properties, and literals. Secondly, we extended the definition of quotient graphs both to process and produce multigraphs, enabling RDF graphs to be summarized as RDF graphs.

Another contribution of this research is `chilon`, a Rust library and command-line tool to summarize and interact with visualizations of massive RDF graphs. It discovers namespaces using mappings from multiple sources, classifies IRIs with the aliases assigned to them, generates an RDF graph according to a graph summarization ontology, and produces an interactive web-based visualization. Using `chilon`, we validated the proposed approach with 11 KGs of different sizes. This validation empirically confirmed the linear complexity of the algorithm and enabled us to extract relevant information from the resulting interactive visualizations.

`chilon` is currently targeted to RDF graphs, but in the future may be extended to KGs in different formats and even to other kinds of massive graphs. Its results are presently focused on graph visualization, but the summary could also be used for source graph selection or query result size estimation. The cornerstone of this approach is the quick classification of identifiers, which in RDF graphs is achieved through namespaces. However, most identification schemata have similar features that can be exploited for node and edge classification.

Acknowledgments. This work is financed by National Funds through the Portuguese funding agency, FCT - Fundação para a Ciência e a Tecnologia, within project LA/P/0063/2020. André Fernandes dos Santos: Ph.D. Grant SFRH/BD/129225/2017 from Fundação para a Ciência e Tecnologia (FCT), Portugal.

References

1. Alexander, K., Cyganiak, R., Hausenblas, M., Zhao, J.: Describing linked datasets with the VoID vocabulary (2011)
2. Beckett, D.: RDF 1.1 N-Triples (2014). https://www.w3.org/TR/n-triples/
3. Beckett, D., Berners-Lee, T., Prud'hommeaux, E., Carothers, G.: RDF 1.1 Turtle (2014)
4. Bergman, M.K.: A Knowledge Representation Practionary. Springer, Cham (2018). https://doi.org/10.1007/978-3-319-98092-8
5. Berners-Lee, T.: Linked data - design issues (2006). http://www.w3.org/DesignIssues/LinkedData.html
6. Bizer, C., Heath, T., Berners-Lee, T.: Linked data: the story so far. In: Semantic Services, Interoperability and Web Applications: Emerging Concepts. IGI global (2011)
7. Bonifati, A., Dumbrava, S., Kondylakis, H.: Graph summarization. arXiv preprint arXiv:2004.14794 (2020)
8. Čebirić, Š, et al.: Summarizing semantic graphs: a survey. VLDB J. **28**, 295–327 (2019). https://doi.org/10.1007/s00778-018-0528-3
9. da Costa, A.R.S.L.: Sumariação de grafos semânticos de grande dimensão usando espaços de nomes. Master's thesis, Faculty of Sciences of the University of Porto (2022)

10. da Costa, A.R.S.L., Santos, A., Leal, J.P.: Large semantic graph summarization using namespaces. In: 11th Symposium on Languages, Applications and Technologies, SLATE 2022. Schloss Dagstuhl-Leibniz-Zentrum für Informatik (2022)

11. Cyganiak, R., Wood, D., Lanthaler, M., Klyne, G., Carroll, J.J., McBride, B.: RDF 1.1 concepts and abstract syntax. W3C Recommendation, 25 February 2014

12. Debattista, J., Lange, C., Auer, S., Cortis, D.: Evaluating the quality of the LOD cloud: an empirical investigation. Semant. Web **9**(6), 859–901 (2018)

13. Duerst, M., Suignard, M.: RFC 3987: Internationalized Resource Identifiers (IRIs) (2005)

14. Färber, M.: The Microsoft academic knowledge graph: a linked data source with 8 billion triples of scholarly data. In: Ghidini, C., et al. (eds.) ISWC 2019. LNCS, vol. 11779, pp. 113–129. Springer, Cham (2019). https://doi.org/10.1007/978-3-030-30796-7_8

15. Färber, M., Menne, C., Harth, A.: A linked data wrapper for CrunchBase. Semant. Web **9**(4), 505–515 (2018)

16. Haller, A., Fernández, J.D., Kamdar, M.R., Polleres, A.: What are links in linked open data? A characterization and evaluation of links between knowledge graphs on the web. J. Data Inf. Qual. (JDIQ) **12**(2), 1–34 (2020)

17. Hassanzadeh, O., Consens, M.P.: Linked movie data base. In: LDOW (2009)

18. Hofmann, A., Perchani, S., Portisch, J., Hertling, S., Paulheim, H.: DBkWik: towards knowledge graph creation from thousands of Wikis. In: ISWC (2017)

19. Janowicz, K., Hitzler, P., Adams, B., Kolas, D., Vardeman, C., II.: Five stars of linked data vocabulary use. Semant. Web **5**(3), 173–176 (2014)

20. Kondylakis, H., Kotzinos, D., Manolescu, I.: RDF graph summarization: principles, techniques and applications (tutorial). In: EDBT/ICDT 2019–22nd International Conference on Extending Database Technology-Joint Conference (2019)

21. Krishnan, A.: Making search easier (2018). https://www.aboutamazon.com/news/innovation-at-amazon/making-search-easier

22. Lehmann, J., et al.: DBpedia-a large-scale, multilingual knowledge base extracted from Wikipedia. Semant. Web **6**(2), 167–195 (2015)

23. Ley, M.: DBLP: some lessons learned. VLDB Endow. **2**(2), 1493–1500 (2009)

24. Liu, Y., Safavi, T., Dighe, A., Koutra, D.: Graph summarization methods and applications: a survey. ACM Comput. Surv. (CSUR) **51**(3), 1–34 (2018)

25. Matuszek, C., Witbrock, M., Cabral, J., DeOliveira, J.: An introduction to the syntax and content of Cyc. UMBC Computer Science and Electrical Engineering Department Collection (2006)

26. McCrae, J., Fellbaum, C., Cimiano, P.: Publishing and linking wordnet using lemon and RDF. In: Proceedings of the 3rd Workshop on Linked Data in Linguistics (2014)

27. Pellissier Tanon, T., Weikum, G., Suchanek, F.: YAGO 4: a reason-able knowledge base. In: Harth, A., et al. (eds.) ESWC 2020. LNCS, vol. 12123, pp. 583–596. Springer, Cham (2020). https://doi.org/10.1007/978-3-030-49461-2_34

28. Singhal, A., et al.: Introducing the knowledge graph: things, not strings. Official Google blog, 16 May 2012

29. Tchechmedjiev, A., et al.: ClaimsKG: a knowledge graph of fact-checked claims. In: Ghidini, C., et al. (eds.) ISWC 2019. LNCS, vol. 11779, pp. 309–324. Springer, Cham (2019). https://doi.org/10.1007/978-3-030-30796-7_20

30. Vrandečić, D., Krötzsch, M.: Wikidata: a free collaborative knowledgebase. Commun. ACM **57**(10), 78–85 (2014)

Towards a Flexible and Scalable Data Stream Algorithm in FCA

Nicolás Leutwyler[1,2,3,4]([⊠]) [iD], Mario Lezoche[1] [iD], Diego Torres[2,3] [iD],
and Hervé Panetto[1] [iD]

[1] University of Lorraine, CNRS, CRAN, 54000 Nancy, France
{nicolas.leutwyler,mario.lezoche,herve.panetto}@univ-lorraine.fr
[2] LIFIA, CICPBA-Facultad de Informática, UNLP, La Plata,
1900 Buenos Aires, Argentina
{nicolas.leutwyler,diego.torres}@lifia.info.unlp.edu.ar
[3] Dto. CyT, UNQ, Bernal, 1876 Buenos Aires, Argentina
[4] SNMSF, 38240 Meylan, France

Abstract. The amount of different environments where data can be exploited have increased partly because of the massive adoption of technologies such as microservices and distributed architectures. Accordingly, approaches to treat data are in constant improvement. An example of this is the Formal Concept Analysis framework that has seen an increase in the methods carried out to increment its capabilities in the mentioned environments. However, on top of the exponential nature of the output that the framework produces, the data stream processing environment still poses challenges regarding the flexibility in the usage of FCA and its extensions. Consequently, several approaches have been proposed to deal with them considering different constraints, such as receiving unsorted elements or unknown attributes. In this work, the notion of *flexibly scalable* for FCA distributed algorithms consuming data streams is defined. Additionally, the meaning of different scenarios of lattice merge in a particular data stream model is discussed. Finally, a pseudo-algorithm for merging lattices in the case of disjoint objects is presented. The presented work is a preliminary result and, in the future, it is expected to cover the other aspects of the problem with real data for validation.

Keywords: Formal Concept Analysis · Lattice Merge · Scalability · Incremental Algorithm · Data Stream

1 Introduction

Formal Concept Analysis (FCA), introduced by Wille in [16], is a method for knowledge extraction from a dataset consisting of instances and their attributes. The knowledge it allows to extract is a set of formal concepts, which can be

Partly funded by SNMSF.

understood as natural clusters of instances sharing certain properties. For example, as depicted in Table 1 and Fig. 1, in a dataset with electronic devices, there would probably be a concept with the attribute "screen" in which the instances of *television* and *mobile phone* would belong to. In addition, there is the notion of *sub-concept* by inclusion of attributes, e.g., following the last example, there could be a sub-concept with the attributes "screen" and "battery" that would include *mobile phone* and, unlike its *super-concept*, it would not include the instance of *television*. These formal concepts can give additional information with the form of "having X attributes implies also having Y", e.g., "instances with batteries also have screen with a certain confidence". Notice that the structural output is bounded to the input, meaning that the mentioned result does not imply that all instances with batteries also have a screen in the *real world*.

Table 1. Electronic devices dataset

Objects	Attributes	
	Screen	Battery
Television	X	
Mobile Phone	X	X

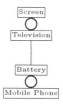

Fig. 1. Electronic devices conceptual hierarchy

Over the last decades, FCA has been used in several areas such as knowledge discovery, information retrieval, machine learning, or automatic software modelling, among others. Additionally, it has been extended in a plethora of ways to deal with the arising problems posed in the mentioned different areas. To name a few, Relational Concept Analysis (RCA) [13], is one extension that allows dealing with multi-relational data-mining (MRDM) [4]. Fuzzy Formal Concept Analysis (FFCA) [8] is the extension that looks to model the uncertainty in data by considering that the instances can have attributes with a degree of certainty in the range of $[0, 1]$, instead of their traditional binary nature, i.e., either having an attribute or not. And Temporal Concept Analysis (TCA) [17], that is the theory of temporal phenomena described with tools of FCA. All these extensions add some degree of flexibility to the FCA method by incrementing the amount of applications it can naturally interact with. However, one of the main pitfalls of FCA is that the amount of formal concepts is exponential in the size of the input in the worst case, making even the best algorithms not directly usable with huge datasets. This poses a problem for scalability because as the input grows bigger, algorithms and computers would require exponentially more resources in order to handle the calculation of the entire set of formal concepts.

Moreover, the need for processing large datasets is becoming more and more common nowadays and a considerable effort has been put into allowing FCA to be applied in such datasets. For organization purposes, we consider three ways of addressing the mentioned problem: reducing the size of the input [1], reducing the size of the output [12, 14], and allowing the algorithm to scale in resources and capabilities [2,5,6]. In this work, we focus on the third one, although it is important to understand that the approaches are not mutually exclusive, e.g., there could be a method for reducing both the input and output, or any other combination. Moreover, although there could be other approaches to address the problem, they are out of the scope of this paper.

There are several reasons why reducing the input or the output is sometimes not enough. On the one hand, not all datasets are made of relevant and not relevant data, for example, we could consider a large dataset that has already been reduced to the minimum, i.e., there is only relevant information left. In addition, even though reducing the size of the output could work very well, the information loss could be not acceptable in some situations. Hence, it is important to have ways of scaling without reducing the size of the input or the output. On the other hand, not all environments for knowledge discovery are the same, in some of them it is reasonable to work with static data and also to wait a considerable amount of time until the algorithm finishes. However, there are other scenarios in which the data is dynamic and there is the need for processing it in a short span of time as it arrives. For this reason, we will focus on the online real-time data streams processing environment.

To deal with the aforementioned problem, as mentioned before, many approaches have been proposed and are currently used both in the industry and the academy. Firstly, one of them is the reduction of the input size by considering only a part of, for example, the attributes [1]. Secondly, another way of dealing with the exponential size of the formal concepts is to calculate only a subset of them, as it is in the case of Iceberg Lattices [14] and AOC-posets [12]. Lastly, a huge effort has also been put in developing distributed algorithms in order to take advantage of parallelization when possible [2,5,6]. Nevertheless, to the best of our knowledge, there is still no algorithm, distributed or not, that can be *flexibly* used to extract knowledge from *infinite* data streams (i.e., once the data stream starts, it never stops producing data). Despite some algorithms being able to process data streams, and even if they are incremental, this does not scale well because at some point even adding one row to the formal context would be computationally too costly. Thus, in this work, we present the definition of a problem to solve in order to have a more flexible scalability in the environment of FCA and its extensions considering the *infinite* constraint in data stream processing.

As for the structure of the paper, in Sect. 2, a set of relevant works in the area of distributed algorithms for FCA for data stream processing are presented and contrasted. In Sect. 3, the definitions and the problem are precisely defined. In Sect. 4 the first approach of a solution is proposed. Finally, in Sect. 5 the conclusion, future work, and final discussions are given.

2   Related Works

Many distributed algorithms have been proposed [2,5,6,18], with their main advantage being the ability to compute in parallel and in that way reducing the amount of time it takes to process the output. Most of the distributed algorithms use the MapReduce framework [3] which is appealing to practitioners mainly because they are easily implementable into cloud infrastructures.

In this section, we direct our attention to three main works in the field of distributed algorithms in FCA: one presenting the incremental distributed algorithm based on AddIntent in an iterative fashion, other considering the constraint of not knowing the attributes in advance, and the last one being the only work, to the best of our knowledge, that can run infinitely by forgetting concepts as it processes the data stream. Thanks to an ongoing state-of-the-art study on the characteristics of formal methods for knowledge extraction, and to the best of our knowledge, we detected that these articles represent well the state of the art in data stream processing algorithms for FCA (a subset of the reviewed articles can be found in [7]).

Firstly, Xu et al. [18] contribute with the *iterative distributed* implementations of some known lattice calculation algorithms such as Ganter and Ganter+ which they call MGanter and MGanter+. They present theoretical properties about partitioning the input and working with the partitions instead of the entire formal context. And finally, they use the properties to argue about the correctness of their MapReduce algorithms. The strengths of this approach are that it uses a well accepted framework such as MapReduce, and that it is incremental, which means that it updates the final lattice as the new rows arrive. This also means it is possible to adapt it to process streams.

Secondly, Goel et al. [5] present a MapReduce algorithm that updates the final lattice without assuming prior knowledge of the attributes and thus allows the *arbitrary distribution* of the formal context. They calculate the lattice from a *snapshot* taken at a particular time, and leave the merging step of several *snapshots* out of the scope. Additionally, the algorithm is more suitable for sparse context than for dense ones.

Lastly, De Maio et al. [2] present an incremental distributed algorithm based on AddIntent [10], and suitable for online stream processing. It uses time interval windows in which only one observation is taken into account from each node. Moreover, the proposed algorithm uses Temporal FFCA instead of plain FCA, in order to maintain a reasonably small lattice by taking full advantage of the concepts' support. In the algorithm, they also forget old concepts when there have not been many occurrences of an object in it in a certain time window.

$$\text{Supp}(C) = \frac{|\text{extent}(C)|}{|G|} e^{-\lambda(t-t_{lio})} \tag{1}$$

The mechanic of "forgetting" is calculated based on a *decay factor* $0 \leq \lambda \leq 1$ that decreases the support of a formal concept C based on how much time has passed since the last object has been inserted into it. In the Eq. 1, G is the set of all objects, t is the current timestamp and t_{lio} is the timestamp of the last inserted object into the concept C.

All these distributed algorithms have their advantages and disadvantages, and particularly, the ones presented in [5,18] are not directly prepared for infinite data stream processing, contrary to [2] which, although it is an online data stream processing algorithm, it is based on an extension of FCA [8], and it is not trivial to migrate it into its FCA version.

3   Flexibly Scalable FCA for Data Streams

The goal of this section is to present a discussion about how to provide enough *flexibility* in terms of scalability for stream processing. As presented in the previous section, there are several algorithms that are able to process data streams, and some of them can run infinitely by "forgetting" some information. However, doing so risks losing important concepts. For instance, let us suppose an FCA algorithm that runs in a data stream to study temporal phenomena in smart cities. By forgetting concepts without an object contributing to it in the defined threshold λ, it is possible to lose concepts representing scenarios that rarely occur, but have a huge impact when they do occur. Such a concept could be the one representing a flood in a certain neighborhood or a protest that block certain streets. Therefore, the ideal scenario would be to be able to perform FCA on a data stream infinitely, without compromising *too much* the amount of information lost.

As illustrated in Fig. 2, and defined in [9], a *data stream* is a *countably infinite* sequence of elements.

Fig. 2. Data stream over time

Regarding the usage of FCA in data stream processing, the model this work considers is the one in which elements represent observations (instances) occurring at a certain point in time, having certain properties (attributes). This model has been addressed in [2,11], where the goal is to extract relevant knowledge from the relations between events (concepts) in time (temporal paths). In these works, the models were based on FCA and FFCA respectively. We call it Ordered Temporal Model (OTM) because the observations occur ordered in time.

3.1   Merge Lattices

A way of dealing with both the necessity of running infinitely, and the ability to regain a part of the lost information, is to consider an algorithm that keeps the size of the lattice bounded, and another algorithm that can perform the union or merge of the lattices calculated in different points in time. Doing so would give the practitioners the flexibility to choose the size they are able to maintain given their resources, without the worry of losing *all* the information outside the lattice they are maintaining. This, however, comes at the cost of having to store the snapshots in a certain way, which goes outside the scope of this paper.

Definition 1. *Let G and M be the objects and attributes of a formal context respectively. The content of a* **Formal Context data stream** *in a given moment $k \in \mathbb{N}$ is defined as an indexed family $S_k = (r_j)_{j \in 1..k}$ where $r_j \subseteq G \times M$.*

Definition 2. *Given a Formal Context data stream S_k, we define the underlying traditional Formal Context $K = (G, M, I)$, where $G = \{\pi_1(r) \mid r \in S_k\}$, $M = \{\pi_2(r) \mid r \in S_k\}$, $gIm \iff \langle g, m \rangle \in S_k$, and both π_1 and π_2 are the functions that return the first and second element of the tuple respectively.*

Definition 3. *A* **snapshot** *of a Formal Context data stream between moments $k, l \in \mathbb{N}$ is the sequence of tuples $S_{k,l} = S_l \setminus S_k$.[1] For convenience, we will use the notation $\mathcal{L}_{k,l}$ when speaking about the underlying lattice from $S_{k,l}$.*

In particular, there are three cases we consider important to highlight for merging different lattice snapshots. The first one, depicted in Fig. 3, is the one in which the goal is to merge $\mathcal{L}_{k,l}$ with $\mathcal{L}_{l+1,m}$. The second one, depicted in Fig. 4, is the one where the goal is to merge $\mathcal{L}_{k,l}$ and $\mathcal{L}_{n,m}$ and $l < n$ i.e., there is at least one element outside the covered range. And the last one, depicted in Fig. 5, is the one in which the goal is to merge two snapshots $\mathcal{L}_{k,l}$, and $\mathcal{L}_{n,m}$, where $k \leq l$, $n \leq m$, and $n < l$. The separation in cases is thought with two things in mind (1) Computation: in case there is repeated information between the two snapshots, the computation cost of merging might be reduced in comparison with the case in which both snapshots are completely disjoint. (2) Interpretation: what should be the interpretation of the result when merging two snapshots that are not contiguous?

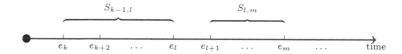

Fig. 3. Contiguous lattice snapshots merge.

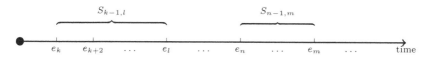

Fig. 4. Spaced lattice snapshots merge case.

---

[1] Notice that $l \leq k$ implies $S_{k,l} = \varnothing$.

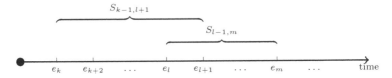

Fig. 5. Intersected snapshots merge case.

Regarding the model, the main problem is that although we could use incremental algorithms to calculate their lattices, at some point the k would be so large that even performing one more update would be too costly, either in time or in space. Thus, for a flexible method whose goal is to run infinitely, it is mandatory to consider "forgetting" objects, attributes, or concepts. Nevertheless, doing so implies potentially losing relevant information, meaning that it is equally necessary to have a way of merging different *snapshots* of the stream, as suggested in [5]. Although one option is to simply join the intervals, remove duplicates, and apply the algorithm to the result, it could be possible that there are not enough resources to run the algorithm with such an input. Moreover, considering that a lattice for each interval has already been calculated, maybe working with them would be more efficient than recalculating everything from the ground up.

Considering this, we say that a method is *flexibly scalable* for knowledge extraction in data stream processing, if it allows running in the data stream infinitely, and it provides a way of considering "forgotten" information without the necessity to *recalculate* or *traverse* the whole lattice.

Merge Problem in the OTM. As defined in [2] and in the previous section, the data stream model merges FCA with Conceptual Time Systems by indexing the timestamped objects adding a time variable to the subject of the formal context, i.e., g_{t_i} with $g \in G$. In this definition, t represents a time window, $i \in \mathbb{N}$, and g_{t_i} is the latest observation g occurring in the time window assigned to that specific time variable. The larger the time window, the more general the study, the smaller, the more detailed it is. Formally (based on [11]):

- g represents a type of observation, e.g., change in temperature of the environment,
- t_i is the i-th element in a discretization of time with the time window t,
- g_{t_i} is the last occurrence of g in the time t_i,
- t_i precedes t_j if $i < j$ for any two $i, j \in \mathbb{N}$.

Definition 4 *(Definition 3.4 in [2]). The intention of an object O at time t_i is defined as*

$$i\{O_{t_i}\} = \{m \mid m \in M \land O_{t_i} I m\}$$

which is the set of all attributes of that particular object at time t_i.

Definition 5. *A **Temporal Lattice** $\mathcal{L}^t$ is a pair $(\mathcal{L}, E^t)$ where $\mathcal{L} = (\mathcal{C}, \leq)$ is a concepts lattice and E^t is a set of temporal edges (see Definition 6).*

Definition 6 *(Based on the definition 3.7 in [2]). Given the set of concepts $\mathcal{C}$, a **Temporal Edge** $e^t_{ij} \in E^t$ is a pair $(C_i, C_j) \in \mathcal{C} \times \mathcal{C}$ iff there exist two objects $g_{t_s} \in C_i$ and $g_{t_k} \in C_j$ such that the time t_s precedes the time t_k.*

The temporal edges have a weight associated with the time granule size function $\Delta t : E^t \to \mathbb{R}$ defined by $\Delta t(e^t_{ij}) = 1/|t_{s'} - t_{k'}|$. Furthermore, they define a function that filters edges that are not so representative, called Temporal Edge Support (TES). For the purpose of this work, we would consider the function, but without any particular definition.

Definition 7 *(Definition 3.9 in [2]). A **temporal path** is defined as a path $\pi = (C_s, \ldots, C_t) \in \mathcal{C} \times \mathcal{C} \times \ldots \mathcal{C}$, such that there exist a temporal edge $e^t_{ij} \in E^t$ for $s \leq i \leq j \leq t$.*

In this context, the merge problem is defined by, given two temporal lattice snapshots $\mathcal{L}^t_{k,l} = (\mathcal{L}_1, E^t_1)$, $\mathcal{L}^t_{n,m} = (\mathcal{L}_2, E^t_2)$, return a lattice $\widehat{\mathcal{L}}^t = (\widehat{\mathcal{L}}, \widehat{E}^t)$ such that $\widehat{\mathcal{L}} = \mathcal{L}_1 \mid \mathcal{L}_2$ (see Definition 8), and $\widehat{E}^t$ is the set of temporal edges in the new lattice with a TES support above the given threshold.

Definition 8. *Given two lattices $\mathcal{L}_1$, and $\mathcal{L}_2$ coming from the contexts $K_1 = (G_1, M_1, I_1)$, and $K_2 = (G_2, M_2, I_2)$, their merged lattice $\mathcal{L}_1 \mid \mathcal{L}_2$ is defined as the resulting lattice from the following formal context:*

$$K_1 \mid K_2 = (G_1 \cup G_2, M_1 \cup M_2, I_1 \cup I_2) \tag{2}$$

Notice that in the worst case, the $|G_1 \cup G_2| = (l - k) + (n - m)$, so the merge algorithm that calculates it will still be bounded by its size, that could be up to $2^{\max(|G_1 \cup G_2|, |M_1 \cup M_2|)}$.

4   Merge Lattice Snapshots

In this section, the different cases and particularities in the implementation of lattice snapshot merge in the OTM data stream model are discussed. Moreover, a pseudo-algorithm for the lattice snapshot merge in the disjoint data streams case is presented.

4.1   Interpretation

In the *contiguous* and *intersected* merge cases, the model should have the interpretation: after performing the merge, the resulting lattice represents the same as if the incremental algorithm had run from point k to m. However, that is not the case when there are elements in the middle that are lost between l and n. In OTM, there would be some g_{t_i} where g either has been previously introduced or not. On the one hand, if it was not previously introduced (i.e., $i = 1$) there would be no impact in the temporal paths, besides losing the first part of them (see Fig. 6). On the other hand, if g was previously introduced, it would simplify the path in the erased part by taking much less granular edges (see Fig. 7).

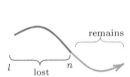

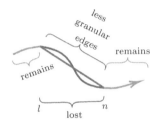

Fig. 6. Temporal path after merging when g_{t_i} occurs for the first time between l and n

Fig. 7. Temporal path after merging when g_{t_i} occurs before l

4.2   Computation

Computing the merge of lattices needs to be treated differently depending on the model. Particularly, in the OTM, the implementation should consider the repeated objects that could belong to different concepts in the two lattices in the intersected snapshots merge case. Additionally, in the other cases, it is possible that the snapshot had objects with incomplete attributes, i.e., if the snapshot had been taken some time later, some objects in it would have more attributes. The rest of the section from now on focuses on the OTM when objects are disjoint, i.e., spaced, and contiguous snapshots merge cases without incomplete attributes.

Given two concept lattices $\mathcal{L}_1 = (\mathcal{C}_1, \leq)$ and $\mathcal{L}_2 = (\mathcal{C}_2, \leq)$, whose formal context are $K_1 = (G_1, M_1, I_1)$ and $K_2 = (G_2, M_2, I_2)$ respectively. When G_1 and G_2 are disjoint, we claim that each intent would remain *unchanged* after the merge since closures at most would have more objects. Moreover, the only new intents that *could* be added to the merged lattice are: $\varnothing$ and $M_1 \cup M_2$, and the ones resulting from the intersection of two intents in $\mathcal{L}_1$ and $\mathcal{L}_2$.

Lemma 1. *Let* $K_1 = (G_1, M_1, I_1), K_2 = (G_2, M_2, I_2), K_s = K_1 \mid K_2$ *be three formal contexts where* $G_1 \cap G_2 = \varnothing$. *Let* $\mathcal{L}_1 = (\mathcal{C}_1, \leq), \mathcal{L}_2 = (\mathcal{C}_2, \leq), \mathcal{L}_s = \mathcal{L}_1 \mid \mathcal{L}_2 = (\mathcal{C}_s, \leq)$ *be their respective lattices. Then, given a concept* $(X, Y) = C_1 \in \mathcal{C}_1$, *such that* $Y \neq \varnothing$ *and* $X \neq \varnothing$, *there exist a* $(Z, Y) \in \mathcal{C}_s$, *where* $X \subseteq Z$.

Proof. For reading purposes, we will say $Y = Y_1 = Y_2 = Y_s$. Y_1' will be used when speaking about the derivation in the context of $\mathcal{L}_1$. Similarly, Y_2' will be used when speaking about the derivation in the context of $\mathcal{L}_2$, and Y_s' when speaking about the derivation in the context of $\mathcal{L}_s$. Analogously, we will use the same notation for the set of objects $X = X_1 = X_2 = X_s$.

Since (X, Y) is a formal concept in $\mathcal{C}_1$, $X_1' = Y$ and $Y_1' = X$.

1. If X_1 at least has one element, it would be an element of G_1, i.e., $g \in G_1$. Then $X_s' = Y$, because the merge does not change the attributes held by any of the G_1 objects.

2. $Y'_s = \{g \in G_1 \cup G_2 \mid gI_s m, \forall m \in Y_s\} = \{g \in G_1 \mid gI_s m, \forall m \in Y\} \cup \{g \in G_2 \mid gI_s m, \forall m \in Y\} = Y'_1 \cup Y'_2$. Then $Y''_s = (Y'_1 \cup Y'_2)' = (X \cup Y'_2)' = X' \cap Y''_2$.

3. Since $Y'_s = Y'_1 \cup Y'_2$ (because of step 2), then $Y'_1 \subseteq Y'_s$. Therefore, $X \subseteq Y'_s$.

4. Since $X' = X'_s = Y$ (because of the step 1)., $Y''_s = X' \cap Y''_2 = Y \cap Y''_2 \implies Y''_s \subseteq Y$.

5. Since $Y \neq \varnothing$, let $m \in Y$. Let us suppose that $m \notin Y''_s$, then, there exist an object $x \in Y'_s$ such that $x \cancel{I_s} m$, which is **absurd** because $Y'_s = \{g \in G_1 \mid gI_s m, \forall m \in Y\} \cup \{g \in G_2 \mid gI_s m, \forall m \in Y\}$, $I_s = I_1 \cup I_2$ and objects are disjoint, thus $gI_1 m$ implies $gI_s m$. Analogously, $gI_2 m$ implies $gI_s m$. Therefore, $m \in Y''_s$, which means $Y \subseteq Y''_s$.

6. Since $Y''_s \subseteq Y$ and $Y \subseteq Y''_s$, then $Y = Y_s = Y''_s$ (steps 4 and 5). Thus, $(Z, Y) = (Y'_s, Y_s) \in \mathcal{C}_s$, and $X \subseteq Z$ (step 3).

$\square$

Lemma 2. *Let $K_1 = (G_1, M_1, I_1), K_2 = (G_2, M_2, I_2), K_s = K_1 \mid K_2$ be three formal contexts where $G_1 \cap G_2 = \varnothing$. Let $\mathcal{L}_1 = (\mathcal{C}_1, \leq), \mathcal{L}_2 = (\mathcal{C}_2, \leq), \mathcal{L}_s = \mathcal{L}_1 \mid \mathcal{L}_2 = (\mathcal{C}_s, \leq)$ be their respective lattices. Let $(X, Y) \in \mathcal{C}_s, Y \neq \varnothing, Y \neq M_1 \cup M_2$ be a formal concept such that its intent Y is not empty nor the whole set of attributes, and it is not an intent of $\mathcal{C}_1$ nor in $\mathcal{C}_2$, then $Y = Z_1 \cap Z_2$ where Z_1 is an intent in $\mathcal{C}_1$ and Z_2 is an intent in $\mathcal{C}_2$.*

Proof. Let $Y'_1 = \{g \in G_1 \mid gI_1 m, \forall m \in Y\}$ and $Y'_2 = \{g \in G_2 \mid gI_2 m, \forall m \in Y\}$. By definition $Y' = Y'_1 \cup Y'_2$. Since Y is not an intent in $\mathcal{C}_1$ nor in $\mathcal{C}_2$, both Y'_1 and Y'_2 yield a set of objects whose derivatives are larger than Y, i.e., $Y \subset Y''_1$ and $Y \subset Y''_2$. Then $Y = Y''_1 \cap Y''_2$. Since Y is an intent of $\mathcal{C}_s$, $Y = Y''$ and $X = X''$. Moreover, $Y'_1 \subset X$ and $Y'_2 \subset X$ because otherwise, their derivative could not possibly yield more attributes. Let us suppose that Y''_1 is not an intent of $\mathcal{C}_1$, then $Y''_1 \subset Y''''_1$ which is absurd because $B' = B'''$ for any attribute set in the same context (proofed in Sect. 1.1, Proposition 10 of [15]). Similarly, Y''_2 is an intent in $\mathcal{C}_2$. If we rewrite $Y''_1 = Z_1$ and $Y''_2 = Z_2$, we have that $Y = Z_1 \cap Z_2$. $\square$

Considering these properties, a naive algorithm to compute the merged lattice could be the one presented in Algorithm 1. Firstly, it initializes the set of different intents between the two given sets of concepts, and the set of concepts of the new lattice with the top and bottom ones (commonly referred to as $\top$ and $\bot$). Secondly, for each different intent Y, it adds a concept (X, Y) to the $\mathcal{C}_s$ set, where Y is exactly the intent being iterated and X is the union of extents of the respective concepts in each lattice including that intent. For reading purposes, we say that $\mathcal{C}[Y]$ is the concept $(X, Z) = C \in \mathcal{C}$ such that $Y \subseteq Z$ and Z is minimal (i.e., $\nexists (U, V) \in \mathcal{C}$ such that $Y \subseteq V \wedge |V| < |Z|$). If no such concept exists, it returns a tuple $(\varnothing, \varnothing)$, so that $\pi_1(C) = \varnothing$. Lastly, for each pair of formal concepts in both lattices, if their intersection is not $\varnothing$, the formal concept $\{(X_1 \cup X_2, Y_1 \cap Y_2)\}$ is added.

As an example, let us suppose two different lattice snapshots calculated from the formal context defined in Table 1 and Table 2. The merged underlying context is shown in Table 3. For the sake of readability, let us rename Television = o_1,

---

Algorithm 1. Merge $\mathcal{L}_1 = (\mathcal{C}_1, \leq)$ and $\mathcal{L}_2 = (\mathcal{C}_2, \leq)$

1: $All\_Intents \leftarrow \{Y \mid (X, Y) \in \mathcal{C}_1 \cup \mathcal{C}_2 \wedge X \neq \varnothing \wedge Y \neq \varnothing\}$
2: $\mathcal{C}_s \leftarrow \{\top, \bot\}$
3: **for** $Y \in All\_Intents$ **do**
4:     $\mathcal{C}_s \leftarrow \mathcal{C}_s \cup \{(\pi_1(\mathcal{C}_1[Y]) \cup \pi_1(\mathcal{C}_2[Y]), Y)\}$ Lemma 1
5: **end for**
6: **for** $(X_1, Y_1) \in \mathcal{C}_1$ **do**
7:     **for** $(X_2, Y_2) \in \mathcal{C}_2$ **do**
8:         **if** $Y_1 \cap Y_2 \neq \varnothing$ **then**
9:             $\mathcal{C}_s \leftarrow \mathcal{C}_s \cup \{(X_1 \cup X_2, Y_1 \cap Y_2)\}$ Lemma 2
10:         **end if**
11:     **end for**
12: **end for**
13: **return** $(\mathcal{C}_s, \leq)$

Mobile Phone $= o_2$, Remote Control $= g_1$ and Notebook $= g_2$ for the objects, and for the attributes Screen $= a_1$, Battery $= a_2$, Camera $= a_3$. Considering this, the concepts of their respective lattices are $\mathcal{C}_1 = \{(\{o_1, o_2\}, \{a_1\}), (\{o_2\}, \{a_1, a_2\})\}$ on the one hand, and on the other $\mathcal{C}_2 = \{(\{g_1, g_2\}, \{a_2\}), (\{g_2\}, \{a_2, a_3\})\}$. Following, if we run the algorithm with the input $\mathcal{L}_1 = (\mathcal{C}_1, \leq), \mathcal{L}_2 = (\mathcal{C}_2, \leq)$, in the line 1, $All\_Intents = \{\{a_1\}, \{a_2\}, \{a_1, a_2\}, \{a_2, a_3\}\}$. Then, in the line 2, $\mathcal{C}_s = \{(\{o_1, o_2, g_1, g_2\}, \varnothing), (\varnothing, \{a_1, a_2, a_3\})\}$. Then, the iterations between line 3 and line 5 go in order:

1. $(Y = \{a_1\})$: $\mathcal{C}_s = \mathcal{C}_s \cup \{(\{o_1, o_2\}, \{a_1\})\}$
2. $(Y = \{a_1, a_2\})$: $\mathcal{C}_s = \mathcal{C}_s \cup \{(\{o_2\}, \{a_1, a_2\})\}$
3. $(Y = \{a_2\})$: $\mathcal{C}_s = \mathcal{C}_s \cup \{(\{o_2\} \cup \{g_1, g_2\}, \{a_2\})\}$
4. $(Y = \{a_2, a_3\})$: $\mathcal{C}_s = \mathcal{C}_s \cup \{(\{g_2\}, \{a_2, a_3\})\}$

Afterwards, between line 6 and line 12, the only combination with a non-empty intersection is $(\{o_2\}, \{a_1, a_2\})$ and $(\{g_2\}, \{a_2, a_3\})$, adding the formal concept $(\{o_2\} \cup \{g_1, g_2\}, \{a_2\})$ which was already added. This shows how the naive algorithm potentially repeats calculations, and that there is room for improvement.

Finally, in line 13, the returned value is

$$\mathcal{C}_s = \{(\{o_1, o_2, g_1, g_2\}, \varnothing), (\varnothing, \{a_1, a_2, a_3\}), (\{o_1, o_2\}, \{a_1\}),$$
$$(\{o_2\}, \{a_1, a_2\}), (\{o_2, g_1, g_2\}, \{a_2\}), (\{g_2\}, \{a_2, a_3\})\}$$

and its line diagram representation is depicted in Fig. 8.

Considering the given algorithm for merging lattices in the case of disjoint objects, it would be possible to use a method that runs maintaining a bounded size, as done in [2], but adapted to the case in which elements are like the ones defined in Definition 1.

Table 2. Extended Formal Context on electronic devices

Objects	Attributes	
	Battery	Camera
Remote Control	X	
Notebook	X	X

Table 3. Merged Formal Context on electronic devices

Objects	Attributes		
	Screen	Battery	Camera
Television	X		
Mobile Phone	X	X	
Remote Control		X	
Notebook		X	X

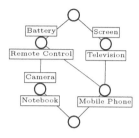

Fig. 8. Merged lattice $\mathcal{L}_s$

5   Conclusion and Future Work

In this paper, the problem of scalability in algorithms for data stream knowledge extraction with FCA has been approached by starting a discussion from several points of view. On the one hand, the notion of *flexibly scalable* for FCA distributed algorithms consuming data streams has been defined in Sect. 3. Furthermore, in the same section, the work formalized the notion of lattice snapshot between times $k \in \mathbb{N}$ and $l \in \mathbb{N}$, and opened a discussion about the meaning of merging two snapshots in three different cases as a way of dealing with the loss of information when keeping a bounded-sized lattice. Additionally, in Sect. 4, the *interpretation* and *computation* of the three different merge cases is discussed considering the model OTM. Finally, a pseudo-algorithm for merging lattices in the case of disjoint objects has been presented, with the addition of the properties that prove its correctness.

The contributions of this paper can be summarized as: (1) The starting point of the discussion about having a general and flexible method for practitioners in order to find a balance between scalability and losing information. (2) A first result in a very specific but real scenario: the intents in the merged lattice when objects are disjoint between the respective formal contexts are composed of all the intents in the two lattice snapshots plus their intersections. (3) The presentation of a naive pseudo-algorithm to compute the lattice in the case of disjoint objects.

For the future work, the study about the non-disjoint objects should be addressed. In addition, it would be interesting to understand whether it is possible to compute the merge using a distributed algorithm to increase the flexibility even further. Particularly, we will work on the study of the rest of the cases to understand their properties and to implement the needed algorithms. Additionally, we plan on working in the study of the merge applied to the multi-relational extensions of the FCA framework (Relational Concept Analysis, Polyadic Concept Analysis, Graph-FCA), to understand whether it could add flexibility there as well or not.

Furthermore, concerning the given properties about the merge with disjoint objects, they should be dual in the sense that they work also with disjoint attributes. However, we did not present the particular proofs for that, so it would be interesting to add them in an extension of the work.

Finally, the study of the time complexity of the algorithm is also needed. For that reason, part of the plan is to study and compare different implementations of Algorithm 1 big-o complexities. Furthermore, we plan on performing benchmarking tests using a real-world case study in the field of e-commerce applied to ski lessons.

Acknowledgements. This work has been funded with the help of the French National Agency for Research and Technology (ANRT) and French National Syndicate of Ski Teachers (SNMSF).

References

1. Co, V., Taramasco, C., Astudillo, H.: Cheating to achieve formal concept analysis over a large formal context. In: CEUR Workshop Proceedings, vol. 959 (2011)
2. De Maio, C., Fenza, G., Loia, V., Orciuoli, F.: Distributed online temporal fuzzy concept analysis for stream processing in smart cities. J. Parallel Distrib. Comput. **110**, 31–41 (2017). https://doi.org/10.1016/j.jpdc.2017.02.002. https://www.sciencedirect.com/science/article/pii/S0743731517300503
3. Dean, J., Ghemawat, S.: MapReduce: simplified data processing on large clusters. Commun. ACM **51**(1), 107–113 (2008). https://doi.org/10.1145/1327452.1327492. https://doi.org/10.1145/1327452.1327492
4. Džeroski, S.: Multi-relational data mining: an introduction. ACM SIGKDD Explor. Newslett. **5**(1), 1–16 (2003). https://doi.org/10.1145/959242.959245. https://doi.org/10.1145/959242.959245
5. Goel, V., Chaudhary, B.D.: Concept discovery from un-constrained distributed context. In: Kumar, N., Bhatnagar, V. (eds.) BDA 2015. LNCS, vol. 9498, pp. 151–164. Springer, Cham (2015). https://doi.org/10.1007/978-3-319-27057-9_11
6. Krajca, P., Vychodil, V.: Distributed algorithm for computing formal concepts using map-reduce framework. In: Adams, N.M., Robardet, C., Siebes, A., Boulicaut, J.-F. (eds.) IDA 2009. LNCS, vol. 5772, pp. 333–344. Springer, Heidelberg (2009). https://doi.org/10.1007/978-3-642-03915-7_29
7. Leutwyler, N., Lezoche, M., Torres, D.: Systematic Literature Mapping - Selected Articles Data Extraction (2022). https://doi.org/10.5281/zenodo.7307957
8. Majidian, A., Martin, T., Cintra, M.: Fuzzy Formal Concept Analysis and Algorithm (2011). pages: 7
9. Margara, A., Rabl, T.: Definition of Data Streams. In: Sakr, S., Zomaya, A.Y. (eds.) Encyclopedia of Big Data Technologies, pp. 648–652. Springer, Cham (2019). https://doi.org/10.1007/978-3-319-77525-8_188

10. van der Merwe, D., Obiedkov, S., Kourie, D.: AddIntent: a new incremental algorithm for constructing concept lattices. In: Eklund, P. (ed.) ICFCA 2004. LNCS (LNAI), vol. 2961, pp. 372–385. Springer, Heidelberg (2004). https://doi.org/10.1007/978-3-540-24651-0_31

11. Neouchi, R., Tawfik, A.Y., Frost, R.A.: Towards a temporal extension of formal concept analysis. In: Stroulia, E., Matwin, S. (eds.) AI 2001. LNCS (LNAI), vol. 2056, pp. 335–344. Springer, Heidelberg (2001). https://doi.org/10.1007/3-540-45153-6_33

12. Osswald, R., Petersen, W.: A logical approach to data-driven classification. In: Günter, A., Kruse, R., Neumann, B. (eds.) KI 2003. LNCS (LNAI), vol. 2821, pp. 267–281. Springer, Heidelberg (2003). https://doi.org/10.1007/978-3-540-39451-8_20

13. Rouane-Hacene, M., Huchard, M., Napoli, A., Valtchev, P.: Relational concept analysis: mining concept lattices from multi-relational data. Ann. Math. Artif. Intell. **67** (2013). https://doi.org/10.1007/s10472-012-9329-3

14. Stumme, G., Taouil, R., Bastide, Y., Pasquier, N., Lakhal, L.: Computing iceberg concept lattices with Titanic. Data Knowledge Engineering **42**(2), 189–222 (2002). https://doi.org/10.1016/S0169-023X(02)00057-5. https://linkinghub.elsevier.com/retrieve/pii/S0169023X02000575

15. Tamrakar, E.S.: Formal concept analysis: mathematical foundations (1997). https://www.academia.edu/3362029/Formal_concept_analysis_mathematical_foundations

16. Wille, R.: Restructuring lattice theory: an approach based on hierarchies of concepts. In: Rival, I. (ed.) Ordered Sets. NATO Advanced Study Institutes Series, pp. 445–470. Springer, Dordrecht (1982). https://doi.org/10.1007/978-94-009-7798-3_15

17. Wolff, K.E.: Temporal Concept Analysis (2001)

18. Xu, B., de Fréin, R., Robson, E., Ó Foghlú, M.: Distributed formal concept analysis algorithms based on an iterative MapReduce framework. In: Domenach, F., Ignatov, D.I., Poelmans, J. (eds.) ICFCA 2012. LNCS (LNAI), vol. 7278, pp. 292–308. Springer, Heidelberg (2012). https://doi.org/10.1007/978-3-642-29892-9_26

Modelling and Explanation

Postmodern Human-Machine Dialogues: Pedagogical Inquiry Experiments

Marie Bocquelet[(✉)], Fabien Caballero, Guillaume Bataille, Alexandre Fleury, Thibault Gasc, Norman Hutte, Christina Maurin, Lea Serrano, and Madalina Croitoru

University of Montpellier, Montpellier, France
`marie.bocquelet@etu.umontpellier.fr`

Abstract. In the classical Human-Machine Dialogue (HMD) setting, existing research has mainly focused on the objective quality of the machine answer. However, it has been recently shown that humans do not perceive in the same manner a human made answer and respectively a machine made answer. In this paper, we put ourselves in the context of conversational Artificial Intelligence software and introduce the setting of postmodern human machine dialogues by focusing on the factual relativism of the human perception of the interaction. We demonstrate the above-mentioned setting in a practical setting via a pedagogical experiment using ChatGPT3.

1 Background and Contribution

In the classical Human-Machine Dialogue (HMD) [23] existing research in symbolic Artificial Intelligence has classically been focused on the objective quality of the machine answer (its correctness with respect to the formal representation of the problem at hand, the famous trade-off of expressivity/tractability [21], the speed and memory requirements for finding one/all correct answers etc.). However, one aspect that becomes more and more prevalent in modern days is the quality of the human experience within the dialogue process [29]. This, of course, has a lot to do with what the given answer is, but not only. Perception plays a very important role, as us, humans, are notoriously and hopelessly biased [11]. It has been recently shown that humans do not react in the same way to the same human made or machine made answer when they are aware of the source of the answer to be a human, respectively a machine. For instance, it has been shown that when faced to credit application, humans applicants prefer the approval of the human decision maker as opposed to that of the machine [30]. This concept has yet to be explored in the context of Artificial Intelligence as it is very different, at its core, from the Turing test principle proposed by Alan Turing over 80 years ago [12]. In the vision of Alan Turing the perceived intelligence of the machine was, certainly, made with respect to a human observer, but always within two main differences. First, and very importantly, the original imitation game was a third-party interaction where two entities are observed by a third trying to distinguish given perceived qualities based on their dialogue

M. Ojeda-Aciego et al. (Eds.): ICCS 2023, LNAI 14133, pp. 121–128, 2023.
https://doi.org/10.1007/978-3-031-40960-8_10

(originally gender and then artificial-ness). Albeit highly relevant as setting in the context of post-modern Artificial Intelligence, third party interactions are outside the scope of this paper (as it has been shown that the observation of a process alters the process as such). Second, the test proposed by the famous '50s paper when Alan Turing posed the problem of computers thinking puts the spotlight on how the human observer can be "tricked" into believing its dialogue partner to also be human [27]. But please note what we are interested in this paper is different at the core. The act of tricking a partner into having certain qualities can be possibly pleasant to the partner (in certain conditions) but it is neither a necessary nor a sufficient condition to ensure that this dialogue runs smooth, feels good, natural, interesting and engaging. Instead, we should really focus on the human partner experience of the process and try to measure it. This paper is a call for arms into this yet unexplored but essential aspect of HMD.

Since most work in Artificial Intelligence has been done in the symbolic realm [20], explanation has been a core concept that researchers have put forward (historically, and, recently, with doubled-up enthusiasm) regarding the usability of HMD software [26]. While explanation capabilities in the machine certainly push for the humans to engage more, it also means that the humans overwrite more easily proposed decisions of the machine [28]. Our interest in explanation should go beyond usability and far deeper into how the interaction wholly affects the human decision-making.

In this paper we put ourselves in the modern context of conversational Artificial Intelligence software that currently passes the classical Turing test (such as ChatGPT, Bart, etc.). It is a highly hyped and dynamic setting as, since the launch of ChatGPT in November 2022, not a week goes by without a new Generative Artificial Intelligence (GAI) software being released. Since the beginning of the year Silicon Valley saw more than 500 GAI start-ups newly created; not to mention Meta's LLAMA, Baidu's Ernie, Google's Bard, Anthropic's Claude, GPT 2,3 or 4 etc. All of these softwares fall within the HMD setting and are using as backbone GAI techniques. They are being used by school kids to cheat on their homework, by judges to pass on moral decisions, by researchers to write up papers. Our interest here lies precisely with how the human participant to a two party dialogue with such software experiences the interaction. Against this background, our contribution is twofold:

– Introduce the setting of "postmodern human machine dialogues" by focusing on the factual relativism of the human perception of the interaction.
– Demonstrate the interest of formalising the above-mentioned setting in a practical pedagogical experiment carried out at the University of Montpellier using ChatGPT3.

To conclude this introductory section, we would also like to highlight that the paper is highly relevant to the ICCS community. Since its 1992 kick off workshop [6], the ICCS community gathered a unique blend of logicians, philosophers, mathematicians, and engineers. Such a community would thus be a first class candidate for fostering discussions on our proposal.

2   Proposed Setting

The most important motivation for the study of interactional relations stems from a knowledge representation perspective. So far, knowledge representation took the stance of representing things that "are". Ontologies (in their broad sense, even if the term has been widely used in computer since mainly for the past 20 years) were employed as a formal conceptualisation of shared knowledge [17]. Controversially, in this paper, our research hypothesis claims that "shared knowledge" is not a realistic concept in cognitive human interactions. Moreover, such assumption will hinder the development of meaningful interactions from the artificial side. We claim that it is high time for a complete rethink of what a knowledge representation paradigm should encompass in order to aim to achieve successful interactions with humans. The assumption behind a unique and universally valid truth is also the main reason the Turing test is fundamentally different from our proposal. It makes sense that if the human is the owner of the supreme truth, then the only way that the machine can aspire to any truthful behaviour is by imitating the human. But here we do not make such assumption. This is due to two main factors. First, it has been shown by research in neuroscience that the universally truthful perception does not exist [10]. And this not only applies to relative things (such as morality) but also to what we consider "objective" things, such as colour or taste [2]. Second, and closely related, is that the observer will always alter the perception object [14]. Therefore, the perception of the same dialogue will be different from one human to the other. Such differences need to be captured and analysed.

Our proposal for the introduced notion of postmodern Artificial Intelligence relies on the fact that postmodernism is associated with relativism that considers "reality" to be a mental construct [8]. It rejects the possibility of absolute reality and asserts that all interpretations are contingent on the perspective from which they are made. This notion of perspective contingency has been long explored by social sciences, starting from the imago concept of Jung [1]. But the first, partly subconscious image of a given concept, while highly personal and relative, is not enough within the context of this paper. The interaction process of the dialogue, i.e. the engagement, is also crucial for how the perception is being transformed.

Walter Truett Anderson described postmodernism as a world view in which truth is defined through methodical, disciplined inquiry [7]. Peter Drucker suggested the post-modern world is based on the notions of purpose and process rather than a primordial cause [4]. These authors and many more show that our claim of knowledge as a product of the interaction is not novel. Even more recently, the introduction of relational quantum mechanics solved many formalisation problems by making explicit the fact that a universal observer (holder of the truth) does not exist [3]. In their view the state is the relation and the interaction process between the observer and the system.

In this paper, we introduce the setting of postmodern human machine dialogues. Within this setting, for simplification, it is accepted that there is a world but that absolute world it is not accessible to the observers. Instead, every agent (human or artificial) has a personal view on the world which corresponds to the information it has access to, the language it has for representing this knowledge, experiences etc. This is represented in Fig. 1.

Fig. 1. Relative world representations

Of course, when interacting, we also make a mental model of the agent in front of us (natural or artificial), based on what we think their model of the world is. At their turn, they also make a model about our vision of the world, and, recursively, our vision of their world. Please note that this process is fundamentally different from epistemic logic [15]. The fundamental difference lies in our rejection of universal truth. It is not the case that I know that the agent in front of me does not know that the Earth is flat (while the Earth being flat is an undisputed truth and the lack of knowledge of the agent can be remediated to this effect). In our setting, each agent has a mental model of the shape of the Earth, which is, for them only, the undisputed truth. This is illustrated in Fig. 2.

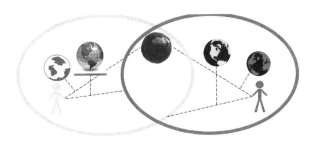

Fig. 2. Recursive relative world representations

In this setting, we claim that argumentation [25] is the main backbone to be used as reasoning facility. This is due to the dual aspect of the argumentation process. On the one hand, argumentation allows for reasoning with inconsistent knowledge (by means of extension based semantics [16] or ranking based semantics [22]) and, on the other, the dialogue process is an inherent part of the argumentation method [5]. While the dialogue will allow for the exchange of information needed within the HMD setting, the reasoning mechanism will attempt, if required, to restore consistency within the agent's models. This is depicted in Fig. 3.

Fig. 3. Dialogue induced alteration of participant world representations

It has been shown that certain argumentation semantics coincide with inconsistent tolerant semantics in logic based models [19]. Dialogue games exist of argumentation semantics, and they have been adapted for reasoning in presence of inconsistency in ontology based data access settings [24]. The dialogue based aspect of reasoning is investigated and practically evaluated in the next section.

3   Inquiry Dialogue Based Evaluation

Argumentation dialogues have been long investigated for reasoning with conflicting information [5]. According to Walton, we can distinguish amongst five kinds of dialogues types (that could mix and match during the dialogue between two agents): persuasion, negotiation, deliberation, inquiry, and explanation. All of them have been formalised in terms of turn taking games [13]. In this section, we will illustrate how the inquiry dialogue can be practically evaluated in the newly proposed setting of HMD.

In the proposed experiment, we have used ChatGPT3 in an advanced algorithmic class of 20 Master students in Computer Science at the University of Montpellier (France). The aim of the algorithmic class was for the students to investigate and analyse three classical problems [20]: the TIC-TAC-TOE game, the puzzle 12 game and the cannibals and missionaries problem. The algorithms were investigated over the course of three weeks, one algorithm per week, during a three-hour practical session (no course was available, the students had to use existing resources to learn about the problem and subsequently implement a solution). None of the students had any experience with the above-mentioned problems beforehand.

The students were split into two groups. The first group of students had to implement the above-mentioned algorithms, from scratch, using the programming language of their choice. The second group had to implement the algorithms solely relying on their interaction with ChatGPT3. They were using an inquiry dialogue for obtaining the code necessary for solving the problem. The postmodern setting of HMD (of Fig. 1) was demonstrated by the students having a model of the problem to be solved themselves, having a model of ChatGPT's model for solving the problem and then trying to find the right "prompt" to extract their perceived model from the ChatGPT agent.

All the students in the first group (the business as usual algorithmic class) implemented the games without any difficulty, using either Python or C++ as the programming language of choice during the time duration of the class. One student used JavaScript. The other students, interacting with ChatGPT, reported the following results.

First, all groups managed to implement the TIC-TAC-TOE algorithm without problems. The implementation was done in Python. As a rule of thumb, ChatGPT is much better at implementing problems in Python rather than other languages. The students tried to obtain an implementation of Puzzle12 in C++ that definitely did not work. The same failure was noticed for JavaScript implementation. The main explanation for this, apart from the lack of examples available for learning (which we think it is not the case for JavaScript algorithms) is the fact that a limitation of the number of characters replied is imposed by ChatGPT. For the other two algorithms (the cannibals and missionaries, respectively, Puzzle 12) the success was less flagrant. Actually, for cannibals and missionaries, all the three groups failed to obtain a working code despite numerous tries. For Puzzle 12 two of the three groups managed to get a working Python code.

When the code gets too large, ChatGPT3 "cuts" the program. When asked to continue, the previously started program ChatGPT does not perform correctly. Actually, the higher the number of interactions with the student, the less reliable the answers are. It is clear that the interaction as such is not obtained, ChatGPT behaving much better in a one shot query answering setting rather than HMD. Please note that this is also consistent with the way ChatGPT has been portrayed in publicity (passing the bar exam, passing medical exams etc.), all interactions that are a one shot interaction rather than a elaborated dialogue.

Most intriguingly, the manner the students referred to the software changed within the same interaction and during the weeks. Their interaction was very much cautioned by frustration (due to the time limitation and the requirement of solely using ChatGPT for code) with initial requests carefully formulated and last requests harsh and, sometimes, abusive. A deeper analysis of these phenomena is definitely the first item on our future work, as it fully aligns with our hypothesis of explicitly examining the perceived quality of the interaction by the human.

Apart from illustrating the novel setting proposed by the paper, we believe that, purely from a pedagogical point of view, the use of ChatGPT in this class was actually very beneficial for two main reasons. First, students understood the limitations and eventual benefits of the technology and second, "mistakes" provided by ChatGPT generated code were excellent starting points for in-depth conversations about formal analysis of the algorithms.

4   Conclusion

In this paper, we present a novel human machine dialogue setting based on interaction and the notion of relative truth. The aim of this new view on the interaction between an artificial agent and a human agent lies in the new era of software clearly passing the Turing test, but that require further attention in terms of the quality of the interaction with the human counterpart. Basically, the setting allows attempting measuring when an interaction with a machine would "feel off" to the human. This setting is solely presented in a simplified version in this paper. We can easily extend the setting by considering how the mental model of the human participant is affected if the artificial agent is embodied [18]. We can also extend this work to capture three-person games [9], essential in the context of ubiquitous Artificial Intelligence future.

References

1. Jung, C.G., Hinkle, B.M.: Symbolism of the mother and of rebirth (1925)
2. Brian, C.R., Goodenough, F.L.: The relative potency of color and form perception at various ages. J. Exp. Psychol. **12**(3), 197 (1929)
3. Hugh Everett, I.I.I.: "Relative state" formulation of quantum mechanics. Rev. Modern Phys. **29**(3), 454 (1957)
4. Drucker, P.: "Landmarks of tomorrow: a report on the new" post-modern. World (1959)
5. Walton, D.N.: Dialogue theory for critical thinking. Argumentation **3**, 169–184 (1989)
6. Pfeiffer, H.D., Nagle, T.E. (eds.): Conceptual Structures: Theory and Implementation. LNCS, vol. 754. Springer, Heidelberg (1993). https://doi.org/10.1007/3-540-57454-9
7. Walter Truett Anderson: The moving boundary: art, science, and the construction of reality. World Futures: J. General Evol. **40**(1–3), 27–34 (1994)
8. Grenz, S.J.: A Primer on Postmodernism. Wm. B. Eerdmans Publishing (1996)
9. Anderson, A.H., et al.: Multi-mediating Multi-party Interactions. In: Interact, pp. 313–320 (1999)
10. Hu, Y., Goodale, M.A.: Grasping after a delay shifts size-scaling from absolute to relative metrics. J. Cogn. Neurosci. **12**(5), 856–868 (2000)
11. Kahneman, D.: A perspective on judgment and choice: mapping bounded rationality. Am. Psychol. **58**(9), 697 (2003)
12. Turing, A.: Intelligent Machinery (1948), p. 395. B. Jack Copeland (2004)
13. Prakken, H.: Formal systems for persuasion dialogue. The Knowl. Eng. Rev. **21**(2), 163–188 (2006)
14. Stapp, H.P.: Mindful Universe: Quantum Mechanics and the Participating Observer, vol. 238. Springer, Heidelberg (2007). https://doi.org/10.1007/978-3-540-72414-8
15. Van Ditmarsch, H., van Der Hoek, W., Kooi, B.: Dynamic Epistemic Logic, vol. 337. Springer, Dordrecht (2007). https://doi.org/10.1007/978-1-4020-5839-4
16. Dunne, P.E., Wooldridge, M.: Complexity of abstract argumentation. In: Simari, G., Rahwan, I. (eds.) Argumentation in Artificial Intelligence, pp. 85–104. Springer, Heidelberg (2009). https://doi.org/10.1007/978-0-387-98197-0_5

17. Guarino, N., Oberle, D., Staab, S.: What is an ontology? In: Staab, S., Studer, R. (eds.) Handbook on Ontologies, pp. 1–17. Springer, Heidelber (2009). https://doi.org/10.1007/978-3-540-92673-3_0

18. Hoffman, G.: Embodied cognition for autonomous interactive robots. Top. Cogn. Sci. **4**(4), 759–772 (2012)

19. Croitoru, M., Vesic, S.: What can argumentation do for inconsistent ontology query answering? In: Liu, W., Subrahmanian, V.S., Wijsen, J. (eds.) SUM 2013. LNCS (LNAI), vol. 8078, pp. 15–29. Springer, Heidelberg (2013). https://doi.org/10.1007/978-3-642-40381-1_2

20. Russel, S., Norvig, P., et al.: Artificial Intelligence: A Modern Approach, vol. 256. Pearson Education Limited, London (2013)

21. Germano, S., Pham, T.-L., Mileo, A.: Web stream reasoning in practice: on the expressivity vs. scalability tradeoff. In: ten Cate, B., Mileo, A. (eds.) RR 2015. LNCS, vol. 9209, pp. 105–112. Springer, Cham (2015). https://doi.org/10.1007/978-3-319-22002-4_9

22. Bonzon, E., Delobelle, J., Konieczny, S., Maudet, N.: A comparative study of ranking-based semantics for abstract argumentation. In: Proceedings of the AAAI Conference on Artificial Intelligence, vol. 30 (2016)

23. Mallios S., Bourbakis, N.: A survey on human machine dialogue systems. In: 2016 7th international conference on information, intelligence, systems & applications (IISA), pp. 1–7. IEEE (2016)

24. Arioua, A., Croitoru, M., Vesic, S.: Logic-based argumentation with existential rules. Int. J. Approximate Reasoning **90**, 76–106 (2017)

25. Baroni, P.,Gabbay, D., Giacomin, M., Van der Torre, L.: Handbook of Formal Argumentation (2018)

26. Miller, T.: Explanation in artificial intelligence: insights from the social sciences. Artif. Intell. **267**, 1–38 (2019)

27. Gonçalves, B.: Machines will think: structure and interpretation of Alan turing's imitation game (2020)

28. La Torre, D., Colapinto, C., Durosini, I.,Triberti, S. : Team formation for human-artificial intelligence collaboration in the workplace: a goal programming model to foster organizational change. IEEE Trans. Eng. Manag. (2021)

29. Shneiderman, B.: Human-Centered AI. Oxford University Press, Oxford (2022)

30. Yalcin, G., Lim, S., Puntoni, S., van Osselaer, S.M.J.: How do customers react when their requests are evaluated by algorithms? MIT Sloan Manage. Rev. **63**(3), 1–3 (2022)

Conceptual Modelling
with Euler$^+$ Diagrams

Uta Priss$^{(\boxtimes)}$ (iD)

Fakultät Informatik, Ostfalia University, Wolfenbüttel, Germany
u.priss@ostfalia.de
https://www.upriss.org.uk

Abstract. This short paper introduces Euler$^+$diagrams as an enhanced version of traditional Euler diagrams and discusses how these can be utilised for conceptual modelling. Instead of the traditional interpretation of Euler diagrams as Boolean logic, Euler$^+$diagrams are considered 3-valued logic diagrams that are interpreted as First Order Logic (FOL) expressions. It is argued that such diagrams have a good usability because they are sufficiently simple yet reasonably expressive. Conditions for a translation between Euler$^+$diagrams and logical expressions and some consistency rules are provided. Questions still remain with respect to a detailed explanation of visual reasoning algorithms.

1 Introduction

Venn and Euler diagrams are frequently used as a tool for visualising logical and set theoretical expressions. A common interpretation of such diagrams evaluates existing zones into True and missing or shaded zones into False resulting in Boolean algebra. But set theory is more complex because the operations $\cup$ and $\cap$ result in sets, whereas $\subseteq$, $\subset$ and $=$ result in truth values. For example, $A \subseteq B$ is equivalent to (NOT A) $\cup$ B as a set-valued (Boolean) expression but to $\forall(x)\, x \in A \Rightarrow x \in B$ as a truth-valued, FOL expression. These two possible interpretations are not equivalent to each other because their negations are different as shown in Sect. 3. For a truth-valued interpretation, Euler diagrams should be assumed to be filled with 3 states: 'none', 'at least one' or 'any number of' elements. This enhanced version of Euler diagrams is introduced in this paper as 'Euler$^+$diagrams' which can additionally express functions and relations. Visually, the enhancement is simple: a quantifier and arrows are added to the diagrams. Furthermore in order to reduce complexity, diagrams can be split and concatenated using 'AND' and 'OR'. Last but not least, truth-valued set statements can also be added to Euler$^+$diagrams in a textual format.

One motivation for this paper were Chapman et al.'s (2011) 'Concept Diagrams' which present a different form of enhanced Euler diagrams used for modelling ontologies. Amongst several differences between Concept Diagrams and Euler$^+$diagrams, Concept Diagrams use a notation where dots represent variables which, in our opinion, is more difficult to visually parse. Nevertheless the visual reasoning algorithms described by Chapman et al. are relevant for Euler$^+$diagrams as well. A second motivation for this paper were discussions

© The Author(s), under exclusive license to Springer Nature Switzerland AG 2023
M. Ojeda-Aciego et al. (Eds.): ICCS 2023, LNAI 14133, pp. 129–137, 2023.
https://doi.org/10.1007/978-3-031-40960-8_11

with students about Euler diagrams while teaching an introductory mathematics class. It highlighted the need for using simple notations that the students are already familiar with or learning anyway during the class. Students tend to be very critical users that point out any difficulties encountered when learning a notation. Previous experience showed that conventional diagrams for concept lattices (Ganter & Wille 1999) are not intuitive for students and require more teaching time (Priss 2017). Euler diagrams can express the same content as concept lattices (Priss 2023) but appear to be easier to read. Because students sometimes perceive diagrams for functions as in Fig. 1c also (incorrectly) as Euler diagrams, the idea arose to include arrows for functions in Euler$^+$diagrams as well. Apart from teaching purposes, we envision illustrations of scientific results for a general audience as a possible application of Euler$^+$diagrams.

Euler$^+$Diagrams support conceptual modelling because sets can be considered concepts as they have both an extensional listing of elements as well as an intensional, logical definition. For example, $\{x \mid x \in \mathbb{N} \text{ AND } x < 4\}$ has an extension $\{1, 2, 3\}$ and an intension 'natural numbers smaller than 4'. Set operations can be interpreted as conceptual operations. For example, if sets for 'dog' and 'pet' are defined, then so are 'dog AND pet' and 'dog OR pet'. Thus Euler$^+$diagrams visualise methods of concept formation and are also suitable for representing concept lattices (Priss 2023).

This short paper introduces Euler$^+$diagrams without presenting a detailed mathematical or logical description (which will be left for a future paper). Rodgers (2014) provides an overview of existing Euler diagram research. Later results can be found mostly in the DIAGRAMS conference series[1]. Stapleton, Shimojima & Jamnik (2018) discuss some aspects of existential quantifiers for Euler diagrams, but we believe that a clear distinction between (Boolean) Euler diagrams and more expressive Euler$^+$diagrams as presented in this paper is more convincing and more usable.

Section 2 presents a short definition of Euler$^+$diagrams and their semantics. Section 3 explains details and challenges of using Euler$^+$diagrams. Section 4 discusses how to add functions and relations to the diagrams. Section 5 presents some short examples of visual reasoning with Euler$^+$diagrams. The paper finishes with a conclusion.

2   Definition of Euler$^+$Diagrams

This section introduces Euler$^+$diagrams as an enhanced version of Euler diagrams (Fig. 1a and b). Euler diagrams consist of closed curves with labels representing sets. In this paper, Euler diagrams fulfil the 'well-formedness' condition that each visible area of the diagram is in one-to-one correspondence to a distinct intersection of sets. The areas are called 'zones' in this paper. For example, in Fig. 1a, exactly and only the zone just inside the outer zone corresponds to 'partial function $\cap$ NOT function'. Rodgers (2014) defines further terminology and well-formedness conditions which are not relevant for this paper. Venn diagrams are Euler diagrams that contain 2^n zones for n sets corresponding to all possible intersections (such as, $\emptyset$,

---

[1] http://diagrams-conference.org/.

A, B and $A \cap B$ for $n = 2$). In Euler diagrams, empty sets, such as a zone 'function AND NOT partial function' in Fig. 1a are left off or shaded as in Fig. 1b. It is not always possible to draw an Euler diagram without shading. For fewer than 4 sets, the curves of Euler diagrams can be drawn as circles but for more than 3 sets, other curve shapes may be required. Priss (2023) explains that rounded rectangular curves as used in this paper have some advantages over the other shapes with respect to the number of diagrams that can be drawn.

Euler$^+$ diagrams are Euler diagrams with the following enhancements:

D1 Diagrams can be combined using AND and OR and also with textual statements (truth-valued set expressions or definitions of sets using ':=' and set operations or relations).
D2 Elements of the sets can be written into the curves (as labels).
D3 Zones have 3 possible states: shaded, 'don't care' (nothing is written into the zone) or 'existential' (contains at least one element or an $\exists$).
D4 Arrows can be added between two zones or between two elements.

Some conditions are required:

C1 If a zone occurs more than once in a combined diagram, it must have the same state.
C2 The state of the outer zone must always be 'don't care'.
C3 Each curve and arrow must have exactly one label. Labels can occur more than once but only for the same item. The sets of labels for curves, sets and elements must be mutually disjoint. If it is clear what is meant, labels can sometimes be omitted.

The semantics of Euler$^+$ diagrams is defined as follows:

S1 Labels of elements, curves and arrows are names of elements, sets and relations, respectively.
S2 For a combined diagram, each component is translated separately into a statement by interpreting each missing or shaded zone as a statement about not existing elements, each existential zone as a statement about existing elements and ignoring all 'don't care' zones. The resulting FOL statements are then combined with AND.
S3 Textual statements are interpreted as FOL statements.
S4 Arrows between zones are interpreted as binary relations. Arrow heads are in the middle of the lines for relations and at the end of the lines for functions. Arrows between elements are relation instances. An arrow head indicates a direction of a relation, for example, $a \leftarrow b$ corresponds to a pair (b, a). Relations and functions are interpreted as not empty and as total, i.e. all elements in the sets at both ends of the arrows must occur at least once in the relation.
S5 The negation of shaded or missing zones is existential zones and vice versa and the negation of 'don't care' is 'don't care'.

With further conditions:

C4 The set of drawn or deducible arrows is complete, i.e. whenever some elements in a zone relate to another zone, an arrow must exist between the two zones or be deducible from textual statements.

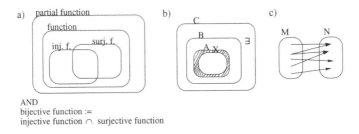

Fig. 1. Euler$^+$diagrams (left and middle) and a diagram of a function (right)

C5 Because relations are not empty, zones connected by arrows must be existential, i.e. contain an ∃-quantifier.

The conditions are not sufficient for avoiding contradictory diagrams but FOL also does not have conditions that stop a user from writing '$A = B$ AND $A \neq B$'. Thus, a diagram is non-contradictory if all its statements combine to an FOL statement that is free of contradictions. Further details about what is meant by some of the points of this definition are explained in the remainder of the paper. The focus of this paper is on the graphical aspects not on a more detailed description of formal semantics which is left for a future paper.

A challenge for Euler diagrams is that they can easily become too complex to be usable. Euler$^+$diagrams overcome this challenge by allowing to split a diagram into many parts which are then combined with AND and OR. Furthermore, textual statements (that are equivalent to Euler$^+$diagrams) are allowed because sometimes a diagram is simpler, sometimes a textual expression is simpler. Obviously this poses a new question as to how to split a diagram in a manner that still supports visual reasoning about facts that are distributed across different parts. The condition C1 avoids some problems. For example, it would not be useful to split $A = B$ into $A \subseteq B$ in one component and $B \subseteq A$ in another. Most likely OR should be used extremely sparingly for combining diagrams. NOT is only allowed as a set operation but not for combining statements. Combining and splitting diagrams is discussed, for example, by Priss (2021 and 2023).

3   Expressing Logical Statements with Euler$^+$Diagrams

Figure 1a displays an Euler$^+$diagram visualising conceptual information, such as the fact that functions are partial functions. It is a typical diagram that might be used in the context of teaching showing students that functions are partial functions contrary to natural language where a noun modified by an adjective tends to denote a subconcept of the unmodified noun. The diagram also expresses a definition of 'bijective function' but as a textual statement because otherwise an intersection would need to be labelled which is difficult to visually parse. Figure 1b demonstrates transitivity of the set containment relation ($A \subseteq B$ AND $B \subseteq C \implies A \subseteq C$). The existence quantifier indicates that $B \subset C$. Whether

$A \subset B$ is not known (i.e. 'don't care'). The diagram further shows an example of shading. If curves have exactly one label (C3), then showing the equality of sets $(A = X)$ either requires shading or a textual statement 'AND $X := A$'. A textual statement would be clearer in this case.

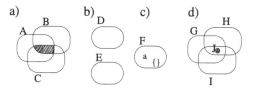

Fig. 2. Euler diagrams and the empty set

Elements of sets can be written into the zones as in Fig. 2c $(a \in F)$. Sets can only be shown as subsets but not as elements of other sets unless they are written as strings $(\{\} \in F)$. Figure 2 highlights difficulties expressing empty sets in Euler diagrams which also affect Euler$^+$diagrams. An empty set can either be shaded $(A \cap B \cap C = \emptyset)$ or missing $(D \cap E = \emptyset)$. The empty set J is a subset of $G \cap H \cap I$. But there are no graphical clues showing that J must not be drawn in any other location than the intersection of all other sets, that it is a subset of $G \cap H \cap I$ even if not shown in the diagram and that all empty sets are equal to each other. These challenges may not be caused by the diagrams but by the fact that 'empty' tends to be a difficult concept.

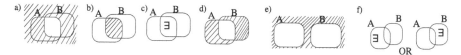

Fig. 3. Euler diagram negation: binary or truth-valued

Figure 3 shows the difference between set- and truth-valued diagrams with respect to negation. According to C2, Fig. 3a and 3e are Euler diagrams, but not Euler$^+$diagrams because their outer zones are shaded. The set-valued negation of $A \cap B$ (Fig. 3a) is in 3b whereas 3b and 3c are truth-valued negations of each other. The set-valued negation of $A = B$ (in Fig. 3d) is in 3e and its truth-valued negation in 3f, in this case resulting in two diagrams connected with 'OR'. Figure 4 shows all 4 possible quantifiers that can result from translating an Euler$^+$diagram into an FOL statement. A symbol for an all-quantifier is not included in the definition of Euler$^+$diagrams because it is implied by missing zones. According to S2, 'don't care' zones are ignored. If the quantifier in Fig. 4b was missing, then it would contain four 'don't care' zones and be interpreted as an empty FOL statement. Translations between Euler$^+$diagrams and FOL should be equivalent, but are not unique. For example, Fig. 4c can also be expressed as $\forall (x \in B)\, x \notin A$. Furthermore, Euler diagrams can always be drawn in different manners. A proof of logical equivalence of interpretations could follow strategies employed by Chapman et al. (2011) and similar publications but is not included in this short paper.

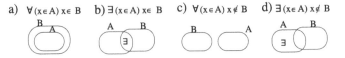

Fig. 4. Expressing quantifiers: a) ALL, b) SOME, c) NONE, d) NOT ALL

4   Euler⁺Diagrams, Functions and Relations

As mentioned in the introduction, operations on sets or concepts support the formation of further concepts. For example, the concepts 'pet' and 'cat' support a discussion about 'pet cats'. If functions or relations are added to the mixture, further sets or concepts can be defined. For example, a relation 'childOf' generates a set of parents and a set of children and a verb 'to see' distinguishes objects that can see or can be seen. For a universal set $\mathbb{U}$ of elements, a relation r and subsets $A, B \subseteq \mathbb{U}$, one can define the sets $r^\triangleleft(B) := \{x \mid x \in \mathbb{U}, \exists (b \in B)(x, b) \in r\}$ and $r^\triangleright(A) := \{x \mid x \in \mathbb{U}, \exists (a \in A)(a, x) \in r\}$. It follows that $r \subseteq r^\triangleleft(\mathbb{U}) \times r^\triangleright(\mathbb{U})$ is a relation that is total on both sides, which means that every element in $r^\triangleleft(\mathbb{U})$ relates to at least one element in $r^\triangleright(\mathbb{U})$ and vice versa. For functions one can write the usual $f(A)$ instead of $f^\triangleright(A)$. It follows that $f^{-1}(B) = f^\triangleleft(B)$ for bijective functions, $r^\triangleleft(\mathbb{U}) = r^\triangleleft(r^\triangleright(\mathbb{U}))$, $r^\triangleright(\mathbb{U}) = r^\triangleright(r^\triangleleft(\mathbb{U}))$ and $f(f^\triangleleft(f(A))) = f(A)$ for functions. But in general $r^\triangleright(r^\triangleleft(r^\triangleright(A))) \neq r^\triangleright(A)$ is possible. For example for a translation relation between English and Irish, one can start with an Irish word, look up its English translation, then their Irish translations and so on - a process that might only stop after many iterations or when $r^\triangleleft(\mathbb{U})$ and $r^\triangleright(\mathbb{U})$ have been reached.

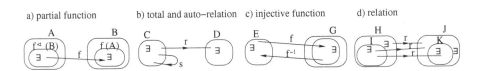

Fig. 5. Euler⁺diagrams for functions and relations

Figure 5a shows a partial function $f : A \twoheadrightarrow B$ with $f : f^\triangleleft(B) \to B$ and $f(A) = f(f^\triangleleft(B)) \subseteq B$. Figure 5b contains a total relation $r \subseteq C \times D$ and a total auto-relation $s \subseteq C \times C$. Because of C5, arrows connect zones that are existential. Furthermore C4 implies that if a zone I has more than one arrow for a single relation r then $J = r^\triangleright(I)$ is true for the union J of the outermost zones (Fig. 5d). For a zone K with one arrow, the zone at the other end of the arrow can be defined using K and r as $I := r^\triangleleft(K)$. For the two outermost zones H and J, C4 implies that $H = r^\triangleleft(r^\triangleright(H)) = r^\triangleleft(J)$ and $J = r^\triangleright(r^\triangleleft(J)) = r^\triangleright(H)$. If these two equations hold, sets H and J are called a 'closed pair' in this paper. Closed pairs can be modelled as concepts using Formal Concept Analysis (Ganter &

Wille 1999) but that is left for another paper. Because of C4, a relation between sets with many subsets will lead to many arrows. Most likely separate diagrams should therefore be used for each function or relation. Instead of labelling each arrow, different colours could be used. Furthermore, a reduced drawing of arrows can be employed drawing only the arrows for closed pairs and adding textual statements that imply the remaining arrows. For example, in Fig. 5d only the arrow between H and J might be drawn and a statement '$I := r^{\triangleleft}(K)$' added. Full and reduced drawing of arrows must not be mixed.

5   Reasoning with Diagrams

This section translates two examples from Chapman et al. (2011) into Euler$^+$ diagrams. A translation of the first example, shown in Fig. 6, yields a function isPetOf: isPetOf$^{\triangleleft}(\mathbb{U}) \rightarrow$ person and a statement 'isPetOf$^{\triangleleft}(\mathbb{U}) \subseteq$ animal AND isPetOf(Rex) = Mick' which implies 'Rex $\in$ animal AND Mick $\in$ person' involving reasoning about the fact that if a function is applicable to instances then the instances must be elements of the domain and codomain of the function. Such reasoning is more easy to see in the diagrams than using the FOL statements. In this case the top right and left diagrams should be mentally combined into one diagram. The bottom right diagram summarises all of the information.

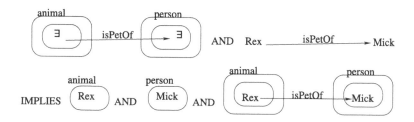

Fig. 6. Example of reasoning with diagrams

A second, slightly more complex example, is shown in Fig. 7. Translated into FOL, it defines a relation drives $\subseteq$ drives$^{\triangleleft}(\mathbb{U}) \times$ drives$^{\triangleright}(\mathbb{U})$ with driver := drives$^{\triangleleft}$(vehicle). The definition of driver is implied by the diagram because there is only one arrow into drives$^{\triangleright}(\mathbb{U}) \cap$ vehicle. Thus drivers are people who drive at least one vehicle and possibly other non-vehicles. The statement 'drives$^{\triangleleft}(\mathbb{U}) \subseteq$ person AND driver $\subseteq$ adult AND ABC1 $\in$ vehicle AND drives(Mick) = ABC1' then implies 'Mick $\subseteq$ adult'. Visual reasoning consists of mentally inserting the diagram about the relation instance (Mick, ABC1) into the top right diagram using the fact that ABC1 is a vehicle and then realising that the top left diagram applies. The same information is contained in the FOL statements but these are more difficult to visually parse and combine without writing down each step.

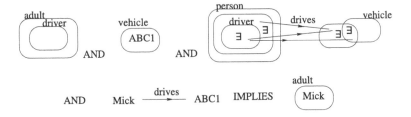

Fig. 7. Further example of reasoning with diagrams

6   Conclusion

This paper introduces Euler$^+$ diagrams as a means for visually representing statements about sets, functions and relations. A goal of this research is to produce simple diagrams for representing set (or conceptual) statements to a general audience of people who are not or not yet trained in mathematics. By splitting information into separate diagrams, complexity issues of larger Euler diagrams can be avoided by Euler$^+$ diagrams. Advantages of Euler diagrams for reasoning are known from the literature (eg. Stapleton et al. 2018) and apply to Euler$^+$ diagrams as well. Euler$^+$ diagrams do not solve consistency checking of statements. But because Euler$^+$ diagrams can be translated into FOL statements, algorithms for consistency checking of FOL statements can also be utilised for Euler$^+$ diagrams - although a more precise translation algorithm still needs to be provided in a future paper. Some rudimentary software for generating Euler diagrams from expressions is currently in development[2]. It is planned to extend this software into a tool for Euler$^+$ diagram generation and modification that is compatible with other software for conceptual structures, such as Formal Concept Analysis, Conceptual Graphs and ontologies.

References

Chapman, P., Stapleton, G., Howse, J., Oliver, I.: Deriving sound inference rules for concept diagrams. In: 2011 IEEE Symposium on Visual Languages and Human-Centric Computing, pp. 87–94 (2011)

Ganter, B., Wille, R.: Formal Concept Analysis: Mathematical Foundations. Springer, Heidelberg (1999). https://doi.org/10.1007/978-3-642-59830-2

Priss, U.: Learning thresholds in formal concept analysis. In: Bertet, K., Borchmann, D., Cellier, P., Ferré, S. (eds.) ICFCA 2017. LNCS (LNAI), vol. 10308, pp. 198–210. Springer, Cham (2017). https://doi.org/10.1007/978-3-319-59271-8_13

Priss, U.: Modelling conceptual schemata with formal concept analysis. In: Proceeding of FCA4AI'21 (2021)

Priss, U.: Representing concept lattices with Euler diagrams. In: Dürrschnabel, D., López Rodríguez, D. (eds.) ICFCA 2023. LNCS, vol. 13934, pp. 183–197. Springer, Cham (2023). https://doi.org/10.1007/978-3-031-35949-1_13

---

[2] https://upriss.github.io/educaJS/.

Rodgers, P.: A survey of Euler diagrams. J. Vis. Lang. Comput. **25**(3), 134–155 (2014)

Stapleton, G., Shimojima, A., Jamnik, M.: The observational advantages of Euler diagrams with existential import. In: Chapman, P., Stapleton, G., Moktefi, A., Perez-Kriz, S., Bellucci, F. (eds.) Diagrams 2018. LNCS (LNAI), vol. 10871, pp. 313–329. Springer, Cham (2018). https://doi.org/10.1007/978-3-319-91376-6_29

Automatic Textual Explanations
of Concept Lattices

Johannes Hirth[1,3]($\boxtimes$) (iD), Viktoria Horn[2,3], Gerd Stumme[1,3] (iD),
and Tom Hanika[4,5] (iD)

[1] Knowledge & Data Engineering Group, University of Kassel, Kassel, Germany
{hirth,stumme}@cs.uni-kassel.de

[2] Gender/Diversity in Informatics Systems, University of Kassel, Kassel, Germany
viktoria.horn@uni-kassel.de

[3] Interdisciplinary Research Center for Information System Design,
University of Kassel, Kassel, Germany

[4] School of Library and Information Science, Humboldt-Universität zu Berlin,
Berlin, Germany
tom.hanika@uni-hildesheim.de

[5] Institute of Computer Science, University of Hildesheim, Hildesheim, Germany

Abstract. Lattices and their order diagrams are an essential tool for communicating knowledge and insights about data. This is in particular true when applying Formal Concept Analysis. Such representations, however, are difficult to comprehend by untrained users and in general in cases where lattices are large. We tackle this problem by automatically generating textual explanations for lattices using standard scales. Our method is based on the general notion of *ordinal motifs* in lattices for the special case of standard scales. We show the computational complexity of identifying a small number of standard scales that cover most of the lattice structure. For these, we provide textual explanation templates, which can be applied to any occurrence of a scale in any data domain. These templates are derived using principles from human-computer interaction and allow for a comprehensive textual explanation of lattices. We demonstrate our approach on the spices planner data set, which is a medium sized formal context comprised of fifty-six meals (objects) and thirty-seven spices (attributes). The resulting 531 formal concepts can be covered by means of about 100 standard scales.

Keywords: Ordered Sets · Explanations · Formal Concept Analysis · Closure System · Conceptual Structures

1 Introduction

There are several methods for the analysis of relational data. One such method is Formal Concept Analysis [4] (FCA). The standard procedure in the realm of FCA is to compute the concept lattice, i.e., a data representation on the ordinal level of measurement [16]. Ordered data structures are comparatively more comprehensible for users than, e.g., Euclidean embeddings. Nevertheless, untrained

M. Ojeda-Aciego et al. (Eds.): ICCS 2023, LNAI 14133, pp. 138–152, 2023.
https://doi.org/10.1007/978-3-031-40960-8_12

users may have difficulties in grasping knowledge from lattices (and lattice diagrams). Moreover, even trained users cannot cope with lattice structures of large sizes. In addition, there are up until now only rudimentary methods to derive basic meaning of lattices that are of standard scale [4, Figure 1.26].

A meaningful approach to cope with both issues is to employ more complex ordinal patterns, e.g., scales composed from standard scales. A recent result by Hirth et al. [9] allows for the efficient recognition of such patterns, there called *ordinal motifs*. Based on these we propose a method to automatically generate textual explanations of concept lattices. For the recognition of ordinal motifs we employ *scale-measures*, i.e., continuous maps between closure spaces. These are able to analyze parts of a conceptual structure with respect to a given set of scale contexts. While this approach is very expressive there may be exponentially many scale-measures. Therefore we introduce an importance measure of ordinal motifs based on the proportion of the conceptual structure that they reflect. With this our method can identify a small number of ordinal motifs that covers most of the concept lattice.

An advantage of employing sets of standard scales is their well-known structural semantic, cf. *basic meaning* Fig. 1.26 [4]. Based on this we constructed textual templates for every standard scale based on principles from human computer interaction. In detail we applied the five goodness criteria [11] for explainability in machine learning to ensure that the textual templates are human comprehensible.

Besides our theoretical investigations we provide an experimental example of a real world data set of medium size. All proposed methods are implemented in conexp-clj [5], a research tool for Formal Concept Analysis. Our approach is not only beneficial for untrained users but also provides explanations of readable size for concept lattices that are too large even for experienced users.

2   Formal Concept Analysis

Throughout this paper we presume that the reader is familiar with standard FCA notation [4]. In addition to that, for a formal context $\mathbb{K} := (G, M, I)$ we denote by $\mathbb{K}[H, N] := (H, N, I \cap H \times N)$ the induced sub-context for a given set of objects $H \subseteq G$ and attributes $N \subseteq M$. If not specified differently the lift of a map $\sigma : G_1 \to G_2$ on $\mathcal{P}(G_1) \to \mathcal{P}(G_2)$ is defined as $\sigma(A) := \{\sigma(a) \mid a \in A\}$ where $A \subseteq G_1$. The second lift to $\mathcal{P}(\mathcal{P}(G_1)) \to \mathcal{P}(\mathcal{P}(G_2))$ is defined as $\sigma(\mathcal{A}) := \{\sigma(A) \mid A \in \mathcal{A}\}$ for $\mathcal{A} \subseteq \mathcal{P}(G_1)$. For a closure system $\mathcal{A}$ on G we call $\mathcal{D}$ a finer closure system, denoted $\mathcal{A} \leq \mathcal{D}$, iff $\mathcal{D}$ is a closure system on G and $\mathcal{A} \subseteq \mathcal{D}$. In this case $\mathcal{A}$ is coarser than $\mathcal{D}$. We call $\mathcal{D}$ a sub-closure system of $\mathcal{A}$ iff $\mathcal{D}$ is a closure system on $H \subseteq G$ and $\mathcal{D} = \{H \cap A \mid A \in \mathcal{A}\}$.

Note that there are other definitions for sub-closure systems in the literature [7].

3   Recognizing Ordinal Motifs of Standard Scale

For the generation of textual explanations we recognize parts of the concept lattice that match an ordinal motif, i.e., are isomorphic to a standard scale. For this task we employ (full) scale-measures as introduced in the following.

Definition 3.1 (Scale-Measure (Definition 91 [4])). For two formal contexts $\mathbb{K}$, $\mathbb{S}$ a map $\sigma : G_\mathbb{K} \to G_\mathbb{S}$ is a *scale-measure* iff for all $A \in \text{Ext}(\mathbb{S})$ the pre-image $\sigma^{-1}(A) \in \text{Ext}(\mathbb{K})$. A scale-measure is *full* iff $\text{Ext}(\mathbb{K}) = \sigma^{-1}(\text{Ext}(\mathbb{S}))$.

We may note that we use a characterization for full scale-measures (Definition 91 [4]) which can easily be deduced. For a scale-measure from a context $\mathbb{K}$ into a scale context $\mathbb{S}$ it holds that the conceptual structure of $\mathbb{S}[\sigma(G_\mathbb{K}), M_\mathbb{S}]$ is entailed in $\mathfrak{B}(\mathbb{K})$. Thus, if we are able to explain $\mathbb{S}$ we can derive a *partial* explanation of $\mathbb{K}$. In contrast, for full scale-measures we can derive an *exact* explanation (up to context isomorphism) of $\mathbb{K}$. Obviously, both scale-measures and full scale-measures differ in their *coverage* of $\text{Ext}(\mathbb{K})$, i.e., partial and exact. However, both morphisms are defined on the entire set of objects G of $\mathbb{K}$ and are therefore of a *global scope*.

Even though global explanations are the gold standard for explainable artificial intelligence, they often elude from human comprehensibility due to their size. Therefore we divide the problem of deriving a single global explanation into multiple local explanations. To *locally* describe a part of context $\mathbb{K}$ a generalization of scale-measures is introduced in Hirth et al. [9].

Definition 3.2 (Local Scale-Measures [9]). For two contexts $\mathbb{K}$, $\mathbb{S}$ a map $\sigma : H \to G_\mathbb{S}$ is a *local scale-measure* iff $H \subseteq G_\mathbb{K}$ and σ is a scale-measure from $\mathbb{K}[H, M]$ to $\mathbb{S}$. We say σ is *full* iff σ is a full scale-measure from $\mathbb{K}[H, M]$ to $\mathbb{S}$.

In the following we construct templates for textual explanations. The basis for these templates are standard scales. Given a context $\mathbb{K}$ and a local (full) scale-measure σ of $\mathbb{K}$ into $\mathbb{S}$ we can replace every instance of an object $g \in G_\mathbb{S}$ in a textual explanation template of $\mathbb{S}$ by its pre-image $\sigma^{-1}(g) \subseteq G$. This yields a textual explanation of $\mathbb{K}$ with respect to σ.

For the standard scales, i.e., *nominal, ordinal, interordinal, crown* and *contranominal*, we show textual templates in Sect. 5. These are designed such that they can be universally applied in all settings. Prior to discussing the textual templates we have to discuss how to recognize standard scales in a given formal context. The general ordinal motif recognition problem was introduced in Hirth et al. [9]. In this work the authors are only concerned with the recognition of ordinal motifs based on scale-measures into standard scales. Nonetheless, we recall the general problem for enumerating scale-measures.

Problem 1 (Recognizing Ordinal Motifs [9]). *Given a formal context $\mathbb{K}$ and an ordinal motif $\mathbb{S}$, find a surjective map from $\mathbb{K}$ into $\mathbb{S}$ that is:*

	global	local
partial	scale-measure	local scale-measure
full	full scale-measure	local full scale-measure

The underlying decision problem of Problem 1 has been proven to be NP-complete [9]. In a moment we will investigate a particular instance of this problem for standard scales. But first we want to give the idea of how the recognition of standard scales relates to the overall explanation task.

In practice we consider families of standard scales for investigating a given formal context $\mathbb{K}$ such that we have explanation templates for each scale. Thus we have to solve the above problem for a family of scale contexts $\mathcal{O}$. Moreover, usually we are not only interested in a single scale-measure into a scale context $\mathbb{S}$ but all occurrences of them.

Fortunately, is for all standard scales, except for crown scales, the existence of local full scale-measures hereditary with respect to subsets of $H \subseteq G$. For example a context for which there exists a local full scale-measure $\sigma : H \to G_\mathbb{S}$ into the ordinal scale of size three does also allow for a local full scale-measure into the ordinal scale of size two by restricting σ to two elements of H. Thus when enumerating all local full scale-measures a large number of candidates does not need to be considered.

Another meaningful restriction for the rest of this work is to consider local full scale-measures only. Thus our methods focus on local full explanations (cf. Problem 1). Moreover, this choice allows to mitigate the enumeration of all scale-measures. For a family of standard scales of a particular type, e.g., the family of all ordinal scales, let $\mathbb{S}_n$ be the scale context of size n. We thus consider only the local full scale-measures $\sigma : H \to G_{\mathbb{S}_n}$ of $\mathbb{K}$ where there is no local full scale-measure $H \cup \{g\} \to G_{\mathbb{S}_{n+1}}$ from $\mathbb{K}$ to $\mathbb{S}_{n+1}$ with $g \in G, g \notin H$. For example, in case that H is of ordinal scale with respect to σ we can infer that all proper subsets of H are of ordinal scale. We remind the reader that we only consider surjective maps (cf. Problem 1).

Proposition 3.1 (Recognizing Standard Scales). *Deciding whether there is for a given formal context $\mathbb{K}$ a full scale-measure into either standard scale $\mathbb{N}_n$, $\mathbb{O}_n$, $\mathbb{I}_n$, $\mathbb{C}_n$ or $\mathbb{B}_n$ is in P.*

Proof WLoG we assume that $\mathbb{K}$ is clarified.

For a contranominal scale $\mathbb{B}_n := ([n], [n], \neq)$ every pair of bijective maps $(\alpha : [n] \to [n], \beta : [n] \to [n])$ is a context automorphism of $\mathbb{B}_n$ ([4]). Thus we can select an arbitrary mapping from G into $[n]$ and check if it is a full scale-measure from $\mathbb{K}$ into the contranominal scale $\mathbb{B}_n$. The verification of full scale-measures is in P [9]. The same reasoning applies to nominal scales $\mathbb{N}_n := ([n], [n], =)$.

For ordinal scales we need to verify that for each pair of objects their object concepts are comparable. Hence, the recognition for ordinal scales is in P.

For an interordinal scale $\mathbb{I}_n := ([n], [n], \leq)|([n], [n], \geq)$ we can infer from the extents of $\mathbb{K}$ of cardinality two two possible mappings $\sigma_\leq, \sigma_\geq$ that are the only candidates to be a full scale-measure. For interordinal scales the extents of cardinality two overlap on one object each and form a chain. From said chain we can infer two order relations of the objects G given by position in which they occur in the chain. From the total order on G we can infer a mapping $\sigma_\leq : G \to [n]$ where the objects are mapped according to their position. We can construct $\sigma_\geq$ analogously by reversing the positions. All maps other than $\sigma_\leq$ and $\sigma_\geq$ would violate the extent structure of the chain. For $\sigma_\leq$ and $\sigma_\geq$ we can verify in P if either is a full scale-measure. Moreover, the extents of cardinality two can be computed in polynomial time using `TITANIC` or `next_closure`. Hence, the recognition for interordinal scales is in P.

For crown scales $\mathbb{C}_n := ([n], [n], J)$ where $(a, b) \in J \iff a = b$ or $(a, b) = (n, 1)$ or $b = a + 1$ we can select an arbitrary object $g \in [n]$ and select repeatedly without putting back a different $h \in [n]$ with $\{g\}' \cap \{h\}' \neq \{\}$. Starting from g there is a unique drawing order. In order to find a full scale-measure we have to find an isomorphic drawing order for the elements of G in the same manner. From this we can derive a map $G \to [n]$ with respect to the drawing order and verify if it is a full scale-measure. The computational cost of the drawing procedure as well as the verification is in P.   □

In the contranominal case, our problem setting is related but different to the question by Dürrschnabel, Koyda, and Stumme [2] for the largest contranominal scale of a context $\mathbb{K}$.

Once we can recognize standard scales we are able to provide contextual explanations that are based on them. One may extend the set of scales to non-standard scales, yet this may be computationally intractable if they cannot be recognized in polynomial time.

While we are able to decide if a context $\mathbb{K}$ is of crown scale, it is NP-hard to decide if it allows for a surjective scale-measure into a crown scale of size $|G|$.

Proposition 3.2. *Deciding for a context $\mathbb{K}$ if there is a surjective scale-measure into a crown scale of size $|G|$ is NP-hard.*

Proof. To show the NP-hardness of this problem we reduce the Hamilton cycle (HC) problem for undirected graphs to it, i.e., for a graph G is there a circle(-path) visiting every node of G exactly ones. This problem is known to be NP-complete.

For the reduction, we map the graph $G := (V, E)$ (WLoG $|V| \geq 2$) to a formal context $\mathbb{K} := (V, \hat{V} \cup E, \in)$ where $\hat{V} := \{\{v\} \mid v \in V\}$. This map is polynomial in the size of the input. The set of extents of $\mathbb{K}$ is equal to $\hat{V} \cup E \cup \{V, \{\}\}$. The context $\mathbb{K}$ accepts a surjective scale-measure into the crown scale of size $|G|$ iff there is a sequence of extents of cardinality two $A_1, \ldots, A_n$ of $\mathbb{K}$ such that $(V, \{A_1, \ldots, A_n\}) \leq G$ is a cycle visiting each object $v \in V$ exactly ones. This is the case iff G has a Hamilton cycle.   □

First experiments [9] on a real world data set with 531 formal concepts revealed that the number of local full scale-measures into standard scales is too large to be humanly comprehended. Thus we propose in the following section two importance measures for selection approaches.

4   Important Ordinal Motifs

Our goal is to cover large proportions of a concept lattice $\mathfrak{B}(\mathbb{K})$ using a small set of scale-measures $\mathcal{S}$ into a given set of ordinal motifs. We say a concept

$(A, B) \in \underline{\mathfrak{B}}(\mathbb{K})$ is covered by $(\sigma, \mathbb{S}) \in S$ iff it is reflected by $(\sigma, \mathbb{S})$, i.e., there exists an extent $D \in \mathbb{S}$ with $\sigma^{-1}(D) = A$.

The above leads to the formulation of the general *ordinal motif covering* problem.

Problem 2 (Ordinal Motif Covering Problem). *For a context $\mathbb{K}$, a family of ordinal motifs $\mathcal{O}$ and $k \in \mathbb{N}$, what is the largest number $c \in \mathbb{N}$ such that there are surjective local full scale-measures $(\sigma_1, \mathbb{O}_1), \dots, (\sigma_k, \mathbb{O}_k)$ of $\mathbb{K}$ with $\mathbb{O}_1, \dots, \mathbb{O}_k \in \mathcal{O}$ and*

$$\left| \bigcup_{1 \leq i \leq k} (\varphi_{\mathbb{K}} \circ \sigma_i^{-1})(\mathrm{Ext}(\mathbb{O}_i)) \right| = c$$

where $\varphi_{\mathbb{K}}$ denotes the object closure operator of $\mathbb{K}$. If $\mathbb{K}$ does not allow for any scale-measure into an ordinal motif from $\mathcal{O}$ the value of c is 0.

We remind the reader that the maps $\varphi_{\mathbb{K}}, \sigma_i$ are lifted to a family of sets (cf. Sec. 2).

We call the set $\{(\sigma_1, \mathbb{O}_1), \dots, (\sigma_k, \mathbb{O}_k)\}$ an ordinal motif covering of $\mathbb{K}$.

If one is able to find an ordinal motif covering that reflects all formal concepts of $\mathbb{K}$ we can construct a formal context $\mathbb{O}$ which accepts a scale-measure $(\sigma, \mathbb{S})$ if and only if $(\sigma, \mathbb{S})$ is a scale-measure of $\mathbb{K}$.

Proposition 4.1 (Ordinal Motif Basis of $\mathbb{K}$). *Let $\mathbb{K}$ be a formal context with object closure operator $\varphi_{\mathbb{K}}$ and ordinal motif covering $\{(\sigma_1, \mathbb{O}_1), \dots, (\sigma_k, \mathbb{O}_k)\}$ that covers all concepts of $\mathbb{K}$, i.e., $c = |\underline{\mathfrak{B}}(\mathbb{K})|$. Let*

$$\mathbb{O} := |_{1 \leq i \leq k} (G, M_{\mathbb{O}_i}, I_{\mathbb{O}_i, \varphi_{\mathbb{K}}}), \ with \ (g, m) \in I_{\mathbb{O}_i, \varphi_{\mathbb{K}}} \iff g \in \varphi_{\mathbb{K}}(\sigma_i^{-1}(\{m\}^{I_{\mathbb{O}_i}}))$$

where $|$ is the context apposition. Then a pair $(\sigma, \mathbb{S})$ is a local full scale-measure from $\mathbb{K}[H, M]$ to $\mathbb{S}$ iff σ is a local full scale-measure from $\mathbb{O}[H, M_{\mathbb{O}}]$ to $\mathbb{S}$. In this case we call $\mathbb{O}$ an ordinal motif basis of $\mathbb{K}$.

Proof We have to show that the identity map is a full scale-measure from $\mathbb{K}$ to $\mathbb{O}$. Hence, we need to prove that all attribute extents of $\mathbb{O}$ are extents in $\mathbb{K}$ [7, Proposition 20] and each extent of $\mathbb{K}$ is an extent of $\mathbb{O}$. For an attribute $m \in M_{\mathbb{S}_i}$ is $\{m\}^{I_{\mathbb{S}_i, \varphi}} \in \mathrm{Ext}(\mathbb{K})$ per definition. The second requirement follows from the fact that $c = |\underline{\mathfrak{B}}(\mathbb{K})|$. □

The just introduced basis is a useful tool when investigating scale-measures of a context $\mathbb{K}$ given a set of ordinal motifs $\mathcal{O}$. One can perceive $\mathcal{O}$ as a set of analytical tools and the existence of $\mathbb{O}$ implies that a found ordinal motif covering $\{(\sigma_1, \mathbb{O}_1), \dots, (\sigma_k, \mathbb{O}_k)\}$ is complete with respect to scale-measures of $\mathbb{K}$.

4.1   Scaling Dimension Complexity

An interesting problem based on the ordinal motif covering for (non-local) scale-measures is to determine the smallest number k such that $c = |\underline{\mathfrak{B}}(\mathbb{K})|$. This number is also the *scaling dimension* [3] of $\mathbb{K}$ with respect to the family of scale contexts $\mathcal{O}$. Note that the scaling dimension for a given context $\mathbb{K}$ and family of scales $\mathcal{O}$ does not need to exist. In the following we recall the scaling dimension problem in the language scale-measures.

Problem 3 (Scaling Dimension Problem [3]). *For a context $\mathbb{K}$ and a family of scale contexts $\mathcal{O}$, what is the smallest number $d \in \mathbb{N}$ of scale contexts $\mathbb{S}_1, \ldots, \mathbb{S}_d \in \mathcal{S}$, if existent, such that $\mathbb{K}$ accepts a full scale-measure into the semi-product*

$$\underset{1 \leq i \leq d}{\times} \mathbb{S}_i.$$

The scaling dimension can be understood as a measurement for the complexity of deriving explanations for a formal context based on scale-measures and a set of ordinal motifs. However, determining the scaling dimension is a combinatorial problem whose related decision problem is NP-complete, as can be seen in the following.

Theorem 4.1 *(Scaling Dimension Complexity)*. *Deciding for a context $\mathbb{K}$ and a set of ordinal motifs $\mathcal{O}$ if the scaling dimension is at most $d \in \mathbb{N}$ is NP-complete.*

Proof To show NP-hardness we reduce the recognizing full scale-measure problem (RfSM) [9] to it.

For two input contexts $\hat{\mathbb{K}}$ and $\hat{\mathbb{S}}$ of the RfSM let context $\mathbb{K} := \hat{\mathbb{K}}$. We map $\hat{\mathbb{K}}$ to $\mathbb{K}$ and $\hat{\mathbb{K}}[S]$ to the set of ordinal motifs $\mathcal{O} := \{\hat{\mathbb{S}}\}$ and set $d = 1$. This map is polynomial in the size of the input.

If there is a full scale-measure from $\hat{\mathbb{K}}$ into $\hat{\mathbb{S}}$ we can deduce that there is a full scale-measure of $\mathbb{K}$ into the semi-product that has only one operand and is thus just one element of $\mathcal{O}$. Hence, this element is $\hat{\mathbb{S}}$ and therefore the scaling dimension is at most one. The inverse can be followed analogously.

An algorithm to decide the scaling dimension problem can be given by non-deterministically guessing d scale contexts $\mathbb{S}_1, \ldots, \mathbb{S}_d \in \mathcal{O}$ and d mappings from $\sigma_i = G_{\mathbb{K}} \rightarrow G_{\mathbb{S}_i}$. These are polynomial in the size of the input. The verification for full scale-measures in P [9]. □

4.2 Ordinal Motif Covering with Standard Scales

The ordinal motif covering problem is a combinatorial problem which is computationally costly, even for standard scales. Thus, we propose in the following a greedy approach which has two essential steps. First, we compute all local full scale-measures $\mathcal{S}$ for standard scales. This step is computationally tame due to the heredity property of local full scale-measures for standard scales, as discussed in Sect. 3. Our goal is now to identify, in a greedy manner, elements of $\mathcal{S}$ that increase c the most. Thus, secondly, we select k full scale-measures where at each selection step i with $1 \leq i \leq k$ we select a scale-measure $(\sigma, \mathbb{O}) \in \mathcal{S}$ that maximizes Eq. 1.

$$\left| \left(\varphi_{\mathbb{K}} \circ \sigma^{-1} \right) \left(\mathrm{Ext}(\mathbb{O}) \right) \setminus \bigcup_{1 \leq j < i} \left(\varphi_{\mathbb{K}} \circ \sigma_j^{-1} \right) \left(\mathrm{Ext}(\mathbb{O}_j) \right) \right| \tag{1}$$

In the above equation $(\sigma_j, \mathbb{O}_j)$ denotes the scale-measure that was selected at step $j \leq i$. The union is the covering number c of the ordinal motif covering $(\sigma_1, \mathbb{O}_1), \ldots, (\sigma_{i-1}, \mathbb{O}_{i-1})$. Overall, the computed cardinality is equal to the number of concepts reflected by $(\sigma, \mathbb{O})$ that are not already reflected by $(\sigma_1, \mathbb{O}_1), \ldots, (\sigma_{i-1}, \mathbb{O}_{i-1})$.

For obvious reasons this approach results in the selection of scale-measures that have the largest number of (so far) uncovered concepts. A downside of this heuristic is that it favors ordinal motifs that have in general more concepts, e.g., contranominal scales over ordinal scales. To compensate for this we propose to normalize the heuristic by the number of concepts of the ordinal motif, i.e., $\left| \sigma^{-1} \left(\mathrm{Ext}(\mathbb{O}) \right) \right|$.

In the first step, the normalized heuristic does not account for the total size of the ordinal motif. The first selected scale-measure covers at least the top extent, i.e., G, and thus the scores for all following ordinal motifs are at most $|\mathrm{Ext}(\mathbb{S})| - 1 / |\mathrm{Ext}(\mathbb{S})|$.

5 Human-Centered Textual Explanations

We want to elaborate on textual explanations of concept lattices based on principles drawn from human-computer interaction for state of the art *human-centered explanations*. One of the most currently applied fields of these explanations in computer science is Explainable AI (XAI) [15]. Developing explainable systems commonly begins with "an assertion about what makes for a good explanation" [13], which are not seldomly based on guidelines or collections of principles. Those principles aim to derive *human-centered textual explanations* that impart complex concepts in a manner that is accessible, relevant, and understandable. They are designed to cater to the individual cognitive and emotional needs of readers, anticipating their concerns and queries. Thereby they aim at fostering the understanding of the reader by exposing reasoning and additional information to accompany data structures they rely on [17]. Moreover, textual explanations based on goodness criteria in the context of computer-generated knowledge and information help to strengthen trust in the computed reasoning results [11].

Mamun et al. [11] proposed five goodness criteria for explainability in the context of machine learning models. We identify them as adaptable to our task for textual explanations of concept lattices. The first criterion is *accuracy*, which requires that an explanation is a valid reflection of the underlying data. [14]. The second criterion is *scope*, which refers to the level of detail in the explanation, which can vary from explaining a single action to a global description of a system, depending on the tasks and needs of the reader. The third criterion relates to the type of question the explanation answers, which is called the *explanation form criterion*. The questions can be of type "what...", "why...",

"why not...", "what if...", or "how to...". This is related to the so-called explanation triggers identified by Mueller et al. [12]. In their study, Mamun et al. [11] found that many explanations in Explainable AI contexts were "what" statements. The fourth criterion is *simplicity*, which emphasizes the importance of making an explanation easy to read and understand (e.g., Kulesza et al. [10]). Mamun et al. [11] suggested testing the appropriate readability level by comparing the grade level of other related content with one's explanations. Finally, the fifth criterion is the *knowledge base criterion*, which emphasizes the importance of providing workable knowledge in the explanation. Thus, explanations should predominantly be written as factual statements [11]. In the following, we first propose our textual explanation templates for standard scales and afterwards discuss how the principles above are implemented in their design.

Nominal Scale: The elements $n_1, \ldots, n_{k-1}$ and n_k are incomparable, i.e., all elements have at least one property that the other elements do not have.

Ordinal Scale: There is a ranking of elements $n_1, \ldots, n_{k-1}$ and n_k such that an element has all the properties its successors has.

Interordinal Scale: The elements $n_1, \ldots, n_{k-1}$ and n_k are ordered in such a way that each interval of elements has a unique set of properties they have in common.

Contranominal Scale: Each combination of the elements $n_1, \ldots, n_{k-1}$ and n_k has a unique set of properties they have in common.

Crown Scale: The elements $n_1, \ldots, n_{k-1}$ and n_k are incomparable. Furthermore, there is a closed cycle from n_1, over $n_2, \ldots n_{k-1}$ and n_k back to n_1 by pairwise shared properties.

We explain how our approach relates to the goodness criteria above.

Accuracy. The generation of textual explanations are based on ordinal motif coverings with scale-measures, i.e., continuous maps between closure spaces. These maps do not introduce any conceptual error [8]. Moreover, ordinal motif coverings can function as a basis for the complete conceptual structure of the data set with respect to Proposition 4.1. Therefore an accurate mapping of an explanation onto the represented information is guaranteed.

Scope. For the scope of the introduced explanations we differed between global and local explanations which is determined by the choice of scale-measures, i.e., local vs non-local. In addition to that we can differentiate between two kinds of `coverage`, i.e., full and non-full scale-measures. However, with our experiments and the ordinal motif covering we focus mainly on local full explanations. Altogether, we can serve different task requirements with the explanations.

Explanation Form. The main question addressed by ordinal motifs is dependent on the type of scale-measure. For full scale-measures we answer the question on *"What is the conceptual relation between a given set of objects."* and for non-full scale-measures we answer *"What is **a** conceptual relation between a given set of objects.".*

Simplicity. The presented explanations are written using terms familiar for readers with basic knowledge about graphs and mathematical descriptions. Formulations that require prior knowledge about conceptual structures have been avoided. In addition to that, the textual structure is kept simple and explanations are composed of at most two short sentences.

Knowledge Base. The generated textual explanations describe the conceptual relations between objects and can thus be considered to be factual statements.

All proposed textual explanations are designed to be applicable in every data domain that is representable by formal contexts. However, different data domains and applications come with different requirements for the design of human-centered textual explanations. Thus, a development of domain specific explanations for a large variety of settings is advisable. Given more general principles of HCI [1], user studies with the prospective users of a system are the gold standard in evaluating any kind of interaction [11]. Since the focus of this work is to introduce the theoretical foundation of how to derive human-centered explanations we deem the execution of a user study future work.

6   Application Example

To show the applicability of our method, we compute the ordinal motif covering for the *spices planner* data set [6]. This context contains fifty-six meals as objects and thirty-seven spices and food categories as attributes. The context has 531 formal concepts and accepts over ten-thousands local full scale-measures into standard scales. In Table 1 we recall results [9] on how many local full scale-measures there are per family of standard scales. The most frequent ordinal motif of the spices planner context is the interordinal motif. The motif having the largest scale size is the nominal scale motif, which includes up to nine objects. There are no non-trivial ordinal scale motifs in the spices planner context, i.e., the size of all local full scale-measure domains into ordinal scales within the spices planner context is one. Therefore we exclude the ordinal scales from the following analysis.

In our experiment we applied the introduced greedy strategy. In Fig. 1 we report the extent sizes of selected ordinal motifs. In the left diagram we depict

Table 1. Results for ordinal motifs [9] of the spices planner context. Every column represents ordinal motifs of a particular standard scale family. Maximal lf-sm is the number of local full scale-measures for which there is no lf-sm with a larger domain. Largest lf-sm refers to the largest domain size that occurs in the set of local full scale-measures.

	nominal	ordinal	interordinal	contranominal	crown
local full sm	2342	37	4643	2910	2145
maximal lf-sm	527	37	2550	1498	2145
largest lf-sm	9	1	5	5	6

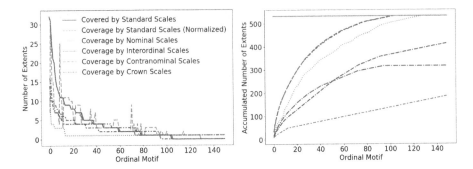

Fig. 1. The extent coverage (left) for the ordinal motif covering computation for all and each standard scale family individually. The right diagram displays the accumulated coverage at each step in the ordinal motif covering computation. The legend of the left diagram does also apply to right diagram with the addition of the total number of extents (pink) in the context. (Color figure online)

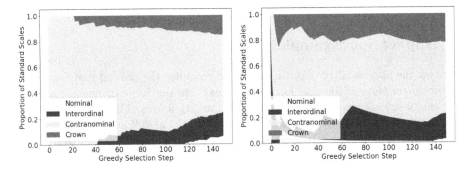

Fig. 2. The ratio of each standard scale family in the ordinal motif covering computation for the standard (left) and normalized heuristic.

in the abscissa the steps of the greedy selection and in the ordinate the number of newly covered concepts. We report the results for the standard scales individually and combined, for the later we also experimented with the normalized heuristic. In the right diagram we depict the accumulated values, i.e., the value c. First we observe that the normalized heuristic does not decrease monotonously in contrast to all other results. From the right diagram we can infer that the crown, interordinal and nominal are unable to cover all extents. The contranominal and the combined scale family took the fewest selection steps to achieve complete extent coverage. This followed by the normalized heuristic on the combined scale family which about thirty percent more steps. Out of the other scale families the crown scales achieved the highest coverage followed by the interordinal and nominal scales.

With Fig. 2 we investigate the influence of the normalization on the greedy selection process. For this we depict the relative proportion of selected scale types up to a step i (abscissa). The left diagram shows the proportions for the standard heuristic and the right reports the proportions for the normalized heuristic. We count ordinal motifs that belong to multiple standard scale families relatively. For example we count the contranominal scale of size three half for the crown family. In the first diagram we see that a majority of the selected ordinal motifs are of contranominal scales. This is not surprising since they have the most concepts among all standard scales. The interordinal and crown scales are almost equally represented and the nominal motifs are the least frequent. In contrast to this the normalized heuristic selects crown and interordinal motifs more frequently (right diagram).

Overall we would argue that while the normalized heuristic produces slightly worse coverage scores it provide a more diverse selection in terms of the standard scales. Therefore, the normalized heuristic may result in potentially more insightful explanations.

We conclude by providing automatically generated textual explanations for the spices planner context. For this we report the top ten selections for the standard and normalized heuristic. First we depict the explanations for the standard heuristic which consist solely of contranominal motifs. Thereafter we will turn to the normalized heuristic results.

1. Each combination of the elements *Thyme, Sweet Paprika, Oregano, Caraway* and *Black Pepper* has a unique set of properties they have in common.
2. Each combination of the elements *Curry, Garlic, White Pepper, Curcuma* and *Cayenne Pepper* has a unique set of properties they have in common.
3. Each combination of the elements *Paprika Roses, Thyme, Sweet Paprika, White Pepper* and *Cayenne Pepper* has a unique set of properties they have in common.
4. Each combination of the elements *Paprika Roses, Thyme, Allspice, Curry* and *Curcuma* has a unique set of properties they have in common.
5. Each combination of the elements *Thyme, Basil, Garlic, White Pepper* and *Cayenne Pepper* has a unique set of properties they have in common.
6. Each combination of the elements *Tarragon, Thyme, Oregano, Curry,* and *Basil* has a unique set of properties they have in common.
7. Each combination of the elements *Vegetables, Caraway, Bay Leef* and *Juniper Berries* has a unique set of properties they have in common.
8. Each combination of the elements *Meat, Garlic, Mugwort* and *Cloves* has a unique set of properties they have in common.
9. Each combination of the elements *Oregano, Caraway, Rosemary, White Pepper* and *Black Pepper* has a unique set of properties they have in common.
10. Each combination of the elements *Curry, Ginger, Nutmeg* and *Garlic* has a unique set of properties they have in common.

These explanations cover a total of 195 concepts out of 531. An interesting observation is that explanation number eight has only four objects compared to the five objects of explanation number nine. Yet, explanation eight was selected first. The reason for this is that number eight has more non-redundant concepts with respect to the previous selections.

The results for the normalized heuristic are very different compared to the standard heuristic. The ten selected motifs cover a total of 125 concepts. They consist of one interordinal motif, four contranominal, one nominal and four motifs that are crown and contranominal at the same time. For the ordinal motifs that are of crown and contranominal scale we report explanations for both.

1. The elements *Thyme*, *Caraway* and *Poultry* are ordered in such a way that each interval of elements has a unique set of properties they have in common.
2. Each combination of the elements *Curry*, *Garlic*, *White Pepper*, *Curcuma* and *Cayenne Pepper* has a unique set of properties they have in common.
3. Each combination of the elements *Allspice*, *Ginger,Mugwort* and *Cloves* has a unique set of properties they have in common.
4. Each combination of the elements *Sweet Paprika*, *Oregano*, *Rosemary* and *Black Pepper* has a unique set of properties they have in common.
5. Each combination of the elements *Sauces*, *Basil* and *Mugwort* has a unique set of properties they have in common.
   The elements *Basil*, *Sauces* and *Mugwort* are incomparable. Furthermore, there is a closed cycle from *Basil* over *Sauces* and *Mugwort* back to *Basil* by pairwise shared properties.
6. Each combination of the elements *Paprika Roses*, *Meat* and *Bay Leef* has a unique set of properties they have in common.
   The elements *Paprika Roses*, *Meat* and *Bay Leef* are incomparable. Furthermore, there is a closed cycle from *Paprika Roses* over *Meat* and *Bay Leef* back to *Paprika Roses* by pairwise shared properties.
7. Each combination of the elements *Saffron*, *Anisey* and *Rice* has a unique set of properties they have in common.
   The elements *Saffron*, *Anisey* and *Rice* are incomparable. Furthermore, there is a closed cycle from *Saffron* over *Anisey* and *Rice* back to *Saffron* by pairwise shared properties.
8. Each combination of the elements *Vegetables*, *Savory* and *Cilantro* has a unique set of properties they have in common.
   The elements *Savory*, *Cilantro* and *Vegetables* are incomparable. Furthermore, there is a closed cycle from *Savory* over *Cilantro* and *Vegetables* back to *Savory* by pairwise shared properties.
9. The elements *Tarragon*, *Potatos* and *Majoram* are incomparable, i.e., all elements have at least one property that the other elements do not have.
10. Each combination of the elements *Paprika Roses*, *Thyme*, *Sweet Paprika*, *White Pepper* and *Cayenne Pepper* has a unique set of properties they have in common.

7   Conclusion

To the best of our knowledge our presented method is the first approach for the automatic generation of textual explanations of concept lattices. It is a first step towards making Formal Concept Analysis accessible to users without prior training in mathematics. Our contribution comprises the theoretical foundations as well as the preparation of human-centered textual explanations for ordinal motifs of standard scale. In particular, we have shown that the recognition of standard scales can be done in polynomial time in the size of the context. This is also the case when the standard scale has exponential many concepts. This is a positive result for the generation of textual explanations of large real world data sets.

Based on ordinal motif coverings we are able to limit the generated textual explanations to a low number of non-redundant conceptual relations. In detail, we proposed a greedy method for the computation of ordinal motif coverings based on two heuristics. To asses the complexity of potential textual explanations of a concept lattice, we showed the relation between ordinal motif coverings and the scaling dimension. For the later we proved that the computational complexity of the related decision problem is NP-complete. Accompanying our theoretical investigation, we derived criteria on how to derive textual explanations for ordinal motifs with principles from human-computer interaction. In addition to that, we demonstrated the applicability of our approach based on a real world data set.

As a next logical step, we envision a participatory user study. This will lead to improved textual explanations for ordinal motifs that are easier to comprehend by humans. Moreover, the development of domain specific textual explanations may increase the number of applications for our proposed methods.

Declarations

Funding and/or Conflicts of interests/Competing interests: This work was funded by the German Federal Ministry of Education and Research (BMBF) in its program "FAIRDIENSTE" under grant number 16KIS1249K. The authors have no competing interests to declare that are relevant to the content of this article.

References

1. Chao, G.: Human-computer interaction: process and principles of human-computer interface design. In: 2009 International Conference on Computer and Automation Engineering, pp. 230–233. IEEE (2009)
2. Dürrschnabel, D., Koyda, M., Stumme, G.: Attribute selection using contranominal scales. In: Braun, T., Gehrke, M., Hanika, T., Hernandez, N. (eds.) ICCS 2021. LNCS (LNAI), vol. 12879, pp. 127–141. Springer, Cham (2021). https://doi.org/10.1007/978-3-030-86982-3_10
3. Ganter, B., Hanika, T., Hirth, J.: Scaling dimension. In: Dürrschnabel, D., López Rodríguez, D. (eds.) ICFCA 2023. LNCS, vol. 13934, pp. 64–77. Springer, Cham (2023). https://doi.org/10.1007/978-3-031-35949-1_5

4. Ganter, B., Wille, R.: Formal concept analysis: mathematical foundations. Springer, Berlin; New York (1999). ISBN 3540627715 9783540627715. http://www.amazon.de/Formal-Concept-Analysis-Mathematical-Foundations/dp/3540627715/ref=sr_1_1?ie=UTF8&qid=1417077494&sr=8-1&keywords=formal+concept+analysis+mathematical+foundations

5. Hanika, T., Hirth, J.: Conexp-Clj - a research tool for FCA. In: Cristea, D., Le Ber, F., Missaoui, R., Kwuida, L., Sertkaya, B., editors, ICFCA (Supplements), volume 2378 of CEUR Workshop Proceedings, pp. 70–75. CEUR-WS.org (2019)

6. Hanika, T., Hirth, J.: Knowledge cores in large formal contexts. Ann. Math. Artif. Intell. Apr (2022a). ISSN 1573–7470. https://doi.org/10.1007/s10472-022-09790-6

7. Hanika, T., Hirth, J.: On the lattice of conceptual measurements. Inf. Sci. **613**, 453–468 (2022b). ISSN 0020–0255. https://doi.org/10.1016/j.ins.2022.09.005. https://www.sciencedirect.com/science/article/pii/S0020025522010489

8. Hanika, T., Hirth, J.: Quantifying the conceptual error in dimensionality reduction. In: Braun, T., Gehrke, M., Hanika, T., Hernandez, N., editors, Graph-Based Representation and Reasoning - 26th International Conference on Conceptual Structures, ICCS 2021, Virtual Event, September 20–22, 2021, Proceedings, volume 12879 of Lecture Notes in Computer Science, pp. 105–118. Springer (2021). https://doi.org/10.1007/978-3-030-86982-3_8

9. Hirth, J., Horn, V., Stumme, G., Hanika, T.: Ordinal motifs in lattices (2023). CoRR, arXiv. 2304.04827

10. Kulesza, T., Burnett, M., Wong, W.-K., Stumpf, S.: Principles of explanatory debugging to personalize interactive machine learning. In: Proceedings of the 20th International Conference on Intelligent User Interfaces, pp. 126–137 (2015)

11. Ibne Mamun, T., Baker, K., Malinowski, H., Hoffman, R.R., Mueller, S.T.: Assessing collaborative explanations of AI using explanation goodness criteria. In: Proceedings of the Human Factors and Ergonomics Society Annual Meeting, vol. 65, pp. 988–993. SAGE Publications Sage CA: Los Angeles, CA (2021)

12. Mueller, S.T., et al.: Explanation in human-AI systems: a literature meta-review, synopsis of key ideas and publications, and bibliography for explainable AI. arXiv preprint arXiv:1902.01876 (2019)

13. Mueller, S.T., et al.: Principles of explanation in human-AI systems. arXiv preprint arXiv:2102.04972 (2021)

14. Papenmeier, A., Englebienne, G., Seifert, C.: How model accuracy and explanation fidelity influence user trust. arXiv preprint arXiv:1907.12652 (2019)

15. Schwalbe, G., Finzel, B.: A comprehensive taxonomy for explainable artificial intelligence: a systematic survey of surveys on methods and concepts. Data Min. Knowl. Discov., pp. 1–59 (2023)

16. Stevens, S.S.: On the theory of scales of measurement. Science **103**(2684), 677–680 (1946). ISSN 0036–8075

17. Tintarev, N., Masthoff, J.: Designing and evaluating explanations for recommender systems. In: Ricci, F., Rokach, L., Shapira, B., Kantor, P.B. (eds.) Recommender Systems Handbook, pp. 479–510. Springer, Boston, MA (2011). https://doi.org/10.1007/978-0-387-85820-3_15

Semantic Web and Graphs

Ontology Population from French Classified Ads

Céline Alec[✉]

Normandie Univ, UNICAEN, ENSICAEN, CNRS, GREYC,
14000 Caen, France
`celine.alec@unicaen.fr`

Abstract. Understanding texts written in natural language is a challenging task. Semantic Web technologies, in particular ontologies, can be used to represent knowledge from a specific domain and reason like a human. Ontology population from texts aims to transform textual contents into ontological assertions. This paper deals with an approach of automatic ontology population from French textual descriptions. This approach has been designed to be domain-independent, as long as a domain ontology is provided. It relies on text-based and knowledge-based analyses, which are fully explained. Experiments performed on French classified advertisements are discussed and provide encouraging results.

Keywords: Ontology population · Knowledge engineering · OWL

1 Introduction

Ontologies [17] are designed to share domain knowledge between humans and machines. They include a hierarchy of classes and relationships between them. Ontology population is the process of adding instances to an ontology. A populated ontology may also be referred to as a knowledge base or knowledge graph.

The approach proposed in this paper is the first part of the DECA project (Detection of Errors and Correction of Annotations). This project deals with annotated descriptions, i.e., descriptions that are in the form of texts to which annotations are appended. For example, this is the case of classified advertisements, annotated with the criteria they meet. Annotations are theoretically meant to describe characteristics of the object or event described in the description. However, this is not always the case. In fact, erroneous annotations may frequently be observed, either due to typing errors or "misuse": descriptions are deliberately wrongly annotated to increase their visibility. For example, one can find a real estate advertisement annotated with the city X, while the description states "30 min from X"; or where the area annotation (in m^2) is 150, whereas the description states "147 m^2". These wrongly annotated descriptions waste a considerable amount of time for users, who must sort through the multiple responses that comply, in theory, with their search criteria. The DECA project deals with this problem. Its goal is to detect and correct erroneous annotations by leveraging the inconsistencies that can be detected based on the content expressed

M. Ojeda-Aciego et al. (Eds.): ICCS 2023, LNAI 14133, pp. 155–170, 2023.
https://doi.org/10.1007/978-3-031-40960-8_13

in the textual description. This requires understanding the text, which is the focus of our contribution. Indeed, our goal is to populate a domain ontology from textual descriptions of objects. Our first use case concerns house sale ads, but the proposed approach must be as generic as possible, i.e., it must be able to populate a domain ontology from descriptions in various domains, whether they are classified ads (car sales, fashion, etc.), or descriptions of a certain type of object (restaurants, hotels, etc.). A domain ontology is considered as input; its design is not the object of our work.

The rest of the paper is organized as follows: Section 2 presents the related work and positions our contribution. Section 3 describes our approach. Section 4 evaluates the approach while Sect. 5 concludes and suggests future work.

2   Related Work and Positioning

Ontology population has been studied in various papers [11]. In this section, we focus only on approaches aiming to extract information from unstructured textual documents and a domain ontology, allowing additions of instances in it, in particular additions of property assertions. Existing systems are based on various rule-based methods using lexico-syntactic patterns (see next paragraph); on methods based on machine learning [9,18]; or on hybrid methods [3]. Some recent approaches use deep learning [2,6]. In general, the use of machine learning techniques requires a large quantity of sentences and their ontological correspondence upstream, which is not the case for our data. We therefore concentrate on approaches exploiting lexico-syntactic patterns.

The ArtEquAKT approach [1] deals with ontology population from the Web in the domain of artists. This approach populates the ontology with property assertions. It uses the verb found in a sentence between two instances of concepts from the ontology. On the same principle, Makki [12] also focuses on verbs in order to populate the ontology with property assertions, but it is semi-automatic and domain-independent. A list of verbs is extracted from the input corpus for each property from the ontology using Wordnet. A set of seven manually written rules is used to recognise subjects and objects of a potential property assertion. Results are then validated by an expert. In [5], a framework is proposed. The goal is to instantiate a concept as well as the relationships that concern it. First, named entities are identified in the text (exploiting also co-references). Second, triggers are considered, i.e., property names as well as their synonyms; and rules are built based on noun phrases preceded or followed by a trigger. The application of these rules leads to the population of the ontology. [15] presents an approach to populate an ontology of criminal events and their causes from Spanish newspaper tweets. It is based on linguistic patterns. [10] aims at extracting property assertions in regulatory documents between incidents and actions (the "hasMeasure" property and its sub-properties) based on rules. They use both co-occurrences of incidents and measures within the same sentence, paragraph or chapter, but this does not distinguish sub-properties, for which lexical patterns are used. [14] presents a rule-based approach to extract relations from musical tidbits to populate a domain ontology. For this, rules based on grammatical labeling are used. The study of these approaches shows several emerging scientific obstacles. In general, rule-based methods have good precision at the expense of recall [4]. Either the rules are domain-specific (lexical patterns and some very precise syntactic patterns), or the rules are generic and cannot be as precise as rules defined for a single domain. Moreover, many of these works require human intervention to validate the propositions. Furthermore, verbs are generally very important in the population of properties, as they strongly characterize relations (e.g., "is married to"). Finally, most approaches deal with named entities as subjects and objects of properties and focus on populating object properties neglecting data properties.

In our case, we aim to apply a similar approach across multiple domains, while remaining in the context of textual descriptions of objects. Since the proposed approach will be the first step towards automated annotation correction, it must be automatic, without any human validation, and sufficiently generic. In general, verbs are not very characteristic of a relation in object descriptions (e.g., "have" or "possess"). Sometimes, there is no verb at all (e.g., "2 bedrooms, 1 bathroom."), which complicates the population. We wish to populate both object and data properties. Subjects and objects are not necessarily named entities. Finally, our context may present ternary properties. Automatic population of n-ary properties has, to our knowledge, never been studied. For all these reasons, the cited works are not adapted to our original problem, which necessitates a novel approach.

3   The KOnPoTe Approach

We present KOnPoTe (Knowledge graph/ONtology POpulation from TExts), an approach to populate a domain ontology from textual descriptions of elements of this domain. It takes as input a corpus of descriptions and a domain ontology and populates the ontology by representing the descriptions of the corpus.

3.1   Initial Data

The input ontology defines the domain. It can be defined as a tuple $(\mathcal{C}, \mathcal{P}, \mathcal{I}, \mathcal{A}, \mathcal{R})$ where $\mathcal{C}$ is a set of classes, $\mathcal{P}$ a set of (object and data) properties characterizing the classes, $\mathcal{I}$ a set of individuals and assertions (potentially empty), $\mathcal{A}$ a set of axioms representable in OWL2 (Web Ontology Language) and $\mathcal{R}$ a set of SWRL (Semantic Web Rule Language) [8] rules (potentially empty). The domain is represented by a class named hereafter *main class*. Data properties taken into account can use boolean values, numerical values or strings. The ontology can contain initial individuals, which are generic. Each entity of the ontology (class, property, individual) has an identifier (URI) and possibly more advanced terminology, via rdfs:label, rdfs:isDefinedBy, as well as a "unit" annotation property, especially created to associate an entity with a unit or a unit expression (exemplified in the following). The ontology may exist beforehand or be created: its design is not part of our contribution. The input corpus is composed of French documents, each of which describes an instance of the *main class*. Figures 2 and 3 show one example of a description.

Fig. 1. Partial vision of the entities of our French house sales ontology

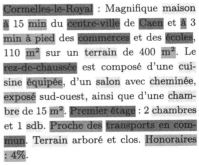

Cormelles-le-Royal : Magnifique maison à 15 min du centre-ville de Caen et à 3 min à pied des commerces et des écoles, 110 m² sur un terrain de 400 m². Le rez-de-chaussée est composé d'une cuisine équipée, d'un salon avec cheminée, exposé sud-ouest, ainsi que d'une chambre de 15 m². Premier étage : 2 chambres et 1 sdb. Proche des transports en commun. Terrain arboré et clos. Honoraires : 4%.

Fig. 2. A French house sale ad

Cormelles-le-Royal : Magnificent house located 15 min from the city center of Caen and 3 min walk from shops and schools, 110 m² on a land of 400 m². The ground floor consists of a kitchen equipped with essential appliances, a living room with fireplace, facing southwest, as well as a bedroom of 15 m². First floor: 2 bedrooms and 1 bathroom. Close to public transport. Wooded and enclosed land. Fees : 4%.

Fig. 3. Translation of Fig. 2

Color legend for the matchings: Individuals Classes Object properties Data properties

The approach is designed to be applicable to different domains. The example unfolded in this paper considers the domain of house sales. Figure 1 represents a partial view of the classes and properties of the ontology used in this domain. It contains classes such as the main class *Property* (denoting real estate), *Room*, *Kitchen*, etc. Among the ontology properties, we can cite the object property *isLocatedIn* linking a real estate property to a municipality, or the data property *areaInM2* connecting a real estate *property part* (land, house, etc.) or a *room* to a numerical value. The initial individuals are generic, e.g., instances of the classes *Municipality* or *HeatingSystem*. The ontology also contains axioms, for example, the fact that a real estate *Property* can only be located in at most one *Municipality*. Units are used, e.g., *areaInM2* with the unit "m²", or *feePercentage* with a unit expression "fees: xxx %". This representation of units is basic and could be improved in a future version.

3.2   Proposed Framework

The proposed approach must be applicable to different types of objects. For a given domain, it is necessary to have as input a domain ontology as well as a corpus of documents, where each document is a text that describes an instance of the *main class*. Thus, the proposed algorithm must not depend on domain-based rules or linguistic models. Therefore, we chose to use domain terminology (from the ontology), syntactic indicators (such as sentences or the order of expressions in the text) and knowledge indicators (such as property domains and ranges).

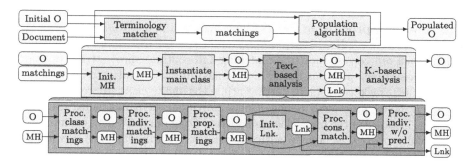

Fig. 4. Outline of the KOnPoTe approach

Figure 4 shows the outline of the approach. The ontology (O), as well as a document from the corpus, are used (top of the Figure) by a terminology matcher. This leads to matchings between text mentions and entities of O. Then, a population algorithm is applied, which is a processing chain (middle of the Figure): an initialisation of an object called "Matching Handler" (MH); an instantiation of the *main class*; a textual analysis, composed of various modules (bottom of the Figure); as well as an analysis based on the knowledge of the ontology. This process is applied on each document of the corpus. At the end, the output populated ontology represents all the descriptions of the corpus. The remaining of this section details each module using the document example from Figs. 2 and 3.

3.3   The Terminology Matcher

The terminology matcher is the first step of the approach. It takes as input the initial ontology and a document, and produces matchings between the textual mentions and entities of the ontology. The text is split into sentences and lemmatized. The ontology's keywords (URI fragments, labels, units) are also lemmatized. Matchings are established between the text and the ontology's keywords. Snake_case and camelCase conventions are taken into account. These also concern unit expressions, e.g., the mention *fees: 4%* matches the unit expression *fees: xxx %*. All matchings contained in another matching are removed. For example, if there is a matching on the mention "city center" and on its sub-mention "city", only the one on "city center" is considered.

In Figs. 2 and 3, matchings concern individuals (e.g., "ground floor" ↔ *groundFloor*), classes ("house" ↔ *House*), object properties ("Close to" ↔

isCloseTo) or data properties ("m^2" ↔ *areaInM2*). Our use case is in French but examples are translated into English in the following.

3.4   The Population Algorithm

Matchings are inputs of the population algorithm. It has four main tasks (see Fig. 4), the first two of which are pre-processing. The third, called text-based analysis, is a population task using matchings and textual indicators. The last task, called knowledge-based analysis, adds property assertions based on the ontology's knowledge. These tasks are described in the remaining of this section.

The Two Pre-processing Tasks. The first task consists in initialising the matching handler $MH = \{mh_1, mh_2, \ldots, mh_n\}$, a set used thorough the algorithm. Each *mh* corresponds to a matching and contains three attributes (individuals, assertions, previous linked individuals) initially empty.

The next task consists in instantiating the main class, to represent the document being processed. Hence, a new individual, hereafter called the *main instance*, instance of the main class, is added to O. In our document example, the individual *property1* is created with the assertion *<property1, isA, Property>* (*Property* being the main class, representing a real estate property).

Text-Based Analysis. This task is detailed at the bottom of Fig. 4. It analyses the matchings, adds individuals and assertions thanks to textual indicators.

Class Matching Processing. Each matching with a class (except the main class) is analyzed, to create a new individual, instance of this class. For the studied document example, the update of MH (added individuals and assertions) can be observed on the rows whose type is "class" in Table 1. These individuals and assertions are added to O. The preceding word(s) of a matching are checked against a list of negation keywords (e.g., "no"), and the matching is disregarded if a negation indicator is detected (e.g., "no garage"). If the preceding word corresponds to a number, multiple individuals are generated accordingly (e.g., "2 bedrooms" creates two instances of the class *Bedroom*).

Individual Matching Processing. Then, MH is updated for the matchings with individuals of O, by adding them. This can be observed on the rows corresponding to the type "individual" in Table 1.

Property Matching Processing. To instantiate a property, we need to determine the subject and object of the assertion. Subject candidate matchings are browsed, starting from the one preceding the property matching, going back to the beginning of the sentence. As soon as a candidate *mh* has individual(s) belonging to the property domain, these individual(s) are subject candidate(s). As for the objects, it depends on the type of the property. For object properties, we consider the matching immediately following the property mention. If such a matching exists, the individuals in its *mh* that are in the property range are considered as

Table 1. MH after dealing with class, individual and property matchings

Matching	Type	Individuals	Assertions	Prev. ind.
Cormelles-le-R.	individual	Cormelles-le-R		
house	class	house1	<house1, isA, House>	
located	object property			
min	data property	distance1	<distance1, isA, Distance>	
			<distance1, minCar, 15>	
city center	individual	city_center		
Caen	individual	Caen		
min walk	data property	~~distance1~~	~~<distance1, minWalk, 3>~~	
		distance2	<distance2, isA, Distance>	
			<distance2, minWalk, 3>	
shops	individual	shops		
schools	individual	schools		
m²	data property	house1	<house1, areaInM2, 110>	
land	class	land1	<land1, isA, Land>	
m²	data property	land1	<land1, areaInM2, 400>	
ground floor	individual	groundFloor		
kitchen	class	kitchen1	<kitchen1, isA, Kitchen>	
equipped	data property	kitchen1	<kitchen1, equipped, true>	
living room	class	livingRoom1	<livingRoom1, isA, LivingRoom>	
fireplace	class	fireplace1	<fireplace1, isA, Fireplace>	
facing	data property	livingRoom1	<livingRoom1, exposure, southwest>	
bedroom	class	bedroom1	<bedroom1, isA, Bedroom>	
m²	data property	bedroom1	<bedroom1, areaInM2, 15>	
First floor	individual	firstFloor		
bedrooms	class	bedroom2	<bedroom2, isA, Bedroom>	
		bedroom3	<bedroom3, isA, Bedroom>	
bathroom	class	bathroom1	<bathroom1, isA, Bathroom>	
Close to	object property	property1	<property1, isCloseTo, pubTransport>	
public transport	individual	pubTransport		property1
Land	class	land2	<land2, isA, Land>	
Fees : 4%	data property	property1	<property1, feePercentage, 4>	

possible objects. For data properties, the options vary based on the range and the matching source (e.g., unit or unit expression).

For each possible subject and object, a property assertion is added, provided that it does not create an inconsistency in O. The mh is updated: the new assertion(s) and their subject individual(s) are added respectively to the attributes *assertions* and *individuals*. The mh representing the object is also updated: the subject of the assertion is added in its attribute *previous linked individuals* (exploited in the following). If no assertion can be added, then the process is repeated with a new instance of the property domain as subject. Once all property matchings have been processed, all individuals in O that are inferred as equivalent are merged, and MH is updated based on this merger.

Table 1 shows the property matching handler on the example (cf. rows whose type is a property). First, the mention "located" refers to the object property *isLocatedIn* whose range is a municipality. It is not followed by a matching on a municipality: the property cannot be instantiated. The matching on "min" refers to the property *minCar* associating a distance to a numerical value in minutes. Its source is a unit ("min" is a unit associated with this property), so we consider the previous word for the value: 15. There is no instance of the class *Distance*, so the set of possible subjects is initially empty, and we take a new instance of *Distance* (*distance*1). Note that new individuals are named according to the class of which they are instances (for example, *distance*1 and *distance*2 for the class *Distance*); if the domain to instantiate is a class expression, then the new individuals are named *indiv*1, *indiv*2, etc. For the matching on "min walk", the process is the same, except that the set of possible subjects considers *distance*1 since it is an individual resulting from a matching preceding the one being processed, from the same sentence, and in the property domain. Therefore, we try to add an assertion $<distance1, minWalk, 3>$ but this one is inconsistent, because *distance*1 already represents 15 min by car. Thus, a new subject individual *distance*2 is created. All the assertions added are in the table. Note that, as the matching on "Close to" leads to the assertion $<property1, isCloseTo, publicTransport>$, *property*1 is a previous linked individual in the *mh* of "public transport".

Initialisation of the Linkabilities. In a descriptive context, verbs are not very meaningful (see Sect. 2). It is very likely to miss property assertions, due to an absence of property matching. The remaining of the population algorithm aims to add property assertions. To this end, we introduce an element called the linkabilities (*Lnk*). Its initialisation consists in creating all the linkabilities $Lnk(i)$ for each individual i from MH. An element of $Lnk(i)$ is a pair *(property, range class expression)*, such that i is linkable (via the property) to an individual belonging to the range class expression. In other words, for an individual i, we look for each property *prop* for which i can be a subject. Then, we look for the range expression to which an object *obj* of a possible assertion $<i, prop, obj>$ must necessarily belong. The set $Lnk(i)$ is automatically built for each i.

In the example, *property*1 belongs to the domain of *contains*, establishing a linkability. Now, *property*1 is an instance of *Property*, which is a subclass of the expression `contains only PartOfProperty`. Thus, the range expression associated with *property*1 and *contains* is the intersection of the range of *contains* (i.e., `PartOfProperty or Rooms`) and the class *PartOfProperty* (based on the definition with `only`). Therefore, the tuple (*contains, PartOfProperty*) is a linkability for *property*1. This means that *property*1 can only serve as the subject of an assertion of *contains* with instances of *PartOfProperty*.

The linkabilities $Lnk(i)$ are used in the following steps to find the most suitable property to link a subject i with an object j. The set $Lnk(i)$ will be browsed until a linkability is found such that j belongs to its range expression. $Lnk(i)$ is a sorted set. When several properties are candidates, finding the best one is not trivial. We give priority to specificity. The first elements are the linkabilities whose range is the most specific, then those whose property domain is the most specific. Otherwise, the sorting is arbitrarily, according to the property URI.

Processing of the Consecutive Matchings. This step checks if it is possible to link the individual(s) resulting from a matching with the one(s) from the following matching in the text, coming from the same sentence. Property assertions are added whenever it is possible. N-ary properties are taken into account. A succession of matchings involving respectively individuals a, b and c may lead to property assertions of the type $<a,...,b>$ and $<a,...,c>$. Here, the goal is to link a and b, which are from consecutive matchings, but also a and c, which are not.

The idea is to check if an individual (*subject*) from the current matching can be connected to an individual (*object*) from the next matching. If there are no associated individuals in the next mh, we move to the next one until we find an individual. If *subject* and *object* are not already connected, there might be a missing assertion. To determine the best property between these individuals, we consider the sorted set $Lnk(subject)$ and select the first property where *object* is in the range expression of the linkability and does not introduce any inconsistencies to O. The assertion is added in the subject's mh, and *subject* is also added as a previous linked individual of the object's mh. If there is no possible assertion between consecutive matchings, we attempt to make an assertion with the previous linked individuals as the subject to facilitate the population of n-ary properties. After examining the entire text, equivalent individuals in O are merged, and MH is updated accordingly.

Table 2. MH of the example after the processing of the consecutive matchings

Matching	Individuals	Assertions	Prev. linked ind.
Cormelles-le-R.	Cormelles-le-R.		
house	house1	<house1, isA, House>	
located			
min	distance1	<distance1, isA, Distance>	
		<distance1, minCar, 15>	
		<distance1, distFromPI, city center> (1)	
city center	city center	<distance1, distFromCity, Caen> (2)	distance1 (1)
Caen	Caen		distance1 (2)
min walk	distance2	<distance2, isA, Distance>	
		<distance2, minWalk, 3>	
		<distance2, distFromPI, shops> (3)	
shops	shops	<distance2, distFromPI, schools> (4)	distance2 (3)
schools	schools		distance2 (4)
...	...	...	...
living room	livingRoom1	<livingRoom1, isA, LivingRoom>	
		<livingRoom1, hasElement, fireplace1> (5)	
fireplace	fireplace1	<fireplace1, isA, Fireplace>	livingRoom1 (5)
...	...	...	

Table 2 shows the MH of the example after this step. First, we try to connect *Cormelles-le-R.* to *house1* (impossible), then *house1* to *distance1* (impossible), etc. We can connect *distance1* to *city center* via the property *distanceFromPointOfInterest* (1). The assertion is added in the subject mh (on the mention "min"). The next mh (on "city center") is updated with the previous linked individual *distance1*. Then, to link the mh on "city center" with the one on "Caen", we cannot connect the associated individuals. Nevertheless, we can link the previous linked individual, *distance1*, to *Caen* (2). And so on, we get (3)-(4)-(5).

Processing of Individuals Without Predecessors. The last step of the text-based analysis deals with individuals without predecessors. Indeed, each document describes an instance of the main class, which should be the starting point of property assertions. It seems quite intuitive to think that every individual considered, except the main instance, must be the object of at least one assertion. Thus, the goal is to find subjects and properties for individuals (except for the main instance) without predecessors, i.e., not being the object of a property assertion. To minimise the risk of linking individuals that have nothing to do with each other, we focus only on the individuals resulting from the matchings of a same sentence. This means that, for each individual without predecessors (*object*) of a sentence, we try to connect another individual from the same sentence (*subject*) to it, in order to obtain the assertion $<subject, prop, object>$, where the property *prop* is the "best" regarding the linkabilities. Finally, any individuals in O that are inferred as equivalent are merged, and MH is updated based on this merger.

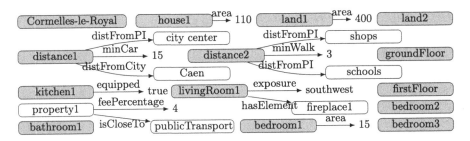

Fig. 5. Individuals and property assertions from the studied example, before the processing of the individuals without predecessors

Figure 5 shows the individuals (nodes) and property assertions (edges) before this step for the studied example. Individuals without predecessors (except the main instance *property*1) are shaded. Table 3 details what is done at this stage. Each row corresponds to a sentence. Individuals without predecessors are in italics. For each of them, we search if it is possible to add an assertion having

Table 3. The processing of the individuals without predecessors in the studied example

#	Individuals	Assertions
1	*Cormelles-le-Royal, house1, distance1,* city center, Caen, *distance2,* shops, schools, *land1*	<del>< distance1, distFromCity, Cormelles-le-R. ></del> <del>< distance2, distFromCity, Cormelles-le-R. ></del> not added because inconsistent
2	*groundFloor, kitchen1, livingRoom1,* fireplace1, *bedroom1*	<kitchen1, isOnFloor, *groundFloor*> <livingRoom1, isOnFloor, *groundFloor*> <bedroom1, isOnFloor, *groundFloor*>
3	*firstFloor, bedroom2, bedroom3, bathroom1*	<bedroom2, isOnFloor, *firstFloor*> <bedroom3, isOnFloor, *firstFloor*> <bathroom1, isOnFloor, *firstFloor*>
4	property1, publicTransport	
5	*land2*	
6	property1	

for subject an individual of the same sentence. The only two possibilities for the first sentence are given in the last column but they are not added because they are inconsistent. This principle is repeated for each sentence. The assertions mentioned in Table 3 are obtained and added in O and MH.

Knowledge-Based Analysis. The last task is based on the knowledge from O. It exploits O, MH and Lnk. Ideally, from the main instance, all the individuals concerned by a document should be reachable. The goal is to add property assertions to establish a connected graph, starting from the main instance. Figure 6(top) shows the individuals (nodes) and object property assertions (edges) of the studied example. Only *publicTransport* is reachable from *property1*.

Individuals are put into batches, each individual being in exactly one batch. Each batch is created from an individual i and contains the individuals reachable from i (either directly or through a sequence of assertions). The *main batch* consists of the main instance and the individuals accessible from it. Then, the remaining individuals are considered: the one with the least predecessors is taken (alphabetical order of URI in case of equality), its batch is created, and the process continues until every individual is in one batch. In the studied example, the first division into batches is shown with frames at the top of Fig. 6. The *main batch* is composed of *property1* and *publicTransport*. The individual with the fewest predecessors (first in alphabetical order) is *bathroom1*. The next batch consists of *bathroom1* and *firstFloor*. And so on, batches are built.

The goal is to access all the individuals from the main instance. To this end, once the batches are built, we try to link the main instance to an individual of each batch (except the main batch). Within a batch, the individuals are sorted in ascending order based on the number of predecessors (and then in alphabetical order). For each batch, we attempt to create an property assertion between the main instance (as the subject) and each individual in the given order (as the object), stopping as soon as a valid property assertion is possible. In the studied example, *distance2* is placed first in the batch {*distance2*, *shops*, *schools*} because it has no predecessors. Using the linkabilities, we determine whether the main instance *property1* can be linked to *distance2*. This is the case via the property *isLocatedAtDistance*. This process is repeated for each batch, resulting in six assertions as shown in the middle of Fig. 6.

Next, individuals that are inferred to be equivalent are merged, and MH is updated based on this merger. In our example ontology, a real estate property can contain only one land. A reasoner identifies *land1* and *land2* as equivalent. They are merged into *land1* (see bottom of Fig. 6).

The same process (creating batches, adding assertions, merging) is repeated, but considering all individuals that are at a distance of 1 from the main instance as subjects, i.e., individuals for which there is an assertion between the main class and them. In other words, the distance of an individual i can be defined as the minimal number of edges between the main instance and i. This distance is progressively incremented. We stop either when the main batch contains all individuals or when we have already attempted to link every individual in

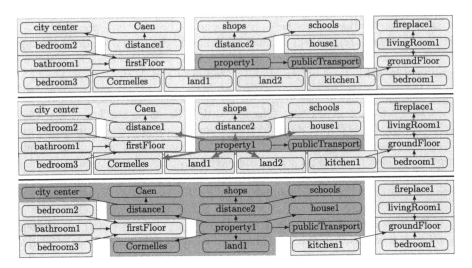

Fig. 6. Knowledge-based analysis: First division into batches (top), first additions of assertions (middle), fusion and second division into batches (bottom)

the main batch. In the example, the batch splitting algorithm is applied again, resulting in the batches shown at the bottom of Fig. 6. We now search for assertions where the subject is at a distance of 1 from the main class (*Cormelles*, *distance*1, *distance*2, *house*1, *land*1 and *publicTransport*). The algorithm enables us to derive six assertions: <*house*1, *contains*, *bathroom*1/*bedroom*1/ *bedroom*2/*bedroom*3/*kitchen*1/*livingRoom*1>. Afterwards, only one batch remains: all elements are accessible from the main instance. The process is stopped.

The example unfolded in this paper is an illustration where KOnPoTe works well. However, the algorithm can generate wrong assertions or miss correct ones. The subsequent section evaluates the algorithm's performance.

4   Experiments and Evaluation

This section reports an evaluation of the proposed approach on one use case: house sale classified ads. KOnPoTe is implemented in Java and uses OWL API [7] to handle the ontology; Stanford NLP [13] to split the texts into sentences; two French lemmatizers: A. Aker's one[1] and TreeTagger [16]; and Openllet reasoner[2]. The experimental protocol and the results obtained are discussed.

4.1   Experimental Protocol

We automatically extracted a corpus from a website[3]. It contains 78 French ads, annotated as sales of a house in Caen. Structured information has been extracted,

---

[1] http://staffwww.dcs.shef.ac.uk/people/A.Aker/activityNLPProjects.html.
[2] https://github.com/Galigator/openllet.
[3] https://www.lecoindelimmo.com/.

but our focus is solely on the textual descriptions of each ad. The ontology, manually built, describes the domain of house sales and adheres to the constraints mentioned in Sect. 3.1. Initially, it contains a few generic individuals, such as *double glazing, public transport,* etc., as well as named entities corresponding to city or village names. On a larger scale, we would require an extensive list of cities, but for this experiment, we chose to represent only those mentioned in the corpus. We constructed a Gold Standard ontology (GS). This GS is the initial ontology manually populated with assertions representing the corpus descriptions. We test KOnPoTe on the initial ontology and each description from the corpus, and then compare the final ontology with the GS, computing precision, recall, and F-measure.

$$Precision = \frac{TP}{TP + FP} \qquad Recall = \frac{TP}{TP + FN} \qquad F\text{-}measure = \frac{2 \times Precision \times Recall}{Precision + Recall}$$

Property assertions are defined as true positives (TP), false positives (FP) or false negatives (FN). A TP is an assertion present in both the GS and the output O. A FP is an assertion present in the output O but absent in the GS. A FN is an assertion present in the GS but absent in the output O. To be as fair as possible in our results, we set three rules. First of all, (1) class assertions are not taken into account because they are often redundant with property assertions, e.g., via domain or range definitions. Moreover, the real issue of our problem lies in the property assertions, as the class assertions are often derived from class matchings. (2) Inferred assertions are taken into account. For example, if the GS contains $<a, prop, b>$ and the resulting ontology contains $<b, inverse(prop), a>$, then we want to realize that these two assertions amount to the same thing. (3) We ignore properties that lead us to count several times a same element. For example, if there is a property and its inverse, we end up with two assertions designating the same thing. The assertions of one of these two are ignored.

Experimental files are available[4]. KOnPoTe creates URIs that are not necessarily the same as the ones from the GS. To evaluate these cases, manual equivalences are defined between the individuals of the GS and those of the output ontology. Furthermore, the approach can generate equivalent individuals, without detecting their equivalence. In this case, we assume that an equivalence axiom (owl:sameAs) is missing and count it as a missing assertion (a FN).

4.2   Results and Discussion

Our problem differs from related work (see Sect. 2), so there are no existing baselines that can be considered for a fair comparison. We evaluate KOnPoTe and analyze the contribution of its main modules. The first baseline we use, called *Baseline*, consists in processing only the class, individual and property matchings (the first three steps of the text-based analysis). Then, in *Baseline+cons.*, we

---

[4] Experimental files (inputs, outputs for all tested approaches, and GS) are at https://doi.org/10.5281/zenodo.5776752. A zip file with a runnable jar for KOnPote with Aker's lemmatizer is at https://alec.users.greyc.fr/research/konpote/.

add the processing of the consecutive matchings (and the initialisation of linka-bilities). In *Text-based analysis*, we include the processing of individuals without predecessors, and finally in *KOnPoTe*, we add the knowledge-based analysis.

Table 4. Results on KOnPoTe and three baselines

Approach	Prec.$_{mac}$	Recall$_{mac}$	F-measure$_{mac}$	Prec.$_{mic}$	Recall$_{mic}$	F-measure$_{mic}$
KOnPoTe$_{Aker}$	**0.9516**	**0.8740**	**0.9079**	**0.9465**	**0.8606**	**0.9015**
KOnPoTe$_{TT}$	0.9496	0.8681	0.9039	0.9446	0.8545	0.8973
Text-based analysis$_{Aker}$	0.8989	0.4648	0.5994	0.8956	0.4726	0.6188
Text-based analysis$_{TT}$	0.8964	0.4579	0.5929	0.8937	0.4662	0.6127
Baseline+cons.$_{Aker}$	0.8911	0.3138	0.4440	0.8741	0.3085	0.4561
Baseline+cons.$_{TT}$	0.8879	0.3081	0.4377	0.8732	0.3036	0.4505
Baseline$_{Aker}$	0.9234	0.1922	0.3099	0.9135	0.1926	0.3182
Baseline$_{TT}$	0.9230	0.1888	0.3054	0.9138	0.1892	0.3135

Table 4 shows the results. Approaches are tested with the two lemmatizers (*Aker* and *TT*). Each metric is computed both macroscopically (*mac*) and micro-scopically (*mic*). The macro-computation is the average of the metrics of each ad (each ad has the same weight), whereas the micro-computation considers the sum of all VP, FP, FN of each ad (each assertion has the same weight).

Aker performs better than *TreeTagger*, but the difference is relatively low. The added modules have a good contribution on the results, since the addition of each one generates a relatively high gain of F-measure. First, the baseline achieves a relatively high precision score (>0.9) but a low recall score (<0.2). Most of the assertions that are made are correct, but a lot of assertions are miss-ing. Adding modules enables us to include mostly correct assertions. Indeed, as modules are added, we are able to increase the recall without losing to much precision. More precisely, the consecutive matching processing introduces some noise (resulting in a slight loss of precision) but increases the recall by half (from ∼0.2 to ∼0.3). Processing individuals without predecessors also increases the recall by half (from ∼0.3 to ∼0.45), without a noticeable decrease in precision (slightly increasing it). Lastly, the knowledge-based analysis makes a significant contribution. It results in an increase in both precision and recall, leading to a 50% increase in F-measure (from ∼0.6 to ∼0.9). These three modules are essen-tial as they add numerous missing assertions while maintaining a low number of false assertions.

5   Conclusion and Future Work

This paper presents KOnPoTe, a fully automatic generic approach to populate a domain ontology from textual descriptions of objects in that domain. KOnPoTe is a processing chain that yields promising results in its initial experiment. Its algorithm is based solely on the context of the problem (textual descriptions of objects) rather than relying on domain-specific linguistic rules.

In future work, we will experiment the approach on new domains: other types of ads (such as boat sales), various descriptions (hotels, restaurants, etc.). Of course, this is time-consuming: constitution of the corpus, of the ontology, of the gold standard, as well as potential equivalences between the gold standard and the KOnPoTe output ontology, and potential missing equivalence links in the output. Another idea is to test KOnPoTe on the same domain and corpus but with different ontologies (same terminology but different representation choices). A deep analysis of such an experiment could lead to a set of guidelines for representing the input ontology. Lastly, our final goal is to use KOnPoTe followed by a reasoning step to address the problem of erroneous annotations mentioned in Sect. 1. The main idea is to deal with inconsistencies between the output triples of KOnPoTe and the annotations. For example, if KOnPoTe states that a house is in $city\_1$, whereas the annotation states it is in $city\_2$ (different from $city\_1$), then this inconsistency needs to be handled.

Acknowledgements. We thank Quentin Leroy and Jean-Philippe Kotowicz for their participation in the ontology design, and Enor-Anaïs Carré and Morgan Gueret for the corpus.

References

1. Alani, H., et al.: Automatic ontology-based knowledge extraction and tailored biography generation from the web. IEEE Intell. Syst. **18**, 14–21 (2003)
2. Ayadi, A., Samet, A., de Bertrand de Beuvron, F., Zanni-Merk, C.: Ontology population with deep learning-based NLP: a case study on the Biomolecular Network Ontology. Procedia Comput. Sci. **159**, 572–581 (2019)
3. Castano, S., et al.: Multimedia interpretation for dynamic ontology evolution. J. Logic Comput. **19**(5), 859–897 (2008)
4. Chasseray, Y., Barthe-Delanoë, A.M., Négny, S., Le Lann, J.M.: A generic metamodel for data extraction and generic ontology population. J. Inf. Sci. **48**(6), 838–856 (2022)
5. Faria, C., Serra, I., Girardi, R.: A domain-independent process for automatic ontology population from text. Sci. Comput. Program. **95**, 26–43 (2014)
6. Gasmi, H., Laval, J., Bouras, A.: Cold-start cybersecurity ontology population using information extraction with LSTM. In: CSET, Doha, Qatar, pp. 1–6 (2019)
7. Horridge, M., Bechhofer, S.: The OWL API: a Java API for working with OWL 2 ontologies. In: OWLED, Aachen, DEU, pp. 49–58 (2009)
8. Horrocks, I., et al.: SWRL: A Semantic Web Rule Language Combining OWL and RuleML. Technical report, World Wide Web Consortium (2004)
9. Jayawardana, V., et al.: Semi-supervised instance population of an ontology using word vector embedding. In: ICTer, September 2017. IEEE (2017)
10. Korger, A., Baumeister, J.: Rule-based semantic relation extraction in regulatory documents. In: LWDA. CEUR Workshop Proceedings, September 2021, vol. 2993, pp. 26–37 (2021)
11. Lubani, M., Noah, S.A.M., Mahmud, R.: Ontology population: approaches and design aspects. J. Inf. Sci. **45**, 502–515 (2019)

12. Makki, J., Alquier, A.M., Prince, V.: Ontology population via NLP techniques in risk management. Int. J. Humanit. Soc. Sci. **3**, 212–217 (2009)
13. Manning, C.D., et al.: The Stanford CoreNLP natural language processing toolkit. In: ACL System Demonstrations, pp. 55–60 (2014)
14. Oramas, S., Sordo, M., Espinosa-Anke, L.: A rule-based approach to extracting relations from music Tidbits. In: WWW, Florence, Italy, pp. 661–666 (2015)
15. Reyes-Ortiz, J.A.: Criminal event ontology population and enrichment using patterns recognition from text. IJPRAI **33**(11), 1940014 (2019)
16. Schmid, H.: Probabilistic part-of-speech tagging using decision trees (1994)
17. Staab, S., Studer, R.: Handbook on Ontologies. Springer, Heidelberg (2009). https://doi.org/10.1007/978-3-540-92673-3
18. Suchanek, F., Ifrim, G., Weikum, G.: LEILA: learning to extract information by linguistic analysis. In: Workshop on Ontology Learning and Population, Sydney, Australia, pp. 18–25 (2006)

Graph Extraction for Assisting Crash Simulation Data Analysis

Anahita Pakiman[1,2(✉)] [iD], Jochen Garcke[1,3] [iD], and Axel Schumacher[2] [iD]

[1] Fraunhofer SCAI, Sankt, Germany
anahita.pakiman@scai.fraunhofer.de
[2] Bergische Universität Wuppertal, Wuppertal, Germany
[3] Institut für Numerische Simulation, Universität Bonn, Bonn, Germany

Abstract. In this work, we establish a method for abstracting information from Computer Aided Engineering (CAE) into graphs. Such graph representations of CAE data can improve design guidelines and support recommendation systems by enabling the comparison of simulations, highlighting unexplored experimental designs, and correlating different designs. We focus on the load-path in crashworthiness analysis, a complex sub-discipline in vehicle design. The load-path is the sequence of parts that absorb most of the energy caused by the impact. To detect the load-path, we generate a directed weighted graph from the CAE data. The vertices represent the vehicle's parts, and the edges are an abstraction of the connectivity of the parts. The edge direction follows the temporal occurrence of the collision, where the edge weights reflect aspects of the energy absorption. We introduce and assess three methods for graph extraction and an additional method for further updating each graph with the sequences of absorption. Based on longest-path calculations, we introduce an automated detection of the load-path, which we analyse for the different graph extraction methods and weights. Finally, we show how our method for the detection of load-paths helps in the classification and labelling of CAE simulations.

Keywords: Automotive · CAE Knowledge · Graph Extraction · Weighted-Directed Graph · Flow Calculation · Load-path Detection

1 Introduction

We live in an interconnected world, and graph theory provides powerful tools for modelling and analysing this interconnectedness. In graph theory, graphs are usually given in advance or easily abstracted from problems. However, for many real-world scenarios, the individual data instantiations of modelled graphs need to be determined from the data before further analysis. Therefore, the construction of high-quality graphs has become an increasingly desirable research problem, resulting in many graph construction methods in recent years [1]. Furthermore, knowledge graph (KG)s have become a new form of knowledge representation and are the cornerstone of several applications for specific use cases

M. Ojeda-Aciego et al. (Eds.): ICCS 2023, LNAI 14133, pp. 171–185, 2023.
https://doi.org/10.1007/978-3-031-40960-8_14

in industry. The graph underlying the abstract structure, which effectively facilitates domain conceptualisation and data management, is the reason for the growing interest in this technology. Moreover, the use of KG is the direct driver of several artificial intelligence applications [2]. Towards vehicle KG, we aim to capture knowledge about vehicle development designs by automatically extracting graphs from a finite element (FE) model representing a vehicle.

The simplest scenario for identifying the connectivity of a graph is when it is associated with a physical problem related to the graph. Such graphs include electrical circuits, power grids, linear heat transfer, social and computer networks, and spring-mass systems [3]. In this work, we are interested in crashworthiness studies in vehicle design, where the transformation of crash simulation data into a graph is a challenging and unexplored area of research. With the resulting representation, we aim to provide an abstraction of the problem that allows the use of graph theory methods for further automated analysis of the simulations.

Computer aided engineering (CAE) analysis, mostly with the finite element method (FEM), enables car manufacturers to analyse many design scenarios, nowadays between 10,000 to 30,000 simulations per week [4]. In crashworthiness analysis, CAE engineers optimise the distribution of impact energy in the vehicle structure to reduce injuries to occupants or vulnerable road users. How to characterise the sequence of absorbed energy, known as the load-path, is a fundamental question in this analysis. The results of crash simulations include several outputs, such as deformations, accelerations and internal energy. However, the load-path is not explicitly calculated in a crash simulation. Therefore, a CAE engineer must visualise the sequence to reveal the load-path. In this work, we propose and investigate graph representations for an automated identification of the load-path from the simulation data.

We consider parts of the FE model entities as vertices of the structural graph following the scheme of [5]. We want to detect the graph edges that resemble the structural connectivity of the vehicle. We propose three approaches to determine this structural graph: component-based graph (CBG), single part-based graph (sPBG) and multi part-based graph (mPBG). The CBG follows two steps: finding the connection of the components (a group of parts) and then identifying the connection of the parts in each component. The sPBG and mPBG graphs have additional steps to convert the component connections to part connections, which requires the detection of the parts that are entangled in the connection that is supporting the flow of energy.

Defining the vehicle structure as a graph is the first step in load-path detection. Secondly, we compute it as the longest path in weighted directed graphs, where the edge weights between the parts shall represent the energy flow during the crash. We study different edge weighting functions for three graph extraction scenarios and analyse the determined load-paths from an engineering perspective. In this work, the investigation is carried out on the frontal structure of a complete vehicle with a multi-scenario load-path in a full frontal load case. But, our approach is applicable to different impact directions and load case scenarios.

In summary, the main contributions of this work are:

- the conversion of a vehicle structure to a weighted directed graph,
- the extraction of features representing the energy flow,
- a further graph segmentation that captures the time sequence of events,
- an automated detection of the load-path,
- the clustering of simulations based on their load-paths.

2 Related Work

Recently, a graph schema to model vehicle development with a focus on crash safety was introduced in [5]. The graph modelling considers the CAE data in the context of the R&D development process and vehicle safety, with the aim to enable searchability, filtering, recommendation, and prediction for crash CAE data during the development process. In [5], the car parts are directly connected to their simulation, and the parts between the simulations have a connection to similar design based on the properties ID (PID) of the parts. But, connections between the parts of one simulation are missing, therefore the vehicle's structure and its connectivity is not modelled. Thus, incorporating the vehicle structure into the graph structure will enrich the data representation.

In crashworthiness, graphs have been used to predict the response of the vehicle [6] or barrier [7] with so-called bond graphs. The bond graphs available for vehicle crashes represent the problem from the perspective of a mass-spring model [6]. Bond graphs are ideal for visualising the essential properties of a system because their graphical nature separates the system structure from the equations [8]. Bond graphs represent the vehicle structure by summarising the physical elements and connections. However, to the best of our knowledge, there is no way of automatically extracting the vehicle structure as a bond graph.

Before the growth of computing power allowed large FEM analysis, there were other modelling techniques that simplified the problem to a mass-spring model. The advantage of the mass-spring model is that it can be easily represented as a weighted graph. SISAME (Structural Impact Simulation And Model-Extraction) is a general-purpose tool for the extraction and simulation of one-dimensional non-linear lumped parameter structural models [9]. Using SISAME, mass element weights and spring element load-paths were optimally extracted directly from the test data accelerations and wall forces [10]. However, the lumped mass spring (LMS) modelling is one-dimensional and focuses mainly on accurately modelling the test data rather than representing the structural performance of the vehicle. Later the deformation space models (DSM) model was introduced [11] to compensate for the limitations of the LMS. It can only roughly capture displacements and energy absorption, neglecting connections and interactions with other components.

Another use of graphs in crash analysis is in the structural optimisation of the vehicle [12,13]. Here, the optimisation method adds vertices and edges to stiffen the structure, starting with a simple graph describing the perimeter of the vehicle. The focus of these studies is to search with a graph for the optimal solution of the vehicle design. As a result, to complete the vehicle design and ensure safety performance, further processes and CAE analysis are required.

To summarise, automatically converting a crash FE model in vehicle development to a graph is still an open research question. Depending on the detail required in a graph, there are several ways to represent an FE model of a vehicle. As a specific application, we investigate how adding connections to the graph will allow a load-path analysis for each simulation. For that, we use and extend the recently introduced energy absorption features [14], which characterize the simulation's behaviour, as edge features to enable the load-path detection.

3   Graph Extraction

It is a challenging task to generate a graph representing the structure of a vehicle from CAE data. Finding the connectivity of the parts is complex due to the number of connections, the variety of FE modelling techniques and the variety of physical types of connections. The best way to obtain this information would be to use the computer aided design (CAD) database, which is more standardised than CAE. However, this data depends on the company's workflow to maintain the link between the CAE and CAD models, which has yet to be well established. In addition, these databases lack information on the dependencies of the part connections, i.e. all parts are connected without any hierarchy. This hierarchy is essential for defining the direction of the edges and for identifying the vertices of the graph as either dead ends or capable of allowing energy to flow through the structure. As a result, we are looking for a method to perform this intelligently using the FE model, based on the location and closeness of parts therein.

The FE model contains mesh faces and volumes with different entities representing the connections. The mesh is defined by nodes and elements, where the element size defines the resolution of the discretization. The nodes can represent the vertices and the elements define the edges for a graph defined as $G(V, E)$ with vertices and edges. Consequently, a FE model mesh itself represents a graph. However, this graph has drawbacks. A small element size, three to five mm, for a complete vehicle will result in a large number of vertices, up to 20 million, which is computationally expensive for graph machine learning (GML) and the lack of semantics makes it difficult to analyse engineering concepts. Coarsening the crash FE mesh is an alternative, which is a topic in FE modelling [15–17]. However, rather than focusing on post-processing aspects, these studies have mainly focused on reducing the compute time of the FE simulation. Nevertheless, the result will still be a disconnected graph because a FE model contains multiple meshes whose connectivity is not element based. Therefore, we focus on linking FE entities to extract the structure of a vehicle as a connected graph.

To determine the connectivity, we split the graph extraction problem into two steps. First, component-level connectivity and then connectivity of parts within a component. Thereby we keep hierarchy information in the graph structure. Previously, we introduced a grouping method for identifying components [18]. Here, we extend this method to search for connections between components. In addition, we add edges to the graph that connect parts that belong to the same component. To include timing in the graph, we also investigate to add a timing segmentation based on the timing of outgoing edges, see Sect. 4.2.

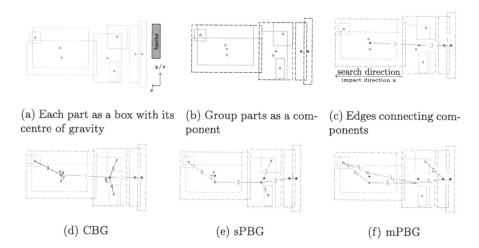

(a) Each part as a box with its centre of gravity

(b) Group parts as a component

(c) Edges connecting components

(d) CBG

(e) sPBG

(f) mPBG

Fig. 1. Abstracted visualization of the stages for graph extraction. While the method works in 3D, we here show a 2D visualisation. Solid squares: part, dashed square: component, circle: part box center of gravity (COG), triangle: component box COG, green edges: component to component, blue edges: component to part, red edges: part to part. (Color figure online)

We consider the parts of the FE entities as vertices of the structural graph of the vehicle, which follows the scheme of [5]. We want to detect the edges that resemble the structural connectivity of the vehicle, and we propose three scenarios to do this: CBG, sPBG and mPBG. We need to extract information from the structure of the vehicle to obtain the connectivity between parts. To do this, we create 3D axis-aligned boxes for each part that contain the volume of the part's geometry, Fig. 1a. Then, based on the overlap of the boxes, we define rules to group them as components, Fig. 1b, and later form the structure of the graph from the overlap of the boxes. In the following three subsections, we will discuss the detailed differences between these methods and for now only describe the general idea. The CBG follows two steps: finding the connections between components, Fig. 1c, and then determining the part connectivity in each component, Fig. 1d. sPBG and mPBG have additional steps to convert component connections to part connections, which requires identifying the parts involved in the connectivity that supports the energy flow. We explore two scenarios for this as single and multi-part-based graphs, Figs. 1e and 1f, respectively. For all these methods, we consider a directed graph whose directions are set to have a positive inner product with the impact axis, direction x in Fig. 1a and Algorithm 1.

Algorithm 1. edge direction for vertices A and B, impact direction x

Input: TVL: Threshold Limit Value

if $\|AB\| < TLV$ then
    if $\overrightarrow{AB} \cdot \overrightarrow{x} > 0$ then
        connect A to B
    else
        connect B to A
    end if
end if

3.1 CBG

The construction of CBG requires first the detection of the components and then the detection of the connections between components. The component detection considers each part to be a box, then groups them together as a component, and finally evaluates the component box. For CBG, in addition to the part vertices, we also introduce component vertices into the graph. The location of these vertices is at the centre of the components and the component parts are connected to them. For example, in Fig. 1a with eight parts, four components are detected and corresponding component boxes are generated, in Fig. 1b. Then, using a threshold value (TLV), our algorithm searches for immediately adjacent components. The thresholding allows having several neighbours. The search algorithm sorts components by impact direction, starting from the impactor/barrier position and moving into the vehicle along the impact direction, e.g. x in Fig. 1c. Finally, we connect all of the parts in each of the components to the component box.

The result at this stage, Fig. 1d, is a connected graph, which is a heterogeneous graph of parts and components. Evaluating the longest path for a heterogeneous graph requires additional evaluation of edge features between vertices of different types. Therefore, our goal is to modify this graph into a homogeneous graph. First, we consider only the components as vertices, delete the vertices of the parts, and evaluate the features of the component vertices based on the parts, as we introduced earlier in [18]. This graph is CBG and doesn't contain the detailed features of all the parts. Another approach is to use the heterogeneous graph as an input to find further connectivities of the parts. We explore this approach in Sects. 3.2 and 3.3.

3.2 sPBG

The sPBG is a basic approach to convert the heterogeneous part-component graph into a part graph by transferring the component vertex and its corresponding edges to a part vertex. Because of the single part selection, we call it sPBG and we consider an alternative multiple part scenario in Sect. 3.3. There are several ways to determine the corresponding part for each component. First, we use a simple scenario and select the largest part, the geometric aspect of the component, as the corresponding vertex for the component connection. For example, in Fig. 1e with this consideration, the ○- 1 -○ remains in the same position as the component-part graph because the connecting components contain a single part. The edges ○- 2,4,5 -○ move from the component box to the largest part, so ○- 6 -○ is removed. Finally, the edge ○- 7 -○ disappears in the last components and edges ○- 8,9 -○ move to the other end of edge seven.

The sPBG graph is characterised by having a main connection from the beginning to the end of vehicles with several dead ends for each master part. We expect that the identification of the energy flow of the simulation will be limited by the existence of many dead ends. Furthermore, for sPBG a single part is the representative of a component and therefore only a single part interacts with the other parts, which in some cases is not appropriate. For example, the side-member, which is a thin-walled structure, has two U-sections welded and several reinforcement plates. In this example, information about the interactions of the other U-profiles and reinforcement plates will be missed if only one part is considered to represent the component. Next, we consider multiple connections between the components with mPBG. Multiple connections reinforce the lack of internal connections compared to sPBG.

3.3   mPBG

The mPBG is an alternative to sPBG by allowing multiple representatives for components. This approach allows for part interactions in the components and between components. Here we transfer and distribute the component vertices using the information from the component discovery process, rather than selecting the largest box. As described in [18], our component detection algorithm has two scenarios for identifying the components: full and partial overlap merge. Full overlap means a box is completely within the parent box, whereas partial overlap addresses partially overlapping scenarios. These two scenarios are treated differently for mPBG extraction. In the case of a full merge, the part is connected to its parent box, similar to sPBG. However, in partial overlap scenarios, both boxes will represent the component. In this case, a component vertex is transferred to all partially overlapped boxes. Nevertheless, each part will retain its connections to the child based on full merges. Figure 1f visualises these two scenarios. The edge ○- 2,3 -○ branches to two edges ○- $2_1,2_2$ -○ and ○- $3_1,3_2$ -○ respectively compared to the sPBG due to a partial merge. Furthermore, the edge ○- 9 -○ branches to ○- $9_1,9_2$ -○ since it is added after the partial merge and belongs to both parent boxes.

4   Load-Path Detection

Understanding how an external load is transferred to a given structure helps to evaluate the performance of different components, improve structural strength and reduce structural weight in structural design and optimisation. The so-called load-path of a component is a concept for tracking the transferred load within a structure, starting from the load points and ending at the support points, which has been studied in structural design for several years [19]. Reviews of different approaches to load-path detection are proposing a new metric to find detailed load-paths at mesh size for better component design. However, we are interested in the load-path in the context of crash analysis, which involves the interaction of several components. Load-paths are typically defined as vehicle parts capable of generating resisting forces during a crash event [20]. To identify load-paths during a crash, nine load-paths were first defined and classified in [20]. These can be easily examined for signs of loading after a crash. On the other hand, this work mainly introduces new measures for evaluating real crashes.

We aim to identify the load-path to be able to compare simulations by high-lighting the importance of different paths during the crash. We use the longest path calculation[1] to find the load-paths involved in absorbing the crash energy. In this calculation, we aim to look at the internal energy absorption of the parts since manufacturers optimise the energy absorption capabilities of the load-paths [20]. To achieve this, we use the so-called internal energy IE features introduced in [14]. Initially, one has an unweighted graph with IE features for vertices. An essential step is to convert vertex features into edge weights. In this way, the edge weights hold the absorption characteristics and instead of the longest unweighted path, we compute the potential load-path.

In the following subsections, we first introduce the edge weights as a single feature of the internal energy flow, f_{IE}, and the time segmentation, s_t. f_{IE} is computed from the vertices maximum absorbed internal energy (IE_{max}) using internal energy flow calculation, see Sect. 4.1. For s_t we update the graph with time segmentation to have absorption time features on the edges, see Sect. 4.2. Finally, in Sect. 4.3 we will present several ways to combine edge features.

4.1   Internal Energy Flow

We consider the flow equation for the propagation of the internal energy maximum IE_{max} feature from the vertices to the edges, f_{IE}. Our graph is a directed weighted graph $G(V, E)$ with vertices V, edges E and a weight $w(e)$ assigned to each edge. We assume that the energy flow from vertex i to j, $w_{i,j}$, is represented by an edge weight between vertices i and j. The energy flow equation relates the absorbed internal energy IE_j of a vertex v_j to the balance of the input and output IE from that vertex to its neighbours:

$$IE_j = \sum_{n \in I(j)} w_{n,j} - \sum_{n \in O(j)} w_{j,n}. \tag{1}$$

For a vertex v in a graph, we denote by $I(v)$ and $O(v)$ the set of in-neighbours and out-neighbours of v, respectively. We start computing edge weights with vertices that only have incoming edges, called dead ends. We compute the flow from the dead ends, backwards along their edge directions, to find the inflow of the dead

---

[1] The longest path in a directed acyclic graph, `dag_longest_path()`, from NetworkX.

ends vertices. The active vertices for the next step calculation are the source vertices to the dead ends. Consequently, if all their outflow energy is available, we can find the inflow energy to the active vertices. Until all its outflows are known, a vertex is withheld from being an active vertex. In addition, there is a different treatment for the dead ends at vertices that have an inflow degree of zero. These source-only vertices reflect where the impact is initiated and where accordingly the kinetic energy input takes place. Therefore, these vertices are not considered when they are marked as active vertices. Instead, the edge weights of these source-only vertices are calculated when their outgoing neighbours are the active vertices. In some cases, the weights of all their outgoing edges have already been evaluated, but the active vertices may have more than one incoming edge. In this case, the energy flow is partitioned to the in-degree, $I(v)$. An unequal stiffness of the structure does not allow an equal distribution. Therefore, equal partitioning can lead to errors in the flow calculation, which we discuss in 5.1.

4.2   Time Segmentation

To convert the vertex absorption times into edge weights is more complex than the handling of IE_{max}. This is because the graph connectivity of the vertices differs from the time sequence of the parts that absorb energy. Moreover, the time information of each vertex is an absorption interval (Δt), initial absorption time t_i to final absorption time t_n, which may overlap with one of its neighbours. In the example shown in Fig. 2, we demonstrate the time segmentation for vertex j with two successors of l and k. In this figure, the absorption period of each vertex is plotted as a vector along the time axis. The overlap of these vectors highlights the need for time segmentation, see Fig. 2a. To overcome this, we segment the time interval of the absorption for each vertex. The segmentation is based on the t_i value of the successors of the vertex.

Accordingly, we add vertices to the graph for each segmented time and connect each successor vertex to the vertex added for time segmentation. In this example, a vertex is added to the graph for each successor vertex, l and k, see Fig. 2b. Note that if some of the successors have the same t_i, then only one vertex will be added. In addition, to include the total absorption, an extra vertex is

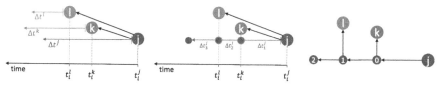

(a) Initial state of the graph before time segmentation.   (b) Adding vertices according to the successors.   (c) The graph after adding time segmentation vertices.

Fig. 2. An example of time segmentation process for a vertex j with two outgoing edges to the successors vertices of k and l. The time axis shows the t_i value for each vertex and absorption time with an arrow in front of each vertex.

added to represent the total absorption vector as the sum of $\delta t^j = \delta t_1^j + \delta t_2^j + \delta t_3^j$, see Fig. 2c. Then we sort the t_i of the successor vertices to find the connection between the new vertices. Finally, the directed edges containing the time sequences and durations are added and the old edges are deleted, see Fig. 2c. Additionally, we add the initial timing t_i^k as a vertex feature for the kth segment, so that all vertices have a t_i. Finally, the edge weight s_t for time segmentation is for a directed edge from m to n defined by $s_t := t_i^m - t_i^n$.

4.3   Feature Combination

We consider two approaches to combine IE_{max} and the timings of part absorption. In the first approach, we modify the vertex feature IE_{max} according to the absorption time before the flow computation from Sect. 4.1. To do this we look at the integration of the IE curve over time, $IE\Delta t$. The start and end of the integration are set to the minimum $t_{i_{min}}$ and maximum $t_{n_{max}}$ of the absorption times, t_i and t_n, respectively, over all parts. To simplify the calculation, we divide the area under the curve IE into three zones. For each zone the area under the curve, A, is calculated:

- $(t_{i_{min}}, \; t_i)$ unload period, $A_1 = 0$
- $(t_i, \; t_n)$ absorption period, $A_2 = IE_{max}(t_n - t_i)/2$
- $(t_n, \; t_{n_{max}})$ saturated period, $A_3 = IE_{max}(t_{n_{max}} - t_n)$

The sum of these areas is the new node feature and we compute, as in Sect. 4.1, the combined edge weight with the flow of $IE\Delta t$, $f_{IE\Delta t}$. In the second approach, we use the time segmentation graph. For this graph, we calculate the energy absorption efficiency, $P_e = IE/\Delta t$, where $\Delta t = s_t$, see Sect. 4.2, and $IE = f_{IE}$, see Sect. 4.1.

5   Result

We use an illustrative example presented in [18] to evaluate our method. This study contains 66 simulations; each model contains 27 parts and 11 components. The model structure is the same, therefore the graph structure remains the same for all simulations. Figure 3 shows the extracted graph for CBG, sPBG and mPBG. Here, in the graph visualisation, the vertices are positioned in the centre of its part or component box. In Fig. 3a for CBG, the vertices of the graph are labelled by these components. For sPBG and mPBG each vertex refers to a part in Figs. 3b and 3c, where the parts corresponding to the vertex of a component are coloured grey. The mPBG has additional edges compared to sPBG that are marked in red, Fig. 3c. While the CBG, sPBG and mPBG graphs are the same for 66 simulations, adding the time segmentation to the graphs can change the structure for each simulation due to different time sequences. Figure 4 shows the differences in two simulations generated by time segmentation for mPBG. In the following sections, we evaluate the computation of the IE flow and the detection of the load-path.[2]

---

[2] The zoomed views use `networkx.kamada_kawai_layout()` with vertex distances and positions to improve the visualisation.

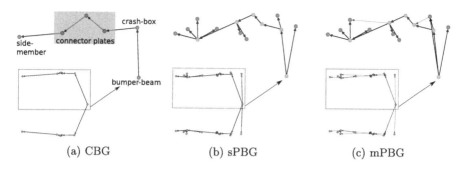

(a) CBG   (b) sPBG   (c) mPBG

Fig. 3. Extracted graphs for the illustrative example [18]. A zoomed view of the upper half is shown for each graph. The additional edges for mPBG compared to sPBG are marked as red in (c) (Color figure online).

Fig. 4. mPBG segmentation differences for simulations (0) and (27) due to different times of absorption.

5.1   Graph Flow

We use the RSME of the inflow and outflow to evaluate the flow calculation as:

$$RSME = \sqrt{\frac{1}{N}\sum_{j=1}^{N} IE_j - \left(\sum_{n \in I(j)} w_{n,j} - \sum_{n \in O(j)} w_{j,n}\right)}. \qquad (2)$$

The flow calculation has a small error in the order of 2 to $3e - 16$ for the three graph extraction methods. The comparatively high spread of the RMSE for CBG indicates that for some simulations the connectivity of the CBG graph is limited, which increases the RMSE for these simulations.

5.2   Load-Path Detection

Here, we first discuss the result of the load-path detection for five reference models, as in [18], and show how the load-path detection characterises the simulations. Then, we use the best method to classify all 66 simulations. In the reference simulations – 3, 30, 31, 60, 61 — the crash-box thicknesses differ as follows. Simulation 3 has the same thickness on both left hand side LHS and

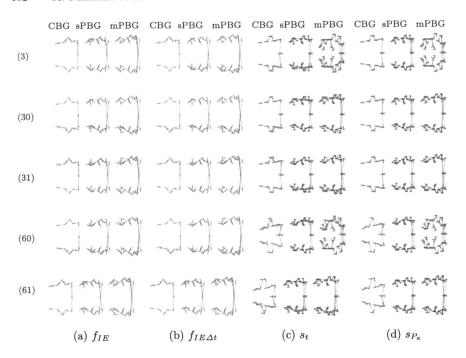

Fig. 5. Load-path detection, marked in red, for the five reference simulations from [18]. LHS and RHS are at the top and bottom, respectively. Each simulation and edge weight setup include results of CBG, sPBG and mPBG. (Color figure online)

right hand side RHS. Compared to 3, simulations 30 and 31 are less stiff on RHS and LHS, respectively. Whereas simulations 60 and 61 are stiffer on LHS and RHS, respectively, compared to 3.

Figure 5 summarises the load-path detection with four edge weights as described in Sect. 4. Columns a and c are the single feature results for f_{IE} and s_t. The other two columns are weighted with combined features $f_{IE\Delta t}$ and s_{P_e}, columns b and d respectively. We show the results of three different graph extraction methods for each scenario and the detected paths are marked in red. Based on the structural stiffness, the expected energy load-path for simulations 30 and 60 is at the RHS (bottom) and for simulations 31 and 61 at the LHS (top).

We expect that for graphs with f_{IE}-edge weight, it is the reverse of graphs with s_t-weight whether we get a top or bottom load-path. This is due to the physics of the problem, i.e. stiffer parts take more time for absorption and deform less, which means lower IE. The only exception we observe is in the result with CBG and s_t weighting. Here the detected path for these simulations does not continue to the side-member and a different side of the structure is detected

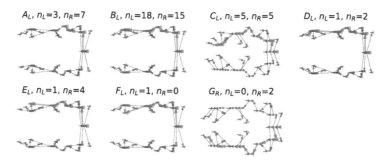

Fig. 6. Identical load-paths, marked in red, that are identified for the simulation dataset from [18]. Only one is shown if there is a symmetric pair. n_L and n_R are the number of occurrences of a load-path in the dataset, respectively. (Color figure online)

compared to sPBG or mPBG. This example shows the limitation of CBG in time feature extraction, i.e., the component level is less sensitive than the part level.

Next for the combined features, $f_{IE\Delta t}$ and s_{P_e}, for most scenarios the detected load-path remains in the expected direction of the structure. The only exception is the CBG graph for simulation 3. Simulation 3 is a symmetric model and lacks a dominant load-path due to its symmetry. Again, the CBG method lacks the detail to realise the effect of time in detecting the load-path. The additional obvious observation is that with s_{P_e} weight the detected path is shorter. This detection describes well that the crash-box influence is much greater than those of the remaining parts. Therefore, this path captures the efficient path of the load rather than the full path along the structure.

Among these approaches, the mpBG with s_t detects the most detailed load-paths, which is better for simulation comparison. As a result, we use it to visually categorise all 66 simulations. This method categorises the data into 12 identical load-paths, where 10 are symmetric pairs, i.e., an LHS path corresponds to an RHS path. Figure 6 summarises the clusters. Most of the simulations, 33, are grouped in cluster B. The biggest difference of the clusters is between cluster A and the rest where the path ends with a crash-box absorption. The remaining clusters have similar absorption for the crash-box and differ in vertex selection for the side-member at the end of the path.

6   Conclusion and Outlook

We considered load-path detection in crash analysis, one of the automotive CAE domains, by using graph approaches. Due to the lack of graphs in the CAE data, we introduced graph extraction methods to convert the CAE analysis of crashes into graphs. To characterise the absorption path of the vehicle structure, we not only abstract the vehicle structure into the graph, but also define edge directions and edge weights. By computing the longest weighted path in a graph an automated detection of load-paths now becomes feasible. Vehicles with the same structural design have an almost similar graph structure, while edge weighting and time segmentation detect differences in load-paths. Our method showed promising results analysing an illustrative example with 66 simulations. Based on our study, it is best to use different graph extraction approaches and edge weights (w) for different applications, as follows:

1. CBG, $w = f_{IE}$: crash mode analysis [18], advantage: simple and stable.
2. mPBG, $w = f_{IE\Delta t}$: IE flow path analysis, advantage: more details.
3. mPBG, $w = s_t$: simulation clustering using load-path, advantage: sensitivity to time sequence.
4. mPBG $w = s_{P_e}$: analyse part or component efficiency.

As well as being useful for the CAE engineers, the load-path clusters from c) can also be used as labels, which opens up new possibilities for using supervised machine learning ML for CAE. We see as a next stage an implementation of graph embedding methods to automatically classify the results.

In addition, posture detection methods can be used to further process the data during the crash [21]. With these methods, part features should remain at the vertex level for active part detection. However, as far as we are aware, there is limited research on directed graphs to find the load-path. Furthermore, converting a whole vehicle into a graph requires additional considerations. For a complete vehicle, graph extraction can often lead to several unconnected graphs due to the existence of larger parts. Our graph extraction works for sub-models, but further heuristics are needed to extend its application, which is beyond the scope of this work. Finally, we extracted a static graph from the undeformed geometry. As the deformed structure may lead to additional contacts between parts that do not exist in the undeformed structure, it may be useful in the future to consider the deformed structures as well.

References

1. Qiao, L., Zhang, L., Chen, S., Shen, D.: Data-driven graph construction and graph learning: a review. Neurocomputing **312**, 336–351 (2018)
2. Abu-Salih, B.: Domain-specific knowledge graphs: a survey. J. Netw. Comput. Appl. **185**, 103076 (2021)
3. Stanković, L., et al.: Data analytics on graphs part III: machine learning on graphs, from graph topology to applications. Found. Trends Mach. Learn. **13**(4), 332–530 (2020)
4. Schwanitz, P.: Towards AI based recommendations for design improvement (AI-B-REDI). Presentation at SIMVEC, Baden-Baden November 2022 (2022)
5. Pakiman, A., Garcke, J.: Graph modeling in computer assisted automotive development. In: 2022 IEEE International Conference on Knowledge Graph (ICKG), pp. 203–210 (2022). arXiv preprint arXiv:2209.14910
6. Granda, J.J.: Automating the process for modeling and simulation of mechatronics systems. In: Bond Graph Modelling of Engineering Systems, pp. 385–430, Springer, New York (2011). https://doi.org/10.1007/978-1-4419-9368-7_11

7. Granda, J.J., Gloekler, T.: Bond graph models for reconstruction of vehicle barrier equivalent speeds. In: Proceedings of the International Conference on Bond Graph Modeling and Simulation, pp. 35–47 (2016)
8. Gawthrop, P.J., Bevan, G.P.: Bond-graph modeling. IEEE Control Syst. Magaz. **27**(2), 24–45 (2007)
9. Mentzer, S.G., Radwan, R.A., Hollowell, W.T.: The sisame methodology for extraction of optimal lumped parameter structural crash models. Tech. rep., SAE Technical Paper (1992)
10. Lim, J.M.: Lumped mass-spring model construction for crash analysis using full frontal impact test data. Int. J. Automot. Technol. **18**, 463–472 (2017)
11. Lange, V.A., Fender, J., Song, L., Duddeck, F.: Early phase modeling of frontal impacts for crashworthiness: from lumped mass-spring models to deformation space models. Proc. Inst. Mech. Eng. Part D: J. Autom. Eng. **233**(12), 3000–3015 (2019)
12. Ortmann, C., Schumacher, A.: Graph and heuristic based topology optimization of crash loaded structures. Struct. Multidiscip. Optimiz. **47**(6), 839–854 (2013)
13. Schneider, D., Schumacher, A.: Finding optimized layouts for ribs on surfaces using the graph and heuristic based topology optimization. In: Schumacher, A., Vietor, T., Fiebig, S., Bletzinger, K., Maute, K. (eds.) WCSMO 2017, pp. 1615–1628. Springer, Cham (2018). https://doi.org/10.1007/978-3-319-67988-4_121
14. Pakiman, A., Garcke, J., Schumacher, A.: Knowledge discovery assistants for crash simulations with graph algorithms and energy absorption features. Appl. Intell. (2023)
15. Bank, R.E., Xu, J.: An algorithm for coarsening unstructured meshes. Numer. Math. **73**(1), 1–36 (1996)
16. Chawla, A., Mukherjee, S., Sharma, A.: Mesh generation for folded airbags. Comput. Aided Des. Appl. **1**(1–4), 269–276 (2004)
17. Montevecchi, F., Venturini, G., Grossi, N., Scippa, A., Campatelli, G.: Finite element mesh coarsening for effective distortion prediction in wire arc additive manufacturing. Addit. Manuf. **18**, 145–155 (2017)
18. Pakiman, A., Garcke, J., Schumacher, A.: Simrank-based prediction of crash simulation similarities. INS Preprint No. 2210. Institut für Numerische Simulation, Universität Bonn (2022)
19. Marhadi, K., Venkataraman, S.: Comparison of quantitative and qualitative information provided by different structural load path definitions. Int. J. Simulat. Multidiscip. Design Optimiz. **3**(3), 384–400 (2009)
20. Lindquist, M., Hall, A., Björnstig, U.: Real world car crash investigations-a new approach. Int. J. Crashworthiness **8**(4), 375–384 (2003)
21. Ma, N., et al.: A survey of human action recognition and posture prediction. Tsinghua Sci. Technol. **27**(6), 973–1001 (2022)

Posters

Factorization of Formal Contexts
from Modal Operators

Roberto G. Aragón$^{(\boxtimes)}$, Jesús Medina, and Eloísa Ramírez-Poussa

Department of Mathematics, University of Cádiz, Cádiz, Spain
{roberto.aragon,jesus.medina,eloisa.ramirez}@uca.es

In [4], the use of two modal operators from possibility theory for decomposing the Boolean relation of a given formal context into independent blocks, whenever it is possible, was studied. For that, it is necessary that the considered context (A, B, R) be normalized, i.e., the corresponding matrix of the relation R has no empty rows and no empty columns, and no object is related to all attributes and no attribute is related to all objects. In particular, Dubois and Prade made use in [4] of the necessity operators $\uparrow_N : 2^B \to 2^A$, $\downarrow^N : 2^A \to 2^B$, defined as follow:

$$X^{\uparrow_N} = \{a \in A \mid \text{for all } b \in B, \text{ if } (a, b) \in R, \text{ then } b \in X\}$$
$$Y^{\downarrow^N} = \{b \in B \mid \text{for all } a \in A, \text{ if } (a, b) \in R, \text{ then } a \in Y\}$$

for all $X \subseteq B$ and $Y \subseteq A$ [3,5–8], to characterize independent subcontexts decomposing the relation R of a given context (A, B, R). From this study, some interesting properties can be deduced from a pair of non-empty subsets $X \subseteq B$, $Y \subseteq A$, that satisfies the following equalities:

$$X^{\uparrow_N} = Y \text{ and } Y^{\downarrow^N} = X, \tag{1}$$

The set of all pairs satisfying Expression (1) is denoted by $\mathcal{C}_N$, that is,

$$\mathcal{C}_N = \{(X, Y) \mid X \subseteq B, Y \subseteq A, X^{\uparrow_N} = Y, \ Y^{\downarrow^N} = X\}$$

New properties were studied and presented in [1]. Notice that, since the context is normalized, the set $\mathcal{C}_N$ is not empty since the pairs (B, A) and $(\varnothing, \varnothing)$ belong to it. In what follows we will exclude these two trivial pairs in order to state the results, so when we consider a pair $(X, Y) \in \mathcal{C}_N$ it will be distinct from (B, A) and $(\varnothing, \varnothing)$. Furthermore, each pair (X, Y) belonging to $\mathcal{C}_N$ determines an independent subcontext of the original context [4]. As a consequence, its complement (X^c, Y^c), where X^c and Y^c are the complements of X and Y respectively, also belongs to $\mathcal{C}_N$ and thus, determines another independent subcontext. Therefore, there may be different ways of factorizing the original context into independent subcontexts depending on the cardinality of the set $\mathcal{C}_N$.

Since we are interested in reducing the complexity in the data processing as much as possible, we should consider the minimal independent subcontexts, but

© The Author(s), under exclusive license to Springer Nature Switzerland AG 2023
M. Ojeda-Aciego et al. (Eds.): ICCS 2023, LNAI 14133, pp. 189–192, 2023.
https://doi.org/10.1007/978-3-031-40960-8_15

the pairs in $\mathcal{C}_N$ do not entail any minimality. In [4], one method of decomposing the context into minimal subcontexts is provided by computing the following intersection:

$$R^* = \bigcap_{(X,Y) \,\in\, \mathcal{C}_N} (X \times Y) \cup (X^c \times Y^c)$$

In this paper, we have studied another point of view for computing these minimal subcontexts and analyzed new properties of the decomposition using necessity operators. Next, several ones have been highlighted and a toy example to illustrate the decomposition and properties is given. First of all, we take into account that the elements of $\mathcal{C}_N$ equipped with operations:

- $(X_1, Y_1) \sqcup (X_2, Y_2) = (X_1 \cup X_2, Y_1 \cup Y_2)$
- $(X_1, Y_1) \sqcap (X_2, Y_2) = (X_1 \cap X_2, Y_1 \cap Y_2)$
- $(X, Y)^c = (X^c, Y^c)$

have the structure of a complete lattice (this was proved in a more general framework in [7]), with the inclusion order on the left argument or on the right argument, that is, $(X_1, Y_1) \leq (X_2, Y_2)$ if $X_1 \subseteq X_2$ or, equivalently, $Y_1 \subseteq Y_2$. Since each element in $\mathcal{C}_N$ defines a subcontext, those elements which are minimal elements of $\mathcal{C}_N$ will determine minimal subcontexts. Furthermore, we can identify these minimal elements of $\mathcal{C}_N$ with the supremum irreducible elements as the following result states.

Proposition 1. *Let (A, B, R) be a formal context and let (X^*, Y^*) be a supremum irreducible element of $(\mathcal{C}_N, \leq)$. There is no element $(X, Y) \in \mathcal{C}_N$ such that $(X, Y) \lneq (X^*, Y^*)$, except the bottom of the lattice, that is, $(\varnothing, \varnothing)$.*

In addition, we can go further and determine the smallest independent subcontexts by means of the supremum irreducible elements of $\mathcal{C}_N$.

Proposition 2. *Given a context (A, B, R), the set of all supremum irreducible elements of $\mathcal{C}_N$ determines partitions of the sets A and B, that is, $A = \bigcup_{i \in I} Y_i^*$ and $B = \bigcup_{i \in I} X_i^*$, where $\{(X_i^*, Y_i^*) \mid i \in I\}$ is the set of all supremum irreducible elements of $\mathcal{C}_N$.*

Example 1. Let us consider the formal context (A, B, R) associated with the data in the table on the left side of Fig. 1. Also, the list of concepts and the Hasse diagram of the concept lattice is shown in Fig. 1.

This context is normalized. Therefore, we can apply Propositions 1 and 2, and compute the elements of the set $\mathcal{C}_N$. The list of elements of $\mathcal{C}_N$ and an isomorphic lattice to $(\mathcal{C}_N, \leq)$ is given in Fig. 2.

We can see that the supremum-irreducible elements are (X_1, Y_1), (X_2, Y_2) and (X_4, Y_4), which do not have any other (supremum-irreducible) concept less than it, as it happens for every supremum-irreducible element in $\mathcal{C}_N$ associated with a normalized formal context (Proposition 1). Moreover, we have that $X_1 \cup X_2 \cup X_4 = B$, as Proposition 2 asserts. Clearly, we can see in Fig. 1 the three blocks associated with (X_1, Y_1), (X_2, Y_2) and (X_4, Y_4).

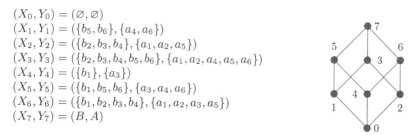

R	b_1	b_2	b_3	b_4	b_5	b_6
a_1	0	1	1	1	0	0
a_2	0	0	0	1	0	0
a_3	1	0	0	0	0	0
a_4	0	0	0	0	1	1
a_5	0	0	1	0	0	0
a_6	0	0	0	0	1	0

$C_0 = (\varnothing, A)$
$C_1 = (\{b_5\}, \{a_4, a_6\})$
$C_2 = (\{b_5, b_6\}, \{a_4\})$
$C_3 = (\{b_1\}, \{a_3\})$
$C_4 = (\{b_4\}, \{a_1, a_2\})$
$C_5 = (\{b_3\}, \{a_1, a_5\})$
$C_6 = (\{b_2, b_3, b_4\}, \{a_1, a_2, a_5\})$
$C_7 = (B, \varnothing)$

Fig. 1. Relation of the context, the list of concepts and concept lattice of Example 1.

$(X_0, Y_0) = (\varnothing, \varnothing)$
$(X_1, Y_1) = (\{b_5, b_6\}, \{a_4, a_6\})$
$(X_2, Y_2) = (\{b_2, b_3, b_4\}, \{a_1, a_2, a_5\})$
$(X_3, Y_3) = (\{b_2, b_3, b_4, b_5, b_6\}, \{a_1, a_2, a_4, a_5, a_6\})$
$(X_4, Y_4) = (\{b_1\}, \{a_3\})$
$(X_5, Y_5) = (\{b_1, b_5, b_6\}, \{a_3, a_4, a_6\})$
$(X_6, Y_6) = (\{b_1, b_2, b_3, b_4\}, \{a_1, a_2, a_3, a_5\})$
$(X_7, Y_7) = (B, A)$

Fig. 2. List of elements and lattice of $\mathcal{C}_N$ of Example 1.

These propositions and other studied results complement those given in [1], providing a complete analysis of the factorization given by the necessity operators and offer the basis for new advances in the fuzzy approach in the near future [2].

Acknowledgment. Partially supported by the 2014-2020 ERDF Operational Programme in collaboration with the State Research Agency (AEI) in projects PID2019-108991GB-I00 and PID2022-137620NB-I00, with the Ecological and Digital Transition Projects 2021 of the Ministry of Science and Innovation in project TED2021-129748B-I00, and with the Department of Economy, Knowledge, Business and University of the Regional Government of Andalusia in project FEDER-UCA18-108612, and by the European Cooperation in Science & Technology (COST) Action CA17124.

References

1. Aragón, R.G., Medina, J., Ramírez-Poussa, E.: Study on the necessity operator to factorize formal contexts in a multi-adjoint framework. Commun. Comput. Inf. Sci. **1601**, 107–117 (2022)
2. Aragón, R.G., Medina, J., Ramírez-Poussa, E.: Possibility theory and thresholds for factorizing multi-adjoint contexts, pp. 8–9. BoA (2022)
3. Dubois, D., de Saint-Cyr, F.D., Prade, H.: A possibility-theoretic view of formal concept analysis. Fund. Inform. **75**(1–4), 195–213 (2007)
4. Dubois, D., Prade, H.: Possibility theory and formal concept analysis: characterizing independent sub-contexts. Fuzzy Sets Syst. **196**, 4–16 (2012)
5. Düntsch, N., Gediga, G.: Modal-style operators in qualitative data analysis. In: 2002 IEEE International Conference on Data Mining, pp. 155–162 (2002)

6. Düntsch, I., Gediga, G.: Approximation operators in qualitative data analysis. In: de Swart, H., Orłowska, E., Schmidt, G., Roubens, M. (eds.) Theory and Applications of Relational Structures as Knowledge Instruments. LNCS, vol. 2929, pp. 214–230. Springer, Heidelberg (2003). https://doi.org/10.1007/978-3-540-24615-2_10
7. Georgescu, G., Popescu, A.: Non-dual fuzzy connections. Arch. Math. Logic **43**(8), 1009–1039 (2004)
8. Yao, Y., Chen, Y.: Rough set approximations in formal concept analysis. In: Peters, J.F., Skowron, A. (eds.) Transactions on Rough Sets V. LNCS, vol. 4100, pp. 285–305. Springer, Heidelberg (2006). https://doi.org/10.1007/11847465_14

Towards Confirmation Measures to Mixed Attribute Implications

Fernando Chacón-Gómez[✉], M. Eugenia Cornejo, and Jesús Medina

Department of Mathematics, University of Cádiz, Cádiz, Spain
{fernando.chacon,mariaeugenia.cornejo,jesus.medina}@uca.es

Abstract. This paper advances in the relationship among formal concept analysis and rough set theory translating the notion of confirmation measure given in rough set theory to formal concept analysis. Consequently, more information of (valid) attribute implications in mixed context is obtained.

Keywords: Formal concept analysis · mixed context · rough set theory · confidence · confirmation measure

1 Introduction

Formal Concept Analysis (FCA) [14] and Rough Set Theory (RST) [9] arose to deal with relational datasets and to extract relevant information from them. The study of dependences among the variables is a very important task in both frameworks [1,15], which is carried out by using attribute implications in FCA and decision rules in RST. This work continues making advances on the contribution presented in [2], relating attribute implications of FCA and decision rules of RST in order to obtain an attribute implication from a decision rule and vice versa. These relationships will allow us to translate the definition of relevance indicators and confirmation measures [7,9], which are studied in RST for the management of decision rules, into the FCA framework for the treatment of attribute implications. Confirmation measures have its origin in Bayesian theory [4,8], which have been considered to quantify how much a piece of evidence confirms a hypothesis.

Confirmation measures have been used in RST [6,7,12,13] to illustrate the impact of the satisfiability of the antecedent on the satisfiability of consequent, providing us with complementary information to the one given by the other measures. This paper will adapt the notion of confirmation measure to the FCA framework in order to enrich the information we can extract from an attribute implication defined on mixed contexts [10,11]. Moreover, some preliminary results will be introduced.

2 Mixed Contexts

This section recall the notions required to define a context in which bipolar attributes are considered [11,14].

© The Author(s), under exclusive license to Springer Nature Switzerland AG 2023
M. Ojeda-Aciego et al. (Eds.): ICCS 2023, LNAI 14133, pp. 193–196, 2023.
https://doi.org/10.1007/978-3-031-40960-8_16

Definition 1. *A context is a tuple* $(A, B, \mathcal{R})$ *where A and B are non-empty sets of attributes and objects, respectively, and $\mathcal{R}$ is a relation between them. From this notion the following ones are obtained.*

- $(\overline{A}, B, \overline{\mathcal{R}})$ *is the* opposite context *to* $(A, B, \mathcal{R})$ *where* $\overline{A} = \{\overline{a} \mid a \in A\}$ *is the set of negative attributes and* $\overline{\mathcal{R}}$ *is defined, for each* $\overline{a} \in \overline{A}$ *and* $b \in B$, *as follows:* $(\overline{a}, b) \in \overline{\mathcal{R}}$ *if and only if* $(a, b) \notin \mathcal{R}$.
- *The* derivation operators $(\Uparrow, \Downarrow)$ *are the mappings* $\Uparrow: 2^B \rightarrow 2^{A \cup \overline{A}}$ *and* $\Downarrow: 2^{A \cup \overline{A}} \rightarrow 2^B$ *defined, for each* $X \subseteq B$ *and* $Y \subseteq A \cup \overline{A}$, *as:*

$$X^{\Uparrow} = \{a \in A \mid (a, b) \in \mathcal{R} \text{ for all } b \in X\} \cup \{\overline{a} \in \overline{A} \mid (a, b) \notin \mathcal{R} \text{ for all } b \in X\}$$
$$Y^{\Downarrow} = \{b \in B \mid (a, b) \in \mathcal{R} \text{ for all } a \in Y\} \cap \{b \in B \mid (a, b) \notin \mathcal{R} \text{ for all } \overline{a} \in Y\}$$

- *Given* $C, D \subseteq A \cup \overline{A}$, *a* mixed attribute implication *is denoted as* $C \Rightarrow D$, *and it is* valid *in* $(A, B, \mathcal{R})$ *if* $C^{\Downarrow} \subseteq D^{\Downarrow}$.

The bipolarity of the attributes in this framework allows to consider that an object can possess an attribute and other object can possess the opposite one. For example, one patient may be cold and another one may not be cold. This is simple but we must take into account that the relationships considered by Ganter and Wille only takes into account the attributes possess by an object [5], that is, in the relation of the context (A, B, R) contains the pair (a, b) if the object b has the attribute a, but if $(a, b) \notin R$, we cannot say that b does not have a [3]. Hence, in order to obtain information from datasets also containing the information of the "negative" attributes considering the theory of FCA, it is important to take into account the mixed contexts.

3   On the Validity of Mixed Attribute Implications

The following definition enables us to analyze mixed attribute implications from a new perspective, by using relevance indicators and confirmation measures. The last definition is an adaptation to FCA of the usual notion of confirmation measure considered in RST, taking into account that the notion of certainty in RST coincides with the notion of confidence in FCA.

Definition 2. *Given a mixed attribute implication* $C \Rightarrow D$.

- *The* support *of* $C \Rightarrow D$ *is a mapping* supp: $A \cup \overline{A} \times A \cup \overline{A} \rightarrow [0, 1]$ *defined as* $supp(C, D) = |C^{\Downarrow} \cap D^{\Downarrow}|$.
- *The* confidence *of* $C \Rightarrow D$ *is a mapping* conf: $A \cup \overline{A} \times A \cup \overline{A} \rightarrow [0, 1]$ *defined as* $conf(C, D) = \dfrac{supp(C, D)}{|C^{\Downarrow}|}$, *when* $|C^{\Downarrow}| \neq 0$.

- A confirmation measure *of $C \Rightarrow D$ is a mapping $cm\colon A \cup \overline{A} \times A \cup \overline{A} \rightarrow [0,1]$ satisfying the following properties:*

$$cm(C, D) > 0 \quad \text{if} \quad \text{conf}(C, D) > \frac{|D^{\Downarrow}|}{|B|}$$

$$cm(C, D) = 0 \quad \text{if} \quad \text{conf}(C, D) = \frac{|D^{\Downarrow}|}{|B|}$$

$$cm(C, D) < 0 \quad \text{if} \quad \text{conf}(C, D) < \frac{|D^{\Downarrow}|}{|B|}$$

Based on these notions, we have analyzed the validity of mixed attribute implications and different examples of confidence measures to be considered in the FCA framework. Next, we only present a small part of the obtained results. The first one extends the relationship between the confidence and validity of attribute implications to mixed attribute implications.

Proposition 1. *Let $(A, B, \mathcal{R})$ be a context and $C \Rightarrow D$ a mixed attribute implication with $C^{\Downarrow} \neq \varnothing$. Then $C \Rightarrow D$ is a valid mixed attribute implication if and only if $\text{conf}(C, D) = 1$.*

Now, we present a novel result relating the validity of mixed attribute implications and confirmation measures.

Proposition 2. *Let $(A, B, \mathcal{R})$ be a context, $C \Rightarrow D$ a mixed attribute implication with $D^{\Downarrow} \neq B$ and $cm\colon A \cup \overline{A} \times A \cup \overline{A} \rightarrow [0,1]$ a confirmation measure. If $C \Rightarrow D$ is a valid mixed attribute implication, then $cm(C, D) > 0$.*

In FCA, it is usual to make more flexible the validity of attribute implications considering association rules, that is, attribute implications with a confidence less than 1. Therefore, confirmation measures can be seen as a complementary value to confidence in FCA to give more information about association rules from another point of view, and so enriching the information obtained from these kind of rules. Thus, the use of confirmation measures in FCA will supply us with a new approach to study attribute implications, being able to detect non-total dependencies between attributes.

4   Conclusions and Future Work

We have adapted the conditions required to a fuzzy measure in order to obtain a confirmation measure in the FCA framework. We have compared the validity of a mixed attribute implication with its confirmation measure and we have obtained that the confirmation should be 1 or at least positive. We have also noted that this value gives an extra information of the association rules. This comparison will be studied in-depth in the future, introducing more properties and useful remarks for the applications.

Acknowledgement. Partially supported by the 2014-2020 ERDF Operational Programme in collaboration with the State Research Agency (AEI) in projects PID2019-108991GB-I00 and PID2022-137620NB-I00, with the Ecological and Digital Transition Projects 2021 of the Ministry of Science and Innovation in project TED2021-129748B-I00, and with the Department of Economy, Knowledge, Business and University of the Regional Government of Andalusia in project FEDER-UCA18-108612, and by the European Cooperation in Science & Technology (COST) Action CA17124.

References

1. Benítez-Caballero, M.J., Medina, J., Ramírez-Poussa, E.: Attribute reduction in rough set theory and formal concept analysis. In: Polkowski, L., et al. (eds.) IJCRS 2017. LNCS (LNAI), vol. 10314, pp. 513–525. Springer, Cham (2017). https://doi.org/10.1007/978-3-319-60840-2_37

2. Chacón-Gómez, F., Cornejo, M.E., Medina, J.: Relating decision rules and attribute implications. In: The 16th International Conference on Concept Lattices and Their Applications (CLA 2022) (2022, in press)

3. Dubois, D., Medina, J., Prade, H., Ramírez-Poussa, E.: Disjunctive attribute dependencies in formal concept analysis under the epistemic view of formal contexts. Inf. Sci. (2021)

4. Fitelson, B.: Studies in Bayesian confirmation theory. Ph.D. thesis, University of Wisconsin, Madison (2001)

5. Ganter, B., Wille, R.: Formal Concept Analysis. Springer, Heidelberg (1999). https://doi.org/10.1007/978-3-642-59830-2

6. Greco, S., Matarazzo, B., Słowiński, R.: Parameterized rough set model using rough membership and Bayesian confirmation measures. Int. J. Approximate Reasoning **49**(2), 285–300 (2008)

7. Greco, S., Pawlak, Z., Słowiński, R.: Can Bayesian confirmation measures be useful for rough set decision rules? Eng. Appl. Artif. Intell. **17**(4), 345–361 (2004)

8. Kyburg, H.E.: Recent work in inductive logic. Am. Philos. Q. **1**(4), 249–287 (1964)

9. Pawlak, Z.: Rough Sets: Theoretical Aspects of Reasoning About Data. Kluwer Academic Publishers, Norwell (1992)

10. Pérez-Gámez, F., López-Rodríguez, D., Cordero, P., Mora, Á., Ojeda-Aciego, M.: Simplifying implications with positive and negative attributes: a logic-based approach. Mathematics **10**(4) (2022)

11. Rodríguez-Jiménez, J., Cordero, P., Enciso, M., Mora, A.: Negative attributes and implications in formal concept analysis. Procedia Comput. Sci. **31**, 758–765 (2014)

12. Szczęch, I.: Multicriteria attractiveness evaluation of decision and association rules. In: Peters, J.F., Skowron, A., Wolski, M., Chakraborty, M.K., Wu, W-Z. (eds.) Transactions on Rough Sets X. LNCS, vol. 5656, pp. 197–274. Springer, Heidelberg (2009). https://doi.org/10.1007/978-3-642-03281-3_8

13. Wieczorek, A., Słowiński, R.: Generating a set of association and decision rules with statistically representative support and anti-support. Inf. Sci. **277**, 56–70 (2014)

14. Wille, R.: Restructuring lattice theory: an approach based on hierarchies of concepts. In: Rival, I. (ed.) Ordered Sets, vol. 83, pp. 445–470. Reidel, Dordrecht (1982). https://doi.org/10.1007/978-94-009-7798-3_15

15. Yao, Y.: Rough-set concept analysis: interpreting RS-definable concepts based on ideas from formal concept analysis. Inf. Sci. **346–347**, 442–462 (2016)

Concept Lattices as a Reduction Tool for Fuzzy Relation Equations

David Lobo[(✉)][iD], Víctor López-Marchante[iD], and Jesús Medina[iD]

Department of Mathematics, University of Cádiz, Cádiz, Spain
{david.lobo,victor.lopez,jesus.medina}@uca.es

Abstract. Recently, a procedure to reduce multi-adjoint relation equations has been published. Such method relies on the strong existing link between fuzzy relation equations and concept lattices, and more specifically, it is based on attribute reduction techniques. In this paper, we illustrate the reduction mechanism for the specific case of fuzzy relation equations on a more general structure than a residuated lattice, in which an adjoint triple is considered instead of a left continuous t-norm and its residuated implication.

Keywords: Fuzzy relation equations · Concept lattices · Attribute reduction · Redundant information

Fuzzy relation equations is a relevant topic from its introduction in the 1980s from a theoretic and applied perspective [5,12–15]. The research conducted in [9] presents a method to reduce the magnitude of a multi-adjoint relation equation (MARE) [7], in the sense of eliminating redundant rows (sub-equations). In this work, we show how to adapt the results in [9] for the reduction of fuzzy relation equations (FRE) [4,6,11] defined with a sup-$\&$ composition operator, where the mapping $\&$ belongs to an *adjoint triple*.

Definition 1. *([3]) Let $(P_1, \preceq_1)$, $(P_2, \preceq_2)$, $(P_3, \preceq_3)$ be posets and $\& : P_1 \times P_2 \to P_3$, $\swarrow : P_3 \times P_2 \to P_1$, $\nwarrow : P_3 \times P_1 \to P_2$ mappings, then $(\&, \swarrow, \nwarrow)$ is called an* adjoint triple *with respect to P_1, P_2, P_3 if*

$$x \preceq_1 z \swarrow y \quad iff \quad x \& y \preceq_3 z \quad iff \quad y \preceq_2 z \nwarrow x$$

for each $x \in P_1$, $y \in P_2$, $z \in P_3$.

Following the terminology employed in [10], we say that a *property-oriented frame* is a triplet of posets endowed with an adjoint triple. Formally:

Definition 2. *Let $(L_1, \preceq_1)$, $(L_2, \preceq_2)$ be two lattices, $(P, \leq)$ a poset and $(\&, \swarrow, \nwarrow)$ an adjoint triple with respect to P, L_2, L_1. The tuple*

$$(L_1, L_2, P, \preceq_1, \preceq_2, \preceq, \&, \swarrow, \nwarrow)$$

is called property-oriented frame.

M. Ojeda-Aciego et al. (Eds.): ICCS 2023, LNAI 14133, pp. 197–200, 2023.
https://doi.org/10.1007/978-3-031-40960-8_17

From here on, consider fixed a fuzzy relation equation of the form

$$R \odot X = T \tag{1}$$

where U, V and W are three finite sets, $(L_1, L_2, P, \preceq_1, \preceq_2, \preceq, \&, \swarrow, \diagdown)$ is a property-oriented frame and $R \in P^{U \times V}$, $T \in L_1^{U \times W}$, $X \in L_2^{V \times W}$ being X unknown.

Basically, the idea of reducing a FRE consists of removing elements in the set U. Notice that, the elimination of elements in U implies the reduction of rows in R and T, which entails the elimination of equations of the system associated with the FRE (1).

Definition 3. *Let* $Y \subseteq U$ *and consider the relations* $R_Y = R_{|Y \times V}$, $T_Y = T_{|Y \times W}$. *The FRE* $R_Y \odot X = T_Y$ *is called* Y-*reduced FRE of* $R \odot X = T$.

Clearly, reducing a solvable FRE in the sense of Definition 3, may give rise to a significant loss of relevant information, resulting in a different FRE whose solution set might have nothing in common with the solutions of the original FRE. In order to avoid this issue, the reduction will only be performed in certain subsets of U, which are consistent sets of a formal context related to the FRE. Therefore, the strategy of the reduction technique consists of associating a property-oriented concept lattice to the FRE (1) and then find consistent sets of attributes.

First of all, we will associate the FRE (1) with the context (U, V, R), where U is usually interpreted as the set of attributes and the set V as the set of objects. Now, denoting $L_1^U = \{f \mid f : U \to L_1\}$ and $L_2^V = \{g \mid g : V \to L_2\}$, the mappings $\uparrow_\pi : L_2^V \to L_1^U$ and $\downarrow^N : L_1^U \to L_2^V$ are defined, for each $f \in L_1^U$ and $g \in L_2^V$, as follows:

$$g^{\uparrow_\pi}(u) = \bigvee_1 \{R(u,v) \,\&\, g(v) \mid v \in V\} \tag{2}$$

$$f^{\downarrow^N}(v) = \bigwedge_2 \{f(u) \diagdown R(u,v) \mid u \in U\} \tag{3}$$

The pair of mappings $(\uparrow_\pi, \downarrow^N)$, which is an isotone Galois connection [10], allows to define the *property-oriented concept lattice* $(\mathcal{M}_{\pi N}(U, V, R), \preceq_{\pi N})$, where

$$\mathcal{M}_{\pi N}(U, V, R) = \left\{ (g, f) \in L_2^V \times L_1^U \mid g = f^{\downarrow^N}, f = g^{\uparrow_\pi} \right\} \tag{4}$$

and $(g_1, f_1) \preceq_{\pi N} (g_2, f_2)$ if and only if $f_1 \preceq_1 f_2$.

The main result that supports the reduction method is given next, and states that the reduction of a solvable FRE via a consistent set of (U, V, R) generates a solvable FRE with the same solution set.

Theorem 1. *Let* $R \odot_\sigma X = T$ *be a solvable FRE and* Y *a consistent set of* (U, V, R). *Then, the* Y-*reduced FRE of* $R \odot_\sigma X = T$ *is solvable and* $\overline{X} \in L_2^{V \times W}$ *is a solution of the* Y-*reduced FRE if and only if it is a solution of the complete FRE.*

Clearly, the process of reducing a FRE is optimized if the consistent set is actually a reduct of (U, V, R), that is, a minimal consistent set of attributes.

Corollary 1. *Let* $R \odot_\sigma X = T$ *be a solvable FRE and* Y *a reduct of* (U, V, R). *Then, the* Y-*reduced FRE of* $R \odot_\sigma X = T$ *is solvable and* $\overline{X} \in L_2^{V \times W}$ *is a solution of the* Y-*reduced FRE if and only if it is a solution of the complete FRE.*

Since the context (U, V, R) may have several reducts with different cardinality, it is natural to assume that the reduct with the minimum number of elements will be the most adequate reduct to proceed with the reduction method. The process of reducing FRE is illustrated by the following example.

Example 1. Consider the sets $U = \{u_1, u_2, u_3, u_4\}$, $V = \{v_1, v_2, v_3, v_4, v_5\}$ and $W = \{w\}$, the discretization of the unit interval $[0, 1]_8$ and the property-oriented frame given by

$$([0, 1]_8, \preceq, \&_G, \nearrow^G, \searrow_G)$$

where $x \&_G y = \min\{x, y\}$. Assume the following FRE

$$R \odot_G X = T \tag{5}$$

where

$$R = \begin{pmatrix} 0.5 & 0.25 & 0.125 & 0.75 & 0.125 \\ 0.5 & 0.375 & 0.5 & 0.625 & 0.25 \\ 0.5 & 0.25 & 0.125 & 0.625 & 0.125 \\ 0.5 & 0.375 & 0.375 & 0.75 & 0.25 \end{pmatrix}, \quad T = \begin{pmatrix} 0.125 \\ 0.25 \\ 0.125 \\ 0.25 \end{pmatrix}$$

and $X \in [0, 1]_8^{V \times W}$ is unknown.

It can be checked that FRE (5) is solvable [7], as $T^{\downarrow^N \uparrow_\pi} = T$. Following the results shown in [2], we obtain that the reducts of the associated context are $Y_1 = \{u_1, u_2\}$ and $Y_2 = \{u_2, u_3\}$.

Hence, by Corollary 1, we can reduce FRE (5) in two different ways. For instance, if we consider the reduct Y_1, then the resolution of the FRE given by

$$R_{Y_1} \odot_G X = T_{Y_1}$$

where

$$R_{Y_1} = \begin{pmatrix} 0.5 & 0.25 & 0.125 & 0.75 & 0.125 \\ 0.5 & 0.375 & 0.5 & 0.625 & 0.25 \end{pmatrix}, \quad T_{Y_1} = \begin{pmatrix} 0.125 \\ 0.25 \end{pmatrix}$$

is equivalent to solving the original one. At this point, the reduced FRE can be solved with any of the procedures that have been developed in the literature, what will lead to a maximum solution and a set of minimal ones. Applying Corollary 1, these are the solutions of FRE (5).□

In the future, more properties of the fruitful relation between concept lattices and FRE will be analyzed and the obtained results will be applied to (real) problems, such as in Digital Forensics [1]. Moreover, the impact of considering different kind of operators in the composition of fuzzy relations is another hot topic to be boosted in the near future [8].

Acknowledgements. Partially supported by the 2014–2020 ERDF Operational Programme in collaboration with the State Research Agency (AEI) in projects PID2019-108991GB-I00 and PID2022-137620NB-I00, with the Ecological and Digital Transition Projects 2021 of the Ministry of Science and Innovation in project TED2021-129748B-I00, and with the Department of Economy, Knowledge, Business and University of the Regional Government of Andalusia in project FEDER-UCA18-108612, and by the European Cooperation in Science & Technology (COST) Action CA17124.

References

1. Digital forensics: Evidence analysis via intelligent systems and practices Dig-ForASP - Action COST CA17124. https://digforasp.uca.es
2. Antoni, L., Cornejo, M.E., Medina, J., Ramirez, E.: Attribute classification and reduct computation in multi-adjoint concept lattices. IEEE Trans. Fuzzy Syst. **29**, 1121–1132 (2020)
3. Cornejo, M.E., Medina, J., Ramírez-Poussa, E.: Algebraic structure and characterization of adjoint triples. Fuzzy Sets Syst. **425**, 117–139 (2021)
4. De Baets, B.: Sup-T equations: state of the art. In: Kaynak, O., Zadeh, L.A., Türkşen, B., Rudas, I.J. (eds.) Computational Intelligence: Soft Computing and Fuzzy-Neuro Integration with Applications. NATO ASI Series, vol. 162, pp. 80–93. Springer, Heidelberg (1998). https://doi.org/10.1007/978-3-642-58930-0_5
5. Di Martino, F., Sessa, S.: A novel image similarity measure based on greatest and smallest eigen fuzzy sets. Symmetry **15**(5), 1104 (2023)
6. Di Nola, A., Sanchez, E., Pedrycz, W., Sessa, S.: Fuzzy Relation Equations and Their Applications to Knowledge Engineering. Kluwer Academic Publishers, Norwell (1989)
7. Díaz, J.C., Medina, J.: Multi-adjoint relation equations: definition, properties and solutions using concept lattices. Inf. Sci. **253**, 100–109 (2013)
8. Lobo, D., López-Marchante, V., Medina, J.: On the impact of sup-compositions in the resolution of multi-adjoint relation equations. Math. Methods Appl. Sci., 1–18 (2023, in press). https://doi.org/10.1002/mma.9414
9. Lobo, D., López-Marchante, V., Medina, J.: Reducing fuzzy relation equations via concept lattices. Fuzzy Sets Syst. **463**, 108465 (2023)
10. Medina, J.: Multi-adjoint property-oriented and object-oriented concept lattices. Inf. Sci. **190**, 95–106 (2012)
11. Peeva, K., Kyosev, Y.: Fuzzy Relational Calculus: Theory, Applications and Software. World Scientific Publishing Company (2004)
12. Rubio-Manzano, C., Alfonso-Robaina, D., Díaz-Moreno, J.C., Malleuve-Martínez, A., Medina, J.: Determining cause-effect relations from fuzzy relation equations. Commun. Comput. Inf. Sci. **1601**, 155–166 (2022)
13. Tiwari, V.L., Thapar, A., Bansal, R.: A genetic algorithm for solving nonlinear optimization problem with max-archimedean bipolar fuzzy relation equations. Internat. J. Uncertain. Fuzziness Knowledge-Based Systems **31**(02), 303–326 (2023)
14. Xiao, G., Hayat, K., Yang, X.: Evaluation and its derived classification in a server-to-client architecture based on the fuzzy relation inequality. Fuzzy Optim. Decis. Making **22**, 213–245 (2023)
15. Yang, X.P.: Random-term-absent addition-min fuzzy relation inequalities and their lexicographic minimum solutions. Fuzzy Sets Syst. **440**, 42–61 (2022)

Analysis of Slovak Court Decisions by Formal Concept Analysis and Machine Learning Methods

Zoltán Szoplák[ID], Dávid Varga[ID], Šimon Horvát[ID], Peter Gurský[ID],
Ľubomír Antoni[(✉)][ID], Ondrej Krídlo[ID], and Stanislav Krajči[ID]

Institute of Computer Science, Faculty of Science,
Pavol Jozef Šafárik University in Košice, 041 80 Košice, Slovakia
{zoltan.szoplak,david.varga}@student.upjs.sk,
{simon.horvat,lubomir.antoni,ondrej.kridlo,stanislav.krajci}@upjs.sk

Abstract. The applications of machine learning and artificial intelligence methods in the natural language processing of court decisions have become an important research topic worldwide. In this paper, we review our datasets and recent results in the field of natural language processing of Slovak court decisions, including the graph-based word embedding methods. We also explore the automated assignment of relevant keywords to Slovak court decisions. Moreover, we applied the methods of Formal concept analysis to Slovak court decisions to explore the relationships between their attributes.

Keywords: Formal Concept Analysis · text analysis · court decisions

1 Introduction

The applications of machine learning and artificial intelligence methods in the decision-making process of courts or the legal profession have become an important research topic worldwide. The decision-making process realized by particular courts requires a thorough understanding of principles, notions, and legal text. Researchers aim to analyze the legal documents (judicial decisions) and to investigate and propose methods to extract fruitful knowledge from them [1,2].

The extracted attributes from the free text of court decisions can be expressed explicitly (i.e. the phrases which are frequently or less frequently used in the court decisions) or implicitly (i.e., phrases which result from the context of the text of the decision itself). The implicit attributes can include the relevance of court legislation, legal labels describing the content of the decision, a summary of the decision, and the similarity of the decision with other court decisions. Machine learning methods have the ability to input a large amount of raw or processed legal data, and based on the patterns and dependencies observed in the text, they can reveal fruitful attributes or additional hidden relationships between them. Regarding the identification of the most representative lexical

M. Ojeda-Aciego et al. (Eds.): ICCS 2023, LNAI 14133, pp. 201–204, 2023.
https://doi.org/10.1007/978-3-031-40960-8_18

units of the general type of documents, Firoozeh et al. [3] published a survey paper based on the methods and issues of keywords extraction, which can be applied in various applications of Information Retrieval, Text Mining, or Natural Language Processing. Moreover, Papagiannopoulou and Tsoumakas [4] reviewed the unsupervised graph-based methods with semantics (knowledge graphs) as the techniques for keyphrase extraction.

Moreno-Schneider et al. [5] developed the service platform Lynx of Legal Knowledge Graph (i.e., a knowledge graph for the legal domain). They demonstrate that the applications of their methods are fruitful for the semantic (content) processing, enrichment, and analysis of documents from the legal domain since they present several use cases based on contract analysis, labor law, or geothermal energy. Several research studies explore the specifics of legal orders and judicial decisions in a particular country. Walter and Pinkal [6] presented a rule-based approach for extracting and analyzing definitions from parsed text and evaluate it on a corpus of German court decisions. Grosz [7] explored the issue of identifying and extracting keywords in Swedish court documents. Martín-Chozas and Revenko [8] proposed the method to extract Hohfeld's deontic relations from legal texts from Spanish labor law.

In this paper, we review our datasets and recent results in the field of natural language processing of Slovak court decisions, including the methods of Formal concept analysis [11]. The automated assignment of relevant keywords to Slovak court decisions has also been explored.

2   Our Recent Datasets and Results

Regarding our fruitful cooperation with the analytical department of the Supreme Court of the Slovak Republic, we can directly access two important datasets for legal texts. The first is the ontology of legal keywords categorized by individual chambers of the Supreme Court, a so-called Repository of Keywords. The second dataset is a set of approximately 14,000 manually annotated Supreme Court judgments, in which multiple attributes and values are assigned to each decision. The presence of relevant keywords from the Repository of Keywords is also one of the annotated attributes of the decision. Moreover, Slovak Law Thesaurus [9], the legislative and information portal of the Ministry of Justice of the Slovak Republic is publicly available. As the second source of data, we have our own tool Morphonary [10], which is a manually annotated database of all possible word forms of the Slovak language, which also retains the root form as well as its lexical and grammatical categories. This tool is publicly available in Slovak language at https://tvaroslovnik.ics.upjs.sk/.

We proposed a novel method for constructing dense vector representation of words from Slovak dictionaries that captures semantic properties. However, our word embedding method is general and can be applied to any other language. Our method is formally described by the directed evaluated graph, whereby the vertices are set of all words, and the edges are relationships between words obtained from the dictionary of synonyms and the classical dictionary. LSTM classification model with our representation vectors obtained 79% accuracy after 30 epochs compared to 65% accuracy based on random initialization.

Moreover, we applied several machine learning methods, including Formal concept analysis, to explore the relationships between attributes of court decisions from their reasoning parts. The various algorithms are implemented to build the models that interpret the dataset's hidden relations. We investigate the typical expressions and phrases for court decisions with a guilty or innocent verdict. We successfully employed several statistical methods and machine learning methods for the representation and classification of the text of more than four million publicly available judicial decisions in criminal matters between 2016 and 2021. Based on the formal context of court decisions and their attributes, we constructed the concept lattice and attribute implications, which show the relationships between the decisions of criminal law, family law, civil law, terms, penalties, and other aspects.

Recently, we explored several unsupervised keyword extraction methods and algorithms on a selected set of court decisions. We applied two unsupervised methods, which combine graph-based weighted PageRank algorithms, tf-idf approach, or autoencoders. The best results were obtained by the autoencoder algorithm, which correctly matched 80% of keywords manually extracted by experts in the law. We found that our method provides even more general legal terms not obtained in the Slovak law thesaurus, and thus it can provide some added value for analysis.

Table 1. Example of top five keywords of court decision obtained by three methods

Method	Keywords
Tf-idf	**bill of exchange**
	form
	first instance court
	first instance
	fill out
Weighted PageRank	assumption
	receiving
	bill of exchange
	form
	stage
Autoencoders	**bill of exchange**
	the first instance court
	to apply the claim
	form of application
	owner of the **bill of exchange**

In Table 1, we present the example of top 5 keyphrases from the selected court decision obtained by three methods tf-idf, weighted PageRank algorithm and by autoencoders. The idf value was computed for all court decisions in our dataset. These keyphrases were indeed included in the abstract of the court decision which a law expert evaluated. The keywords in bold correspond to those also included in the abstract of the court decision. The underlined keywords represent the keywords specified also manually by a law expert.

The natural language processing of court decisions is an interesting research issue. These solutions can help to search keywords from the court decisions, to simplify the manual annotation performed by the Supreme Court, or to detect errors in the manual annotation that had already been performed.

Acknowledgment. This work was supported by the Slovak Research and Development Agency under contract No. APVV-21-0336 Analysis of court decisions by methods of artificial intelligence. This article was supported by the Scientific Grant Agency of the Ministry of Education, Science, Research and Sport of the Slovak Republic under contract VEGA 1/0645/22 entitled by Proposal of novel methods in the field of Formal concept analysis and their application.

References

1. Dale, R.: Law and word order: NLP in legal tech. Nat. Lang. Eng. **25**, 211–217 (2019)
2. Medvedeva, M., Vols, M., Wieling, M.: Using machine learning to predict decisions of the European court of human rights. Artif. Intell. Law **28**, 237–266 (2020)
3. Firoozeh, N., Nazarenko, A., Alizon, F., Daille, B.: Key- word extraction: issues and methods. Nat. Lang. Eng. **1**, 1–33 (2019)
4. Papagiannopoulou, E., Tsoumakas, G.: A review of Keyphrase extraction. Wiley Interdisc. Rev. Data Min. Knowl. Disc. **10**, e1339 (2020)
5. Moreno Schneider, J., Rehm, G., Montiel-Ponsoda, E., et al.: Lynx: a knowledge-based AI service platform for content processing, enrichment and analysis for the legal domain. Inf. Syst. **106**, 101966 (2022)
6. Walter, S., Pinkal, M.: Automatic extraction of definitions from German court decisions. In: Proceedings of the Workshop on Information Extraction Beyond the Document, pp. 20–28 (2006)
7. Grosz, S.: Keyword extraction from Swedish court documents. Master's thesis (2020)
8. Martín-Chozas, P., Revenko, A.: Thesaurus enhanced extraction of Hohfeld's relations from Spanish Labour law. In: Joint Proceedings of the 2nd International Workshop on Deep Learning meets Ontologies and Natural Language Processing, pp. 30–38 (2021)
9. Slovak law thesaurus, legislative and information portal (2022). https://www.slov-lex.sk/web/en
10. Krajči, S., Novotný, R.: Lemmatization of Slovak words by a tool Morphonary. In: NAZOU 2007: Proceedings of Workshop on Tools for Acquisition, Organisation and Knowledge, pp. 115–118 (2007)
11. Ganter, B., Wille, R.: Formal Concept Analysis, Mathematical Foundation. Springer, Heidelberg (1999). https://doi.org/10.1007/978-3-642-59830-2

Correction to: A Note on the Number of (Maximal) Antichains in the Lattice of Set Partitions

Dmitry I. Ignatov ⓘ

Correction to:
Chapter "A Note on the Number of (Maximal) Antichains
in the Lattice of Set Partitions" in: M. Ojeda-Aciego et al.
(Eds.): *Graph-Based Representation and Reasoning*,
LNAI 14133, https://doi.org/10.1007/978-3-031-40960-8_6

The original version of this paper contains errors and typos in the affiliation and reference section. This has been now corrected.

The updated original version of this chapter can be found at
https://doi.org/10.1007/978-3-031-40960-8_6

Author Index

M. Ojeda-Aciego et al. (Eds.): ICCS 2023, LNAI 14133, pp. 205–206, 2023.
https://doi.org/10.1007/978-3-031-40960-8

Printed in the United States
by Baker & Taylor Publisher Services